FUNDAMENTALS OF
English
Grammar

FOURTH EDITION

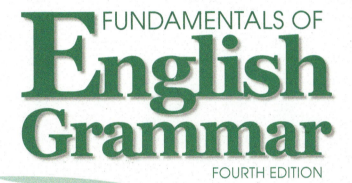

FUNDAMENTALS OF
English
Grammar

FOURTH EDITION

VOLUME A with Essential Online Resources

Betty S. Azar
Stacy A. Hagen

Fundamentals of English Grammar, Fourth Edition
Volume A

Azar Associates: Shelley Hartle, Editor, and Sue Van Etten, Manager

Pearson Education, 221 River Street, Hoboken, NJ 07030

Staff credits: The people who made up the *Fundamentals of English Grammar, Fourth Edition* team, representing editorial, production, design, and manufacturing, are, Dave Dickey, Christine Edmonds, Ann France, Amy McCormick, Robert Ruvo, and Ruth Voetmann.

Text composition: S4Carlisle Publishing Services

Illustrations: Don Martinetti—pages 13, 15, 25, 27, 40, 59, 64, 68, 70, 76, 92, 106, 115, 129, 131, 144, 155, 169, 171, 172, 173, 174, 181, 183, 196, 203;
Chris Pavely—pages 4, 7, 8, 19, 33, 38, 41, 43, 44, 47, 53, 75, 76, 90, 98, 101, 108, 111, 112, 125, 126, 165, 166, 186, 202

Printed in the United States of America

ISBN 10: 0-13-466112-5
ISBN 13: 978-0-13-466112-4

3 2020

To my sister, Jo
B.S.A.

For D. P. and H. B.
with appreciation
S.H.

Contents

Preface to the Fourth Edition

Fundamentals of English Grammar is a developmental skills text for lower-intermediate and intermediate English language learners. It uses a grammar-based approach integrated with communicative methodologies to promote the development of all language skills in a variety of ways. Starting from a foundation of understanding form and meaning, students engage in meaningful communication about real actions, real things, and their real lives in the classroom context. *Fundamentals of English Grammar* functions principally as a classroom teaching text but also serves as a comprehensive reference text for students and teachers.

The eclectic approach and abundant variety of exercise material remain the same as in the earlier editions, but this fourth edition incorporates new ways and means. In particular:

- **WARM-UP EXERCISES FOR THE GRAMMAR CHARTS**
  Newly created for the fourth edition, these innovative exercises precede the grammar charts and introduce the point(s) to be taught. They have been carefully crafted to help students *discover* the target grammar as they progress through each warm-up exercise.

- **LISTENING PRACTICE**
  Numerous listening exercises help students interact with the spoken language in a variety of settings that range from the relaxed, casual speech of everyday conversation to more academic content. The student text audio is available on Essential Online Resources, and a full listening script can be found in the back of the book.

- **READINGS**
  Students can read and respond to a wide selection of readings that focus on the target grammar structure(s).

- **WRITING TASKS**
  New writing activities that practice target structures have been created for every chapter. A writing sample precedes each task so students have a model to follow.

- **EXPANDED SPEAKING ACTIVITIES**
  Students have even more opportunities to share their experiences, express their opinions, and relate the target grammar to their personal lives. The text often uses the students' own life experiences as context and regularly introduces topics of interest to stimulate the free expression of ideas in structured as well as open discussions.

- **CORPUS-INFORMED CONTENT**
  Based on our corpus research, grammar content has been added, deleted, or modified to reflect the discourse patterns of spoken and written English.

Components of Fundamentals of English Grammar, Fourth Edition:

- **Student Book with Essential Online Resources** includes the access code for the audio, self-assessments, and teacher resources with the Student Book answer key.
- **Student Book with MyEnglishLab** that includes the access code to MyEnglishLab, an easy-to-use online learning management system that delivers rich online practice to engage and motivate students.
- A comprehensive *Workbook*, consisting of self-study exercises for independent work.
- An all-new *Teacher's Guide*, with step-by-step teaching suggestions for each chart, notes to the teacher on key grammar structures, vocabulary lists, and expansion activities and *PowerPoint* presentations for key chapters.
- An expanded *Test Bank*, with additional quizzes, chapter tests, and mid-term and final exams.
- *Test-Generator* software that allows teachers to customize their own tests using quizzes and tests from the *Test Bank*.
- *PowerPoint* presentations for key chapters. Based on real-world readings, these lessons are designed for use in the classroom as "beyond-the-book" activities. They can be found in the new *Teacher's Guide* or downloaded from *AzarGrammar.com*.
- A *Chartbook*, a reference book consisting only of the grammar charts.
- *AzarGrammar.com*, a website that provides a variety of supplementary classroom materials and a place where teachers can support each other by sharing their knowledge and experience.

MyEnglishLab

MyEnglishLab provides a range of interactive activities that help motivate and engage students. MyEnglishLab for *Fundamentals of English Grammar*, Fourth Edition includes:

- Rich online practice for all skill areas: grammar, reading, writing, speaking, and listening
- Instant feedback on incorrect answers
- Remediation activities
- Robust assessments that include diagnostic tests, chapter review tests, mid- and end-of-term review tests, and final exams
- Gradebook and diagnostic tools that allow teachers to monitor student progress and analyze data to determine steps for remediation and support
- Student Book answer key in the Teacher Resource Folder

The Azar-Hagen Grammar Series consists of

- *Understanding and Using English Grammar* (blue cover), for upper-level students.
- *Fundamentals of English Grammar* (black), for mid-level students.
- *Basic English Grammar* (red), for lower or beginning levels.

Tips for Using the New Features in this Text

- **WARM-UPS**

The Warm-Up exercises are a brief pre-teaching tool for the charts. They highlight the key point(s) that will be introduced in the chart that follows the Warm-Up exercise. Before beginning the task, teachers will want to familiarize themselves with the material in the chart. Then, with the teacher's guidance, students can discover many or sometimes all of the new patterns as they complete the Warm-Up activity. After students finish the exercise, teachers may find that no further explanation is necessary, and the charts can serve as a useful reference.

- **LISTENING**

The Listening exercises have been designed to help students understand American English as it is actually spoken. As such, it includes reductions and other phenomena that are part of the natural, relaxed speech of everyday English. Because the audio uses English that may be spoken at a rate faster than what students are used to, they may need to hear sentences two or three times while completing a task.

The Listening exercises do not encourage immediate pronunciation (unless they are linked to a specific pronunciation task). Receptive skills precede productive ones, and it is essential that students be able to hear the speech patterns before they begin using them in their own speech.

Students are encouraged to listen to longer passages the first time through without looking at their text. Teachers can then explain any vocabulary that has not already been clarified. During the second listening, students complete the assigned task. Teachers will want to pause the audio appropriately. Depending on the level of the class, pauses may be needed after every sentence, or even within a sentence.

It is inevitable that sound representations in the text will at times differ from the instructor's speech, whether it be due to register or regional variation. As a general rule, if the instructor expects that students will hear a variation, or if students themselves raise the questions, alternate representations can be presented.

A listening script with all the listening exercises can be found at the back of the book.

- **READINGS**

The Readings give students an opportunity to work with the grammar structures in extended contexts. One approach is to have students read the passage alone the first time through. Then they work in small groups or as a class to clarify vocabulary questions. A second reading may be necessary. Varied reading tasks then allow students to check their comprehension, to use the target structures, and to expand upon the topic in speaking or writing.

- **WRITING TASKS**

As students gain confidence in using the target structures, they are encouraged to express their ideas in complete paragraphs. A model paragraph accompanies each assignment and question-prompts help students develop their ideas.

Peer editing can be used for correction. A useful technique is to pair students, have them exchange papers, and then have the *partner* read the paragraph aloud. The writer can *hear* if the content is what he or she intended. This also keeps the writer from automatically self-correcting while reading aloud. (Self-correcting can be a problem if writers are unaware that they are making corrections as they read.)

For classes that have not had much experience with writing, the teacher may want to assign students to small groups. Each group composes a paragraph together. The teacher collects the paragraph and adds comments, and then makes a copy for each group member. Students correct the paragraph *individually*.

When correcting student writing, teachers may want to focus primarily on the structures taught in the chapter.

- **LET'S TALK**

  Each Let's Talk activity is set up as one of the following: **pairwork, small group, class activity, interview,** or **game**. Successful language learning requires social interaction, and these tasks encourage students to speak with others about their ideas, their everyday lives, and the world around them. Students tend to speak more easily and freely when they can connect language to their own knowledge and experiences.

- **CHECK YOUR KNOWLEDGE**

  Toward the end of the chapter, students can practice sentence-level editing skills by correcting errors common to this level. The sentences can be done as homework or in small groups.

  This task can easily be set up as a game. The teacher calls out an item number at random. Students work in teams to correct the sentence, and the first team to edit it correctly wins a point.

  See the *Fundamentals of English Grammar Teacher's Guide* for detailed information about teaching from this book, including expansion activities and step-by-step instructions.

Acknowledgments

We couldn't have done this fourth edition without the many talented professionals who assisted us. We began our revision with the insights and suggestions from these reviewers: Michael Berman, Montgomery College; Jeff Bette, Westchester Community College; Mary Goodman, Everest University; Linda Gossard, DPT Business School, Denver; Roberta Hodges, Sonoma State American Language Institute; Suzanne Kelso, Boise State University; Steven Lasswell, Santa Barbara City College; Diane Mahin, University of Miami; Maria Mitchell, DPT Business School, Philadelphia; Monica Oliva, Miami Sunset Adult Center; Amy Parker, University of Michigan; Casey Peltier, Northern Virginia Community College.

We are fortunate to have an outstanding editorial staff who oversaw this book from planning to production. We'd like to thank Shelley Hartle, managing editor extraordinaire, whose meticulous and perceptive editing shaped every page; Amy McCormick, editorial director, whose vision, attentiveness, and care for the series guided our writing; Ruth Voetmann, development editor, for her keen eye, valuable advice, and unfailing patience; Janice Baillie, our outstanding copy-editor who scrutinized and honed every page; Sue Van Etten, our accomplished and very talented business and web-site manager; Robert Ruvo, our skilled and responsive production manager at Pearson Education.

We'd also like to express our appreciation to the writers of the supplementary texts: Rachel Spack Koch, *Workbook;* Kelly Roberts Weibel, *Test Bank;* and Martha Hall, *Teacher's Guide.* They have greatly enriched the series with their innovative ideas and creativity.

Finally, we'd like to thank the dedicated leadership team at Pearson Education that guided this project: Pietro Alongi, Rhea Banker, and Paula Van Ells.

The colorful artwork is due to the inspired talents of Don Martinetti and Chris Pavely.

Finally, we would like to thank our families, who supported and encouraged us every step of the way. They are a continual source of inspiration.

Betty S. Azar
Stacy A. Hagen

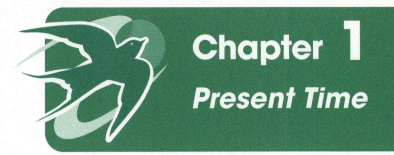

Chapter 1
Present Time

❑ **Exercise 1. Listening and reading.**

Part I. Listen to the conversation between Sam and Lisa. They are college students in California. They are beginning a weeklong training to be resident assistants★ for their dorm. They are interviewing each other. Later they will introduce each other to the group.

SAM: Hi. My name is Sam.

LISA: Hi. I'm Lisa. It's nice to meet you.

SAM: Nice to meet you too. Where are you from?

LISA: I'm from Boston. How about you?

SAM: I'm from Quebec. So, how long have you been here?

LISA: Just one day. I still have a little jet lag.

SAM: Me too. I got in yesterday morning. So — we need to ask each other about a hobby. What do you like to do in your free time?

LISA: I spend a lot of time outdoors. I love to hike. When I'm indoors, I like to surf the Internet.

SAM: Me too. I'm studying Italian right now. There are a lot of good websites for learning languages on the Internet.

LISA: I know. I found a good one for Japanese. I'm trying to learn a little.
Now, when I introduce you to the group, I have to write your full name on the board. What's your last name, and how do you spell it?

SAM: It's Sanchez. S-A-N-C-H-E-Z.

LISA: My last name is Paterson — with one "t": P-A-T-E-R-S-O-N.

SAM: It looks like our time is up. Thanks. It's been nice talking to you.

LISA: I enjoyed it too.

★*resident assistant* = a student who lives in a dormitory and helps other students with everyday life in the dorm; also called an "R.A."

Part II. Read the conversation in Part I. Use the information in the conversation to complete Sam's introduction of Lisa to the class.

SAM: I would like to introduce Lisa Paterson. Lisa is from _Boston_ . She has been here

_____. In her free time, she _____

_____ .

Part III. Now it is Lisa's turn to introduce Sam to the class. What is she going to say? Create an introduction. Begin with *I would like to introduce Sam*.

❑   ## Exercise 2. Let's talk: interview.
Interview a partner. Then introduce your partner to the class. As your classmates are introduced to the class, write their names on a sheet of paper.

Find out your partner's:
   name
   native country or hometown
   free-time activities or hobbies
   favorite food
   reason for being here
   length of time here

❑   ## Exercise 3. Let's write.
Write answers to the questions. Then, with your teacher, decide what to do with your writing. See the list of suggestions at the end of the exercise.

1. What is your name?
2. Where are you from?
3. Where are you living?
4. Why are you here (in this city)?
    a. Are you a student? If so, what are you studying?
    b. Do you work? If so, what is your job?
    c. Do you have another reason for being here?
5. What do you like to do in your free time?
6. What is your favorite season of the year? Why?
7. What are your three favorite TV programs or movies? Why do you like them?
8. Describe your first day in this class.

Suggestions for your writing:
   a. Give it to a classmate to read. Your classmate can then summarize the information in a spoken report to a small group.
   b. Work with a partner and correct errors in each other's writing.
   c. Read your composition aloud in a small group and answer any questions about it.
   d. Hand it in to your teacher, who will correct the errors and return it to you.
   e. Hand it in to your teacher, who will return it at the end of the term when your English has progressed, so you can correct your own errors.

Read the statements and circle *yes* or *no*. Choose responses that are true for you. Share your answers with a partner (e.g., *I use a computer every day.* OR *I don't use a computer every day.*). Your partner will report your information to the class (e.g., *Eric doesn't use a computer every day.*).

1. I use a computer every day.   yes   no

2. I am sitting in front of a computer right now.   yes   no

3. I check emails every day.   yes   no

4. I send text messages several times a day.   yes   no

5. I am sending a text message now.   yes   no

1-1 Simple Present and Present Progressive

Simple Present	(a) Ann *takes* a shower *every day*.	The SIMPLE PRESENT expresses *daily habits* or *usual activities,* as in (a) and (b).
	(b) I *usually read* the newspaper in the morning.	
	(c) Babies *cry*. Birds *fly*.	The simple present expresses *general statements of fact,* as in (c).
	(d) NEGATIVE: It *doesn't snow* in Bangkok.	In general, the simple present is used for events or situations that exist always, usually, or habitually in the past, present, and future.
	(e) QUESTION: *Does* the teacher *speak* slowly?	
Present Progressive	(f) Ann can't come to the phone *right now* because she *is taking* a shower.	The PRESENT PROGRESSIVE expresses *an activity that is in progress (is occurring, is happening) right now.*
	(g) I *am reading* my grammar book *right now*.	The event is in progress at the time the speaker is saying the sentence. The event began in the past, is in progress now, and will probably continue into the future.
	(h) Jimmy and Susie are babies. They *are crying*. I can hear them *right now*. Maybe they are hungry.	FORM: *am, is, are* + *-ing*
	(i) NEGATIVE: It *isn't snowing right now*.	
	(j) QUESTION: *Is* the teacher *speaking* right now?	

1-2 Forms of the Simple Present and the Present Progressive

	Simple Present				Present Progressive			
STATEMENT		I	*work.*			I	*am*	*working.*
		You	*work.*			You	*are*	*working.*
		He, She, It	*works.*			He, She, It	*is*	*working.*
		We	*work.*			We	*are*	*working.*
		They	*work.*			They	*are*	*working.*
NEGATIVE		I	*do*	*not* *work.*		I	*am*	*not* *working.*
		You	*do*	*not* *work.*		You	*are*	*not* *working.*
		He, She, It	*does*	*not* *work.*		He, She, It	*is*	*not* *working.*
		We	*do*	*not* *work.*		We	*are*	*not* *working.*
		They	*do*	*not* *work.*		They	*are*	*not* *working.*
QUESTION	*Do*	I	*work?*		*Am*	I		*working?*
	Do	you	*work?*		*Are*	you		*working?*
	Does	he, she, it	*work?*		*Is*	he, she, it		*working?*
	Do	we	*work?*		*Are*	we		*working?*
	Do	they	*work?*		*Are*	they		*working?*

Contractions

pronoun + *be*	I + *am* = **I'm** working.
	you, we, they + *are* = **You're, We're, They're** working.
	he, she, it + *is* = **He's, She's, It's** working.
do + *not*	*does* + *not* = **doesn't** She **doesn't** work.
	do + *not* = **don't** I **don't** work.
be + *not*	*is* + *not* = **isn't** He **isn't** working.
	are + *not* = **aren't** They **aren't** working.
	(*am* + *not* = am not* I am not working.)

*NOTE: *am* and *not* are not contracted.

❏ **Exercise 5. Listening and grammar.** (Charts 1-1 and 1-2)

Listen to the passage on the next page. Discuss the verbs in *italics*. Is the activity of the verb a usual activity or happening right now (an activity in progress)?

Lunch at the Fire Station

It's 12:30, and the firefighters *are waiting* for their next call. They *are taking* their lunch
                                                    1   2
break. Ben, Rita, and Jada *are sitting* at a table in the fire station. Their co-worker Bruno
                                3
is making lunch for them. He is an excellent cook. He often *makes* lunch. He *is fixing* spicy
   4   5   6
chicken and rice. Their captain *isn't eating*. He *is doing* paperwork. He *skips* lunch on busy
                                      7   8   9
days. He *works* in his office and *finishes* his paperwork.
            10   11

❑ **Exercise 6. Listening.** (Charts 1-1 and 1-2)

Listen to the statements about Irene and her job. Decide if the activity of each verb is a usual
activity or happening right now. Choose the correct answer.

Example: You will hear: Irene works for a video game company.

You will choose: (usual activity)   happening right now

1. usual activity   happening right now

2. usual activity   happening right now

3. usual activity   happening right now

4. usual activity   happening right now

5. usual activity   happening right now

❑ **Exercise 7. Looking at grammar.** (Charts 1-1 and 1-2)

Complete the sentences. Use the simple present or the present progressive form of the verbs
in parentheses.

1. Shhh. The baby (*sleep*) ___is sleeping___. The baby (*sleep*) ___sleeps___ for ten

   hours every night.

2. Right now I'm in class. I (*sit*) _____ at my desk. I usually (*sit*)

   _____ at the same desk in class every day.

3. Ali (*speak*) _____ Arabic. Arabic is his native language, but right

   now he (*speak*) _____ English.

4. A: (*it, rain*) _____ a lot in southern Spain?

   B: No. The weather (*be*) _____ usually warm and sunny.

5. A: Look out the window. (*it, rain*) _____?

   B: It (*start*) _____ to sprinkle.

6. A: Look. It's Yumiko.

   B: Where?

   A: Over there. She (*walk*) _____ out of the café.

7. A: Oscar usually (*walk*) _____ to work.

   (*you, walk*) _____ to work every day too?

   B: Yes.

   A: (*Oscar, walk*) _____ with you?

   B: Sometimes.

❑ **Exercise 8. Let's talk.** (Charts 1-1 and 1-2)
Your teacher will ask one student to perform an action and another student to describe it using the present progressive.

Example: stand next to your desk
To STUDENT A: Would you please stand next to your desk? (*Student A stands up.*)
To STUDENT B: Who is standing next to his/her desk? OR What is (Student A) doing?
STUDENT B: (Student A) is standing next to his/her desk.

1. stand up	7. erase the board
2. smile	8. hold your pen in your left hand
3. whistle	9. knock on the door
4. open or close the door	10. scratch your head
5. read your grammar book	11. count aloud the number of people in the classroom
6. shake your head "no"	12. look at the ceiling

❑ **Exercise 9. Listening.** (Charts 1-1 and 1-2)
Listen to the questions. Write the words you hear.

A problem with the printer

Example: You will hear: Is the printer working?
          You will write: ___*Is*___ the printer working?

1. _____ need more paper?

2. _____ have enough ink?

3. _____ fixing it yourself?

4. _____ know how to fix it?

5. _____ have another printer in the office?

6. Hmmm. Is it my imagination or _____ making a strange noise?

❑ **Exercise 10. Game: trivia.** (Charts 1-1 and 1-2)
Work in small groups. Complete each sentence with the correct form of the verb in parentheses. Then circle "T" for true or "F" for false. The group with the most correct answers wins.*

1. In one soccer game, a player (*run*) _____ seven miles on average.   T   F

2. In one soccer game, players (*run*) _____ seven miles on average.   T   F

3. Right-handed people (*live*) _____ 10 years longer than left-handed people.   T   F

4. Mountains (*cover*) _____ 3% of Africa and 25% of Europe.   T   F

5. The Eiffel Tower (*have*) _____ 3,000 steps.   T   F

6. Honey (*spoil*) _____ after one year.   T   F

7. The letter "e" (*be*) _____ the most common letter in English.   T   F

8. It (*take*) _____ about seven seconds for food to get from our mouths to our stomachs.   T   F

9. A man's heart (*beat*) _____ faster than a woman's heart.   T   F

10. About 145,000 people in the world (*die*) _____ every 24 hours.   T   F

❑ **Exercise 11. Let's talk.** (Charts 1-1 and 1-2)
Work with a partner. Take turns describing your pictures to each other and finding the differences. Use the present progressive. Partner A: Cover Partner B's pictures in your book. Partner B: Cover Partner A's pictures in your book.

Example:

Partner A   **Partner B**

PARTNER A: In my picture, the airplane is taking off.
PARTNER B: In my picture, the airplane is landing.

*See *Trivia Answers,* p. 421.

Partner A

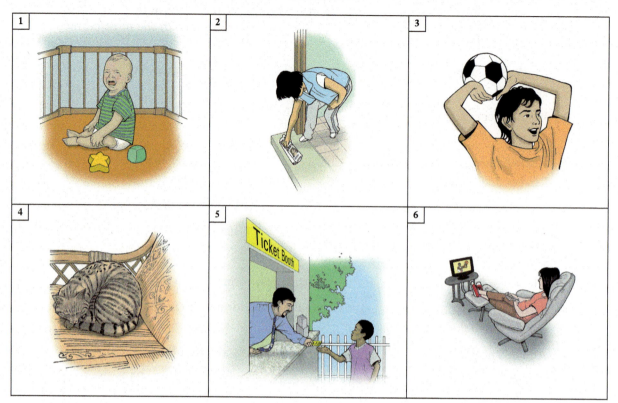

Partner B

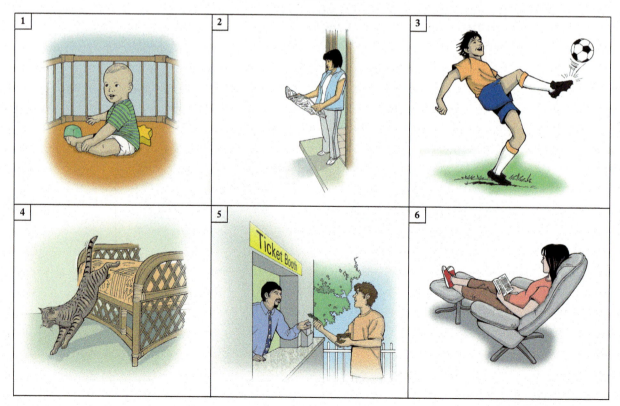

❑ **Exercise 12. Let's read and write.** (Charts 1-1 and 1-2)

Part I. Read the paragraph and answer the questions.

Hair Facts

Here are some interesting facts about our hair. Human hair grows about one-half inch per month or 15 centimeters a year. The hair on our scalp is dead. That's why it doesn't hurt when we get a haircut. The average person has about 100,000 strands of hair.* Every day we lose 75 to 150 strands of hair. One strand of hair grows for two to seven years. After it stops growing, it rests for a while and then falls out. Hair grows faster in warmer weather, and women's hair grows faster than men's hair.

Questions:
1. How fast does hair grow?
2. Why don't haircuts hurt?
3. About how many strands of hair are on your head right now?
4. Where is a good place to live if you want your hair to grow faster?

Part II. Choose one part of the body, for example: fingernails, skin, eyebrows, eyes, heart, lungs, etc. Make a list of interesting facts about this part of the body. Organize the facts into a paragraph. Begin with the given topic sentence. *Note:* If you are researching information on the Internet, search this topic: "interesting _____ facts" (e.g., interesting hair facts).

Topic sentence: Here are some interesting facts about our _____ .

❑ **Exercise 13. Warm-up.** (Chart 1-3)

How often do you do each activity? Give the percentage (0% → 100%). Your teacher will ask which ones you always do, sometimes do, or never do.

1. _____ I take the bus to school.

2. _____ I go to bed late.

3. _____ I skip breakfast.

4. _____ I eat vegetables at lunch time.

5. _____ I cook my own dinner.

6. _____ I am an early riser.**

---

strands of hair = pieces of hair

**early riser* = a person who gets up early in the morning

1-3 Frequency Adverbs

100% ▲
 	
 positive {
 always
 almost always
 usually
 often
 frequently
 generally
 sometimes
 occasionally
 	
 50%
 	
 negative {
 seldom
 rarely
 hardly ever
 almost never
 not ever, never
 	
 0% ▼
	Frequency adverbs usually occur in the middle of a sentence and have special positions, as shown in examples (a) through (e) below.
	
	 The adverbs in **boldface** may also occur at the beginning or the end of a sentence.
	
	    I sometimes get up at 6:30.
	    Sometimes I get up at 6:30.
	    I get up at 6:30 sometimes.
	
	 The other adverbs in the list (not in boldface) rarely occur at the beginning or the end of a sentence. Their usual position is in the middle of a sentence.

S + FREQ ADV + V (a) Karen *always* *tells* the truth.	Frequency adverbs usually come between the subject and the simple present verb except main verb *be*. *INCORRECT: Always Karen tells the truth.*
S + BE + FREQ ADV (b) Karen *is* *always* on time.	Frequency adverbs follow *be* in the simple present (*am, is, are*) and simple past (*was, were*).
(c) Do *you always* eat breakfast?	In a question, frequency adverbs come directly after the subject.
(d) Ann *usually doesn't eat* breakfast.	In a negative sentence, most frequency adverbs come in front of a negative verb (except *always* and *ever*).
(e) Sue *doesn't always eat* breakfast.	***Always*** follows a negative helping verb, as in (e), or a negative form of *be*.
(f) CORRECT: Anna *never eats* meat. *INCORRECT: Anna doesn't never eat meat.*	Negative adverbs (*seldom, rarely, hardly ever, never*) are NOT used with a negative verb.
(g) — *Do* you *ever take* the bus to work? — Yes, I do. I often take the bus.	***Ever*** is used in questions about frequency, as in (g). It means "at any time."
(h) I *don't ever* walk to work. *INCORRECT: I ever walk to work.*	***Ever*** is also used with ***not***, as in (h). ***Ever*** is NOT used in statements.

❑ **Exercise 14. Grammar and speaking.** (Chart 1-3)

Part I. Look at your answers in Exercise 13. Make complete sentences using the appropriate frequency word from Chart 1-3.

Example: 1. 0% = ***I never*** *take the bus to school.* OR

               50% = ***I sometimes*** *take the bus to school.*

Part II. Walk around the room and find people who do the activities with the same frequency as you.

Example:
SPEAKER A: I **always** take the bus to school. Do you **always** take the bus to school?
SPEAKER B: No, I don't. I **sometimes** take the bus to school. Do you **usually** go to bed late?
SPEAKER A: Yes, I do. I **usually** go to bed late.

□ **Exercise 15. Let's talk.** (Chart 1-3)
Answer the questions. Discuss the meaning of the frequency adverbs.

What is something that . . .
1. you seldom do?
2. a polite person often does?
3. a polite person never does?
4. our teacher frequently does in class?
5. you never do in class?
6. you rarely eat?
7. you occasionally do after class?
8. drivers generally do?
9. people in your country always or usually do to celebrate the New Year?

□ **Exercise 16. Looking at grammar.** (Chart 1-3)
Add the given adverbs to each sentence. Put the adverbs in their usual midsentence position.
Make any necessary changes to the sentence.

Example: Emily doesn't get to work on time.
a. usually → Emily **usually** doesn't get to work on time.
b. often → Emily **often** doesn't get to work on time.

1. Kazu doesn't shave in the morning.
   a. frequently   d. always   g. hardly ever
   b. occasionally   e. ever   h. rarely
   c. sometimes   f. never   i. seldom

2. I don't eat breakfast.
   a. usually   c. seldom
   b. always   d. ever

3. My roommate isn't home in the evening.
   a. generally   c. always
   b. sometimes   d. hardly ever

Exercise 17. Looking at grammar. (Chart 1-3)

Complete the sentences using the information in the chart. Use a frequency adverb in each sentence to describe Mia's weekly activities.

Mia's Week	S	M	Tu	W	Th	F	S
1. wake up early				x			
2. make breakfast		x	x		x		
3. go to the gym	x	x		x		x	x
4. be late for the bus		x	x	x	x		
5. cook dinner	x	x	x	x	x	x	x
6. read a book	x	x	x	x		x	x
7. do homework			x			x	
8. go to bed early							

1. Mia ___seldom / rarely wakes___ up early.

2. She _____ breakfast.

3. She _____ to the gym.

4. She _____ late for the bus.

5. She _____ dinner.

6. She _____ a book.

7. She _____ her homework.

8. She _____ to bed early.

□ ## Exercise 18. Let's talk: pairwork. (Charts 1-1 → 1-3)

Work with a partner. Use frequency adverbs to talk about yourself and to ask your partner questions.

Example: walk to school
PARTNER A (*book open*): I usually walk to school. How about you? Do you usually walk to school?
PARTNER B (*book closed*): I usually walk to school too. OR
I seldom walk to school. I usually take the bus.

1. wear a suit to class
2. go to sleep before 11:00 P.M.
3. get at least one email a day
4. read in bed before I go to sleep
5. speak to people who sit next to me on an airplane

Change roles.

6. wear a hat to class
7. believe the things I hear in the news
8. get up before nine o'clock in the morning
9. call my family or a friend if I feel homesick or lonely
10. have chocolate ice cream for dessert

□ **Exercise 19. Warm-up.** (Chart 1-4)
Combine the given words into sentences. Add **-s** where necessary. Do not add any other words.

1. A dolphin \ swim

2. Dolphin \ swim

1-4 Singular/Plural

(a) SINGULAR: *one bird*	SINGULAR = one, not two or more
(b) PLURAL: *two birds, three birds, many birds, all birds, etc.*	PLURAL = two, three, or more
(c) Bird**s** sing.	**A plural noun** ends in **-s**, as in (c).
(d) A bird sing**s**.	**A singular verb** ends in **-s**, as in (d).
(e) A *bird* *sings* outside my window. *It* *sings* loudly. *Ann* *sings* beautifully. *She* *sings* songs to her children. *Tom* *sings* very well. *He* *sings* professionally.	A singular verb follows a singular subject. Add **-s** to the simple present verb if the subject is (1) a singular noun (e.g., *a bird, Ann, Tom*) or (2) *he, she,* or *it.**

**He, she,* and *it* are third person singular personal pronouns. See Chart 6-10, p. 164, for more information about personal pronouns.

□ **Exercise 20. Looking at grammar.** (Chart 1-4)
Look at each word that ends in **-s**. Is it a noun or verb? Is it singular or plural?

Sentence	Noun	Verb	Sing.	Plural
1. Plants grow quickly in warm weather.	x			x
2. Ali lives in an apartment.		x	x	
3. Bettina listens to the radio every morning.				
4. The students at this school work hard.				
5. An ambulance takes sick people to the hospital.				
6. Ambulances take sick people to the hospital.				
7. Cell phones offer text-messaging.				
8. The earth revolves around the sun.				

Exercise 21. Listening. (Chart 1-4)

Listen to the statements. Add **-s** where necessary. Write Ø if no **-s** is needed.

Natural disasters: a flood

1. The weather ___Ø___ cause ___s___ some natural disaster ___s___.

2. Heavy rains sometimes create _____ flood _____.

3. A big flood _____ cause _____ a lot of damage.

4. In town _____, flood _____ can damage building _____, home _____, and road _____.

5. After a flood _____, a town _____ need _____ a lot of financial help for repair _____.

❑ **Exercise 22. Warm-up.** (Chart 1-5)

Write the third person form for each verb under the correct heading. Can you figure out the rules for when to add **-s**, **-es**, and **-ies**?

| mix | speak | stay | study | take | try | wish |

Add **-s** only.   Add **-es**.   Add **-ies**.

_____   _____   _____

_____   _____   _____

_____

1-5 Spelling of Final -s/-es

(a)	visit	→	*visits*	Final **-s**, not **-es**, is added to most verbs.
	speak	→	*speaks*	INCORRECT: *visites, speakes*
(b)	ride	→	*rides*	Many verbs end in **-e**. Final **-s** is simply added.
	write	→	*writes*	
(c)	catch	→	*catches*	Final **-es** is added to words that end in **-ch**, **-sh**, **-s**, **-x**, and **-z**.
	wash	→	*washes*	
	miss	→	*misses*	PRONUNCIATION NOTE:
	fix	→	*fixes*	Final **-es** is pronounced /əz/ and adds a syllable.*
	buzz	→	*buzzes*	
(d)	fly	→	*flies*	If a word ends in a consonant + **-y**, change the **-y** to **-i** and add **-es**, as in (d).
				INCORRECT: *flys*
(e)	pay	→	*pays*	If a word ends in a vowel + **-y**, simply add **-s**,** as in (e).
				INCORRECT: *paies* or *payes*
(f)	go	→	*goes*	The singular forms of the verbs **go**, **do**, and **have** are irregular.
	do	→	*does*	
	have	→	*has*	

*See Chart 6-1, p. 147, for more information about the pronunciation of final **-s/-es**.

**Vowels = a, e, i, o, u. Consonants = all other letters in the alphabet.

Exercise 23. Looking at grammar. (Charts 1-4 and 1-5)

<u>Underline</u> the verb(s) in each sentence. Add final **-s/-es** if necessary. Do not change any other words.

1. A frog <u>jump</u>ˢ.
2. Frogs <u>jump</u>. → (*no change*)
3. A boat float on water.
4. Rivers flow toward the sea.
5. My mother worry about me.
6. A student buy a lot of books at the beginning of each term.
7. Airplanes fly all around the world.
8. The teacher ask us a lot of questions in class every day.
9. Mr. Cook watch game shows on TV every evening.
10. Water freeze at 32°F (0°C) and boil at 212°F (100°C).
11. Mrs. Taylor never cross the street in the middle of a block. She always walk to the corner and use the crosswalk.

Exercise 24. Grammar and listening. (Chart 1-5)

Add **-s/-es/-ies** to the verbs. Check your answers with a partner. Listen to the pronunciation of the verbs.

1. talk ˢ_____
2. fish ᵉˢ_____
3. hope _____
4. teach _____
5. move _____

6. kiss _____
7. push _____
8. wait _____
9. mix _____
10. bow _____

11. study _____
12. buy _____
13. enjoy _____
14. try _____
15. carry _____

Exercise 25. Let's talk: pairwork. (Chart 1-5)

Work with a partner. Look at the pictures and make conversations. Take turns being Partner A and Partner B. Follow this model. Use *he, she,* or *they* as appropriate.

PARTNER A: What is he doing?
PARTNER B: He _____.
PARTNER A: Does he _____ often?
PARTNER B: No, he doesn't. He rarely _____.

❑ **Exercise 26. Game.** (Charts 1-4 and 1-5)
Your teacher will assign each student an item number. (If there are fewer than 24 students, some students will have two numbers. If there are more than 24 students, some students will have the same number.) Find your number in the list and write the words that appear beside it on a slip of paper. Then close your book.

Walk around the classroom and say your words to other classmates. You are looking for the other half of your sentence. When you find the person with the other half, combine the information on both of your slips of paper into a sentence.

Write the sentence on the board or on a piece of paper. Make changes to the verb if necessary.

Example: 1. A star
  2. shine in the sky at night
    → *A star shines in the sky at night.*

1. A car
2. causes air pollution.
3. stretch when you pull on it.
4. A hotel
5. support a huge variety of marine life.
6. A bee
7. Does exercise
8. cause great destruction when it reaches land.
9. A river
10. improves your health?

11. An elephant
12. A hurricane
13. produce one-fourth of the world's coffee.
14. Oceans
15. use its long trunk like a hand to pick things up.
16. Brazil
17. supply its guests with clean towels.
18. A rubber band
19. collects nectar* from flowers.
20. flows downhill.

❑ **Exercise 27. Warm-up.** (Chart 1-6)
Circle the correct completions.

CHARLIE: Shhh! I _____ something on our roof.
    a. hear   b. am hearing

  I _____ there is a person up there.
    a. think   b. am thinking

DAD: I _____.
    a. don't know   b. am not knowing

  It _____ more like a small animal, maybe a cat or squirrel.
    a. sounds   b. is sounding

---

*nectar = a sugary liquid inside flowers

1-6 Non-Action Verbs

(a) I **know** Ms. Chen. INCORRECT: *I am knowing Ms. Chen.* (b) I'm hungry. I **want** a sandwich. INCORRECT: *I am wanting a sandwich.* (c) This book **belongs** to Mikhail. INORRECT: *This book is belonging to Mikhail.*	Some verbs are generally not used in progressive tenses. These verbs are called "non-action verbs."* They express a situation that exists, not an action in progress.

Non-action Verbs

hear	believe	be	own	need	like	forget
see	think	exist	have	want	love	remember
sound	understand		possess	prefer	hate	
	know	seem	belong			agree
	mean	look like				disagree

COMPARE: (d) I **think** that grammar is easy. (e) I **am thinking** about grammar right now. (f) Tom **has** a car. (g) I'**m having** a good time.	***Think*** and ***have*** can be used in the progressive. In (d): When ***think*** means "believe," it is non-progressive. In (e): When ***think*** expresses thoughts that are going through a person's mind, it can be progressive. In (f): When ***have*** means "own" or expresses possession, it is not used in the progressive. In (g): In expressions where ***have*** does not mean "own" (e.g., *have a good time, have a bad time, have trouble, have a problem, have lunch, have a snack, have company, have an operation*), ***have*** can be used in the progressive.

*Non-action verbs are also called "non-progressive" or "stative" verbs.

❑ **Exercise 28. Looking at grammar.** (Chart 1-6)
Choose the correct responses.

1. A: What do you like better: coffee or tea?
   B: I _____ tea.
      a. am preferring (b.) prefer

2. A: Can you help me set the table for dinner?
   B: In a minute. I _____ my report.
      a. am finishing b. finish

3. A: Are you busy?
   B: I _____ a few minutes.
      a. have b. am having

4. A: _____ a good time?
      a. Are you having b. Do you have
   B: Yes, I _____ myself.
      a. am enjoying b. I enjoy

5. A: There's goes Salma on her new racing bike.
    B: Yeah, she really _____ bikes.
        a. is loving   b. loves
    A: That's for sure! She _____ several.
        a. is owning   b. owns

❑ **Exercise 29. Looking at grammar.** (Chart 1-6)
Complete the sentences with the simple present or present progressive form of **think** and **have**.

1. A: How is your new job going?
    B: Pretty good. I (*think*) ___think___ I am doing okay.

2. A: You look upset. What's on your mind?
    B: I'm worried about my daughter. I (*think*) _____ she's in trouble.

3. A: You look far away.* What's on your mind?
    B: I (*think*) _____ about my vacation next week. I can't wait!

4. A: Hey, there! How's the party going?
    B: Great! We (*have*) _____ a lot of fun.

5. A: Could I borrow some money?
    B: Sorry, I only (*have*) _____ a little change** on me.

❑ **Exercise 30. Looking at grammar.** (Chart 1-6)
Complete the sentences. Use the simple present or present progressive form of the verbs in parentheses.

1. Right now I (*look*) ___am looking___ out the window. I (*see*) ___see___ a window washer on a ladder.

2. A: (*you, need*) _____ some help, Mrs. Bernini?

        (*you, want*) _____ me to carry that box for you?

    B: Yes, thank you. That's very nice of you.

3. A: Who is that man? I (*think*) _____ that I (*know*) _____ him, but I (*forget*) _____ his name.

    B: That's Mr. Martinez.

    A: That's right! I (*remember*) _____ him now.

---

*look far away = look like you are thinking about other things; daydream

**change = coins

4. A: (*you, believe*) _____ in ghosts?

   B: No. In my opinion, ghosts (*exist*) _____ only in people's

   imaginations.

5. Right now the children (*be*) _____ at the beach. They (*have*)

   _____ a good time. They (*have*) _____

   shovels, and they (*build*) _____ a sandcastle. They (*like*)

   _____ to build big sandcastles. Their parents (*lie*)

   _____ on the beach and (*listen*) _____

   to music. They (*listen, not*) _____ to their children's

   conversations, but they (*hear*) _____ them anyway.

☐ **Exercise 31. Warm-up.** (Chart 1-7)
Choose the correct response for each question.

1. Does Janet eat fish?
   a. Yes, she does.   b. Yes, she is.   c. Yes, she eats.

2. Do you eat fish?
   a. No, I don't.   b. No, I am not.   c. No, I don't eat.

3. Are you vegetarian?
   a. Yes, I do.   b. Yes, I am.   c. Yes, I like.

1-7 Present Verbs: Short Answers to Yes/No Questions

	Question	Short Answer	Long Answer
QUESTIONS WITH *DO/DOES*	*Does* Bob *like* tea?	Yes, he *does*. No, he *doesn't*.	Yes, he likes tea. No, he doesn't like tea.
	Do you *like* tea?	Yes, I *do*. No, I *don't*.	Yes, I like tea. No, I don't like tea.
QUESTIONS WITH *BE*	*Are* you *studying*?	Yes, I *am*.* No, I'*m not*.	Yes, I am (I'm) studying. No, I'm not studying.
	Is Yoko a *student*?	Yes, she *is*.* No, she'*s not*. OR No, she *isn't*.	Yes, she is (she's) a student. No, she's not a student. OR No, she isn't a student.
	Are they *studying*?	Yes, they *are*.* No, they'*re not*. OR No, they *aren't*.	Yes, they are (they're) studying. No, they're not studying. OR No, they aren't studying.

Am, is, and *are* are NOT contracted with pronouns in short answers.

  INCORRECT SHORT ANSWERS: *Yes, I'm. Yes, she's. Yes, they're.*

❑ ### Exercise 32. Looking at grammar. (Chart 1-7)
Complete the conversations. Use the simple present or present progressive form of the verbs in parentheses. Give short answers to the questions as necessary.

1. A: (*Tanya, have*) __Does Tanya__ have a bike?

    B: Yes, __she does__. She (*have*) __has__ a racing bike.

2. A: (*it, rain*) _____ right now?

    B: No, _____. At least, I (*think, not*) _____ so.

3. A: (*your friends, write*) _____ a lot of emails?

    B: Yes, _____. I (*get*) _____ lots of emails all the time.

4. A: (*the weather, affect**) _____ your mood?

    B: Yes, _____. I (*get*) _____ grumpy when it's rainy.

---

*The word *affect* is a verb: *The weather **affects** my mood.*
  The word *effect* is a noun: *Warm, sunny weather has a good **effect** on my mood.*

5. A: *(Jean, study)* _____ at the library this evening?

    B: No, _____. She *(be)* _____ at the gym. She

      (play) _____ table tennis with her friend.

    A: *(Jean, play)* _____ table tennis every evening?

    B: No, _____. She usually *(study)* _____ at the library.

    A: *(she, be)* _____ a good player?

    B: Yes, _____. She *(play)* _____ table tennis a lot.

    A: *(you, play)* _____ table tennis?

    B: Yes, _____. But I *(be, not)* _____ very good.

❏ **Exercise 33. Listening.** (Chart 1-7)

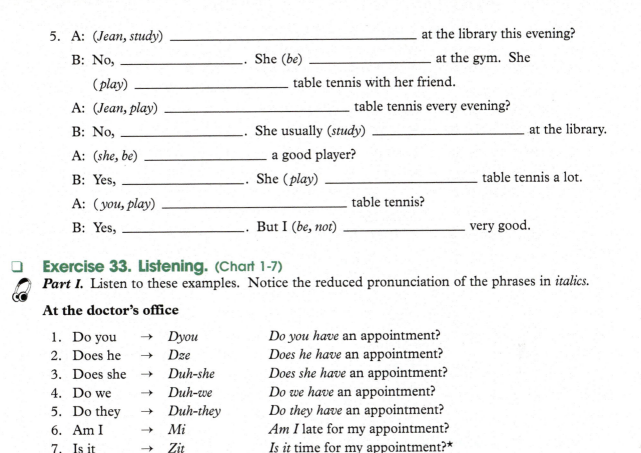

Part I. Listen to these examples. Notice the reduced pronunciation of the phrases in *italics*.

At the doctor's office

1.	Do you	→ *Dyou*	*Do you have* an appointment?
2.	Does he	→ *Dze*	*Does he have* an appointment?
3.	Does she	→ *Duh-she*	*Does she have* an appointment?
4.	Do we	→ *Duh-we*	*Do we have* an appointment?
5.	Do they	→ *Duh-they*	*Do they have* an appointment?
6.	Am I	→ *Mi*	*Am I* late for my appointment?
7.	Is it	→ *Zit*	*Is it* time for my appointment?★
8.	Does it	→ *Zit*	*Does it* hurt?

Part II. Complete each question with the unreduced form of the words you hear.

Example: You will hear: Do you want to tell me what the problem is?

           You will write: _____*Do you*_____ want to tell me what the problem is?

1. _____ have pain anywhere?

2. _____ hurt anywhere else?

3. _____ have a cough or sore throat?

4. _____ have a fever?

5. _____ need lab tests?

6. _____ very sick?

7. _____ serious?

8. _____ need to make another appointment?

9. _____ want to wait in the waiting room?

10. _____ pay now or later?

★See Chapter 5 for more examples of questions with *be* in spoken English.

Exercise 34. Let's talk: interview. (Chart 1-7)
Make questions with the given words. Then walk around the room and ask and answer
questions. Your answers should have both a short and a long response.

Example: be \ Texas \ in South America?
SPEAKER A: Is Texas in South America?
SPEAKER B: No, it isn't. Texas is in North America.

1. the earth \ revolve \ around the sun \ right now?
2. the moon \ revolve \ around the earth \ every 28 days?
3. be \ the sun and moon planets?
4. be \ Toronto in western Canada?
5. whales \ lay \ eggs?
6. your country \ have \ gorillas in the wild?
7. be \ gorillas \ intelligent?
8. mosquitoes \ carry \ malaria?
9. you \ like \ vegetarian food?
10. be \ our teacher \ from Australia?
11. it \ rain \ outside \ right now?
12. be \ you \ tired of this interview?

Exercise 35. Listening. (Chart 1-7)
Choose the correct responses.

Example: You will hear: You look hot and tired. Are you thirsty?
You will choose: (a.) Yes, I am.
b. Yes, I do.

1. a. Yes, I want.   4. a. Yes, we do.
   b. Yes, I do.   b. Yes, we need.

2. a. Yes, I am.   5. a. Yes, he does.
   b. Yes, I do.   b. Yes, he is.

3. a. Yes, it is.   6. a. Yes, they are.
   b. Yes, it does.   b. Yes, they do.

Exercise 36. Looking at grammar. (Chapter 1)
Complete the sentences. Use the simple present or the present progressive form of the verbs
in parentheses.

1. A: My sister (*have*) __*has*__ a new car. She bought it last month.

   B: (*you, have*) __*Do you have*__ a car?

   A: No, I __*don't*__. Do you?

   B: No, but I have a motorcycle.

2. A: What are the children doing? (they, watch) _____ TV?

   B: No, they _____. They (play) _____ outside.

3. A: Jacob, (you, listen) _____ to me?

   B: Of course I am, Mom. You (want) _____ me to take out the garbage. Right?

   A: Yes, and I mean now!

4. A: Hey, Becky, where (be) _____ you?

   B: I (be) _____ in the bedroom.

   A: What (you, do) _____?

   B: I (try) _____ to sleep!

5. A: What (you, think) _____ about at night before you fall asleep?

   B: I (think) _____ about my day. But I (think, not) _____ about anything negative. What (think) _____ about?

   A: I (think, not) _____ about anything. I (count) _____ sheep.*

6. A: A penny for your thoughts.

   B: Huh?

   A: That means: What (you, think) _____ about right now?

   B: I (think) _____ about my homework. I (think, not) _____ _____ about anything else right now.

   A: I (believe, not) _____ you. You (think) _____ about your wedding plans!

7. A: (you, know) _____ any tongue-twisters?

   B: Yes, I _____. Here's one: She sells seashells down by the seashore.

   A: That (be) _____ hard to say! Can you say this: Sharon wears Sue's shoes to zoos to look at cheap sheep?

   B: That (make, not) _____ any sense.

   A: I (know) _____, but it's fun to say.

---

*count sheep = fall asleep naturally by closing your eyes and counting imaginary sheep

❏ **Exercise 37. Reading, grammar, and listening. (Chapter 1)**

Part I. Read the passage and choose the correct completions.

Aerobic Exercise

Jeremy and Nancy believe exercise is important. They go to an exercise class three times a week. They like aerobic exercise.

Aerobic exercise is a special type of exercise. It increases a person's heart rate. Fast walking, running, and dancing are examples of aerobic exercise. During aerobic exercise, a person's heart beats fast. This brings more oxygen to the muscles. Muscles work longer when they have more oxygen.

Right now Jeremy and Nancy are listening to some lively music. They are doing special dance steps. They are exercising different parts of their body.

How about you? Do you like to exercise? Do your muscles get exercise every week? Do you do some type of aerobic exercise?

1. Jeremy and Nancy (*think,*) *are thinking* exercise is good for them.

2. They *prefer, are preferring* aerobic exercise.

3. Aerobic exercise *makes, is making* a person's heart beat fast.

4. Muscles *need, are needing* oxygen.

5. With more oxygen, muscles *work, are working* longer.

6. Right now Jeremy and Nancy *do, are doing* a special kind of dance.

7. *Do you exercise, Are you exercising* every week?

8. *Do you exercise, Are you exercising* right now?

🎧 *Part II.* Listen to the passage and complete the sentences with the words you hear. Cover Part I with a piece of paper.

Aerobic Exercise

Jeremy and Nancy _____ exercise is important. They _____ to
                          1   2
an exercise class three times a week. They _____ aerobic exercise.
                                                3

Aerobic exercise _____ a special type of exercise. It _____ a
                      4   5
person's heart rate. Fast walking, running, and dancing _____ examples of aerobic
                                                              6
exercise. During aerobic exercise, a person's heart _____ fast. This
                                                          7
_____ more oxygen to the muscles. Muscles _____ longer when they
       8   9
_____ more oxygen.
    10

Right now Jeremy and Nancy _____ to some lively music. They
                                      11
_____ special dance steps. They _____ different
            12   13
parts of their body.

How about you? _____ you _____ to exercise? _____ your
                        14   15   16
muscles _____ exercise every week? _____ you _____ some type
                17   18   19
of aerobic exercise?

❑   **Exercise 38. Check your knowledge.** (Chapter 1)
Edit the passage to correct errors in verb tense usage.

Omar's Visit

                                      owns
    (1) My friend Omar ~~is owning~~ his own car now. It's brand new.* Today he driving to a
small town north of the city to visit his aunt. He love to listen to music, so the CD player is
play one of his favorite CDs — loudly. Omar is very happy: he is drive his own car and listen
to loud music. He's look forward to his visit with his aunt.

    (2) Omar is visiting his aunt once a week. She's elderly and live alone. She is thinking
Omar a wonderful nephew. She love his visits. He try to be helpful and considerate in every
way. His aunt don't hearing well, so Omar is speaks loudly and clearly when he's with her.

    (3) When he's there, he fix things for her around her apartment and help her with her
shopping. He isn't staying with her overnight. He usually is staying for a few hours and then is
heading back to the city. He kiss his aunt good-bye and give her a hug before he is leaving.
Omar is a very good nephew.

_____

brand new = completely new

Chapter 2
Past Time

❑ **Exercise 1. Warm-up.** (Chart 2-1)
Check (✓) the statements that are true for you. Share your answers with a partner.

1. _____ I stayed up late last night.
2. _____ I slept well last night.
3. _____ I was tired this morning.

2-1 Expressing Past Time: The Simple Past

(a) Mary **walked** downtown *yesterday*. (b) I **slept** for eight hours *last night*.	The simple past is used to talk about activities or situations that began and ended in the past (e.g., *yesterday, last night, two days ago, in 2010*).
(c) Bob **stayed** home yesterday morning. (d) Our plane **landed** on time last night.	Most simple past verbs are formed by adding **-ed** to a verb, as in (a), (c), and (d).
(e) I **ate** breakfast this morning. (f) Sue **took** a taxi to the airport yesterday.	Some verbs have irregular past forms, as in (b), (e), and (f). See Chart 2-4.
(g) I **was** busy yesterday. (h) They **were** at home last night.	The simple past forms of **be** are **was** and **were**.

Forms of the Simple Past: Regular Verbs

STATEMENT	I, You, She, He, It, We, They **worked** yesterday.
NEGATIVE	I, You, She, He, It, We, They **did not** (**didn't**) **work** yesterday.
QUESTION	**Did** I, you, she, he, it, we, they **work** yesterday?
SHORT ANSWER	Yes, I, you, she, he, it, we, they **did**. OR No, I, you, she, he, it, we, they **didn't**.

Forms of the Simple Past: *Be*

STATEMENT	I, She, He, It **was** in class yesterday. We, You, They **were** in class yesterday.
NEGATIVE	I, She, He, It **was not** (**wasn't**) in class yesterday. We, You, They **were not** (**weren't**) in class yesterday.
QUESTION	**Was** I, she, he, it in class yesterday? **Were** we, you, they in class yesterday?
SHORT ANSWER	Yes, I, she, he, it **was**. Yes, we, you, they **were**. No, I, she, he, it **wasn't**. No, we, you, they **weren't**.

❏ **Exercise 2. Looking at grammar.** (Chart 2-1)
Create your own chart by writing the negative and question forms of the words in *italics*. Omit the rest of each sentence.

	Negative	Question
1. *He needed* water.	He didn't need	Did he need
2. *She drank* tea.		
3. *They played* baseball.		
4. *I left* early.		
5. *They wore* boots.		
6. *We had* time.		
7. *It was* fun.		
8. *You were* late.		

❏ **Exercise 3. Let's talk.** (Chart 2-1)
All of the sentences contain inaccurate information. Make true statements by
   (1) making a negative statement and
   (2) making an affirmative statement using accurate information.

1. Thomas Edison invented the telephone.
   → *Thomas Edison didn't invent the telephone.*
   → *Alexander Graham Bell invented the telephone.*
2. I came to school by hot-air balloon today.
3. The students in this class swam into the classroom today.
4. (*Teacher's name*) is a movie director.
5. I slept in a tree last night.
6. The Internet became popular in the 1970s.

❏ **Exercise 4. Listening.** (Chapter 1 and Chart 2-1)
Listen to each sentence. Choose the correct completion(s). More than one completion may be possible.

Example: You will hear: It snows . . .
           You will choose: (in the winter.)   every day.   now.

1. French.	together.	last week.
2. right now.	yesterday.	last summer.
3. in the evening.	last night.	behind the mountains.
4. at this moment.	our class.	yesterday.
5. two weeks ago.	right now.	at this moment.

❑ **Exercise 5. Listening.** (Chart 2-1)

The differences between **was/wasn't** and **were/weren't** can be hard to hear in spoken English. The "t" in the negative contraction is often dropped, and you may only hear an /n/ sound.

Part I. Listen to these examples.

1. I was in a hurry. I wasn't in a hurry.
2. They were on time. They weren't on time.
3. He was at the doctor's. He wasn't at the doctor's.
4. We were early. We weren't early.

Part II. Circle the words you hear. Before you begin, you may want to check your understanding of these words: *wedding, nervous, excited, ceremony, reception.*

At a wedding

1. was	wasn't		6.	was	wasn't
2. was	wasn't		7.	was	wasn't
3. were	weren't		8.	was	wasn't
4. were	weren't		9.	were	weren't
5. was	wasn't		10.	were	weren't

❑ **Exercise 6. Warm-up.** (Chart 2-2)

Do you know the spelling rules for these verbs?

Part I. Write the **-ing** form of each verb under the correct heading.

die	give	hit	try

Drop final **-e**. Add **-ing**.	Double final consonant. Add **-ing**.	Change **-ie** to **-y**. Add **-ing**.	Just add **-ing**.
_____	_____	_____	_____

Part II. Write the **-ed** form of each verb under the correct heading.

enjoy	tie	stop	study

Double final consonant. Add **-ed**.	Change **-y** to **-i**. Add **-ed**.	Just add **-ed**.	Just add **-d**.
_____	_____	_____	_____

2-2 Spelling of *-ing* and *-ed* Forms

End of Verb	Double the Consonant?	Simple Form	*-ing*	*-ed*	
-e	NO	(a) smile hope	smiling hoping	smiled hoped	*-ing* form: Drop the *-e,* add *-ing.* *-ed* form: Just add *-d.*
Two Consonants	NO	(b) help learn	helping learning	helped learned	If the verb ends in two consonants, just add *-ing* or *-ed.*
Two Vowels + One Consonant	NO	(c) rain heat	raining heating	rained heated	If the verb ends in two vowels + a consonant, just add *-ing* or *-ed.*
One Vowel + One Consonant	YES	**ONE-SYLLABLE VERBS**			If the verb has one syllable and ends in one vowel + one consonant, double the consonant to make the *-ing* or *-ed* form.*
		(d) stop plan	stopping planning	stopped planned	
	NO	**TWO-SYLLABLE VERBS**			If the first syllable of a two-syllable verb is stressed, do not double the consonant.
		(e) vísit óffer	visiting offering	visited offered	
	YES	(f) prefér admít	preferring admitting	preferred admitted	If the second syllable of a two-syllable verb is stressed, double the consonant.
-y	NO	(g) play enjoy	playing enjoying	played enjoyed	If the verb ends in a vowel + *-y,* keep the *-y.* Do not change the *-y* to *-i.*
		(h) worry study	worrying studying	worried studied	If the verb ends in a consonant + *-y,* keep the *-y* for the *-ing* form, but change the *-y* to *-i* to make the *-ed* form.
-ie		(i) die tie	dying tying	died tied	*-ing* form: Change the *-ie* to *-y* and add *-ing.* *-ed* form: Just add *-d.*

*EXCEPTIONS: Do not double "w" or "x": *snow, snowing, snowed, fix, fixing, fixed.*

□ **Exercise 7. Looking at spelling.** (Chart 2-2)
Write the *-ing* and *-ed* forms of these verbs.

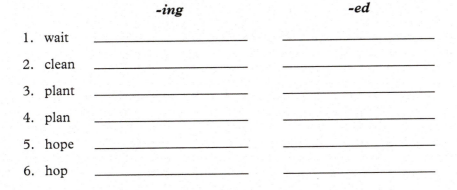

	-ing	*-ed*
1. wait	_____	_____
2. clean	_____	_____
3. plant	_____	_____
4. plan	_____	_____
5. hope	_____	_____
6. hop	_____	_____

7. play   _____   _____

8. study   _____   _____

9. try   _____   _____

10. die   _____   _____

11. sleep   _____   _slept (no -ed)_

12. run   _____   _ran (no -ed)_

❑ **Exercise 8. Listening.** (Chart 2-2)

Complete the sentences with the verbs you hear. Pay special attention to spelling.

1. Shhh. The movie is _____.

2. Oh, no. The elevator door is stuck. It isn't _____.

3. Here's a letter for you. I _____ it accidentally.

4. I'm _____ to the phone message that you already _____ to.

5. Are you _____ to me or telling me the truth?

6. We _____ the party.

7. I'm _____ the nice weather today.

8. You look upset. What _____?

❑ **Exercise 9. Warm-up.** (Charts 2-3 and 2-4)

There are four main parts to a verb. Can you complete the chart?

Simple Form	Simple Past	Past Participle	Present Participle
1. help	_helped_	_helped_	_helping_
2. stay	_____	_____	_____
3. take	_took_	_taken_	_taking_
4. give	_____	_____	_____
5. be	_____	_____	_____

2-3 The Principal Parts of a Verb

Regular Verbs

SIMPLE FORM	SIMPLE PAST	PAST PARTICIPLE	PRESENT PARTICIPLE
finish	finished	finished	finishing
stop	stopped	stopped	stopping
hope	hoped	hoped	hoping
wait	waited	waited	waiting
play	played	played	playing
try	tried	tried	trying

Irregular Verbs

see	saw	seen	seeing
make	made	made	making
sing	sang	sung	singing
eat	ate	eaten	eating
put	put	put	putting
go	went	gone	going

Principal Parts of a Verb

(1) THE SIMPLE FORM	English verbs have four principal forms, or "parts." **The simple form** is the form that is found in a dictionary. It is the base form with no endings on it (no final *-s*, *-ed*, or *-ing*).
(2) THE SIMPLE PAST	**The simple past** ends in *-ed* for regular verbs. Most verbs are regular, but many common verbs have irregular past forms. See the reference list of irregular verbs that follows in Chart 2-4.
(3) THE PAST PARTICIPLE	**The past participle** also ends in *-ed* for regular verbs. Some verbs are irregular. It is used in perfect tenses (Chapter 4) and the passive (Chapter 10).
(4) THE PRESENT PARTICIPLE	**The present participle** ends in *-ing* (for both regular and irregular verbs). It is used in progressive tenses (e.g., the present progressive and the past progressive).

2-4 Common Irregular Verbs: A Reference List

SIMPLE FORM	SIMPLE PAST	PAST PARTICIPLE	SIMPLE FORM	SIMPLE PAST	PAST PARTICIPLE
be	was, were	been	lend	lent	lent
beat	beat	beaten	let	let	let
become	became	become	lie	lay	lain
begin	began	begun	light	lit/lighted	lit/lighted
bend	bent	bent	lose	lost	lost
bite	bit	bitten	make	made	made
blow	blew	blown	mean	meant	meant
break	broke	broken	meet	met	met
bring	brought	brought	pay	paid	paid
build	built	built	put	put	put
burn	burned/burnt	burned/burnt	quit	quit	quit
buy	bought	bought	read	read	read
catch	caught	caught	ride	rode	ridden
choose	chose	chosen	ring	rang	rung
come	came	come	rise	rose	risen
cost	cost	cost	run	ran	run
cut	cut	cut	say	said	said
dig	dug	dug	see	saw	seen
do	did	done	sell	sold	sold
draw	drew	drawn	send	sent	sent
dream	dreamed/dreamt	dreamed/dreamt	set	set	set
drink	drank	drunk	shake	shook	shaken
drive	drove	driven	shoot	shot	shot
eat	ate	eaten	shut	shut	shut
fall	fell	fallen	sing	sang	sung
feed	fed	fed	sink	sank	sunk
feel	felt	felt	sit	sat	sat
fight	fought	fought	sleep	slept	slept
find	found	found	slide	slid	slid
fit	fit	fit	speak	spoke	spoken
fly	flew	flown	spend	spent	spent
forget	forgot	forgotten	spread	spread	spread
forgive	forgave	forgiven	stand	stood	stood
freeze	froze	frozen	steal	stole	stolen
get	got	got/gotten	stick	stuck	stuck
give	gave	given	swim	swam	swum
go	went	gone	take	took	taken
grow	grew	grown	teach	taught	taught
hang	hung	hung	tear	tore	torn
have	had	had	tell	told	told
hear	heard	heard	think	thought	thought
hide	hid	hidden	throw	threw	thrown
hit	hit	hit	understand	understood	understood
hold	held	held	upset	upset	upset
hurt	hurt	hurt	wake	woke/waked	woken/waked
keep	kept	kept	wear	wore	worn
know	knew	known	win	won	won
leave	left	left	write	wrote	written

□ **Exercise 10. Looking at grammar.** (Chart 2-4)
Complete the sentences. Use the simple past of any irregular verb that makes sense.
More than one answer may be possible.

1. Alima walked to the office today. Rebecca _____drove_____ her car. Olga
_____ her bike. Yoko _____ the bus.

2. It got so cold last night that the water in the pond _____.

3. Katya had a choice between a blue raincoat and a brown one. She finally
_____ the blue one.

4. My husband gave me a painting for my birthday. I _____ it on a wall in
my office.

5. Last night around midnight, when I was sound asleep, the telephone _____.
It _____ me up.

6. The sun _____ at 6:04 this morning and _____ at 6:59 last
night.

7. I _____ an email to my cousin after I finished studying last night.

8. Ms. Morita _____ chemistry at the local high school last year.

9. Oh, my gosh! Call the police! Someone _____ my car!

10. The police _____ the car thieves quickly and _____ them
to jail.

11. The earthquake was strong, and the ground _____ for two minutes.

12. A bird _____ into the grocery store through an open door.

13. My dog _____ a hole in the yard and buried his bone.

14. I don't have any money in my wallet. I _____ it all
yesterday. I'm flat broke.*

15. Ann does funny things. She _____ a tuxedo to her
brother's wedding last week.

_____

*flat broke = completely out of money

❑ **Exercise 11. Looking at grammar.** (Charts 2-1 → 2-4)
Create your own chart by writing the simple past, negative, and question forms of the words in *italics*. Omit the rest of each sentence.

	Simple Past	Negative	Question
1. *He skips* lunch.	*He skipped*	*He didn't skip*	*Did he skip*
2. *They leave* early.			
3. *She does* a lot.			
4. *He is* sick.			
5. *We drive* to work.			
6. *You are* right.			
7. *I plan* my day.			

❑ **Exercise 12. Let's talk: pairwork.** (Charts 2-1 → 2-4)
Work with a partner. Answer the questions with **Yes** and a complete sentence.

A broken arm

Imagine that you came to class today with a big cast on your arm. You slipped on some ice yesterday and fell down.

1. Did you have a bad day yesterday? → *Yes, I had a bad day yesterday.*
2. Did you fall down?
3. Did you hurt yourself when you fell down?
4. Did you break your arm?
5. Did you go to the emergency room?

Change roles.
6. Did you see a doctor?
7. Did you sit in the waiting room for a long time?
8. Did the doctor put a cast on your arm?
9. Did you pay a lot of money?
10. Did you come home exhausted?

❑ **Exercise 13. Looking at grammar.** (Charts 2-1 → 2-4)
Complete the conversations with the correct form of the words in parentheses.

1. A: (*you, sleep*) __Did you sleep__ well last night?

   B: Yes, __I did__. I (*sleep*) __slept__ very well.

2. A: (*Ella's plane, arrive*) _____ on time yesterday?

   B: Yes, _____. It (*get*) _____ in at exactly 6:05.

3. A: (*you, go*) _____ away last weekend?

   B: No, _____. I (*stay*) _____ home because I (*feel, not*) _____ good.

4. A: (*you, eat*) _____ breakfast this morning?

   B: No, _____. I (*have, not*) _____ enough time. I was late for class because my alarm clock (*ring, not*) _____.

5. A: (*Da Vinci, paint*) _____ the *Mona Lisa*?

   B: Yes, _____. He also (*paint*) _____ other famous pictures.

❏ **Exercise 14. Looking at grammar.** (Charts 2-1 → 2-4)
Read the facts about each person. Complete the sentences with the correct form of the given verbs.

SITUATION 1: Whirlwind Wendy is energetic and does everything very quickly. Here is her typical morning.

Activities:
   wake up at 4:00 A.M.
   clean her apartment
   ride her bike five miles
   get vegetables from her garden
   watch a cooking show on TV
   make soup for dinner
   bring her elderly mother a meal
   read the day's paper
   fix herself lunch

Yesterday, Wendy . . .

1. ___woke_____ up at 4:00 A.M.

2. ___didn't clean_____ her car.

3. _____ her bike ten miles.

4. _____ vegetables from her garden.

5. _____ a comedy show on TV.

6. _____ soup for dinner.

7. _____ her elderly mother a meal.

8. _____ a book.

9. _____ herself a snack.

SITUATION 2: Sluggish Sam is lazy and slow. He doesn't get much done in a day. Here is his typical day.

Activities:

sleep for 12 hours
wake up at noon
take two hours to eat breakfast
go fishing
fall asleep on his boat

come home
lie on the couch
think about his busy life
begin dinner at 8:00
finish dinner at 11:00

Yesterday, Sam . . .

1. <u> slept </u> for 12 hours.

2. <u> didn't wake </u> up at 5:00 A.M.

3. _____ two hours to eat breakfast.

4. _____ hiking.

5. _____ asleep on his boat.

6. _____ home.

7. _____ on his bed.

8. _____ about his busy life.

9. _____ dinner at 5:00.

10. _____ dinner at 11:00.

❑ **Exercise 15. Let's talk: pairwork.** (Charts 2-1 → 2-4)
Work with a partner. Partner A tells Partner B to perform an action. After Partner B does this, A will ask B a question in the past tense.

Example: Open your book.
PARTNER A: Open your book.
PARTNER B: (*opens his/her book*)
PARTNER A: What did you do?
PARTNER B: I opened my book.

Change roles.

1. Shut your book.
2. Stand up.
3. Hide your pen.
4. Turn to page 10 in your book.
5. Put your book in your lap.
6. Nod your head "yes."
7. Tear a piece of paper.
8. Spell the past tense of "speak."

9. Write your name on the board.
10. Draw a triangle under your name.
11. Shake your head "no."
12. Invite our teacher to have lunch with us.
13. Read a sentence from your grammar book.
14. Wave "good-bye."
15. Ask me for a pencil.
16. Repeat this question: "Which came first: the chicken or the egg?"

□ Exercise 16. Listening. (Charts 2-1 → 2-4)

Part I. **Did** is often reduced at the beginning of questions. The pronoun that follows **did** may also change. Listen to the reduced pronunciations with **did**.

1. Did you   →   *Did-ja*   Did you forget something?
                   Did-ya   Did you forget something?
2. Did I   →   *Dih-di*   Did I forget something?
                   Di   Did I forget something?
3. Did he   →   *Dih-de*   Did he forget something?
                   De   Did he forget something?
4. Did she   →   *Dih-she*   Did she forget something?
5. Did we   →   *Dih-we*   Did we forget something?
6. Did they   →   *Dih-they*   Did they forget something?

Part II. You will hear questions. Complete each answer with the non-reduced form of the verb you hear.

1. Yes, he ___*did*___. He ___*cut*___ it with a knife.

2. Yes, she _____. She _____ it all yesterday.

3. Yes, I _____. I _____ them yesterday.

4. Yes, they _____. They _____ it.

5. Yes, you _____. You _____ it.

6. Yes, she _____. She _____ them.

7. Yes, he _____. He _____ it to him.

8. Yes, I _____. I _____ them yesterday.

9. Yes, he _____. He _____ it.

10. Yes, you _____. You _____ her.

□ Exercise 17. Listening. (Charts 2-1 → 2-4)

Listen to the questions. Complete each answer with the correct form of the verb you hear.

Luka wasn't home last night.

1. Yes, he ___*went*___ to a party last night.

2. Yes, he _____ a good time.

3. Yes, he _____ a lot of food.

4. Yes, he _____ a lot of soda.

5. Yes, he _____ some new people.

6. Yes, he _____ hands with them when he met them.

7. Yes, he _____ with friends.

8. Yes, he _____ with his friends and _____.

Exercise 18. Looking at grammar. (Charts 2-1 → 2-4)
Rewrite the paragraph. Use the past tense. Begin your new paragraph with *Yesterday morning*.

The Daily News

Every morning, Jake reads the newspaper online. He wants to know the latest news. He enjoys the business section most. His wife, Eva, doesn't read any newspapers on her computer. She downloads them on her ebook* reader. She looks at the front pages first. She doesn't have a lot of time. She finishes the articles later in the day. Both Jake and Eva are very knowledgeable about the day's events.

❑ **Exercise 19. Listening.** (Charts 2-1 → 2-4)

Part I. Answer the questions. Then listen to the passage with your book closed.

Did you get the flu** last year?
Were you very sick?
What symptoms did you have?

Part II. Open your book and read the statements. Circle "T" for true and "F" for false.

1. The flu kills a lot of people worldwide every year.   T   F

2. The flu virus from 1918 to 1920 was a usual flu virus.   T   F

3. Most of the people who died were very young or very old.   T   F

Part III. Listen to the passage again. Complete the sentences with the words you hear.

A Deadly Flu

Every year, the flu _____ 200,000 to 300,000 people around the world. But in
                          1

1918, a very strong flu virus _____ millions of people. This flu _____ in
                                 2   3

1918 and _____ until 1920. It _____ around the world, and between
            4   5

20 million and 100 million people _____. Unlike other flu viruses that usually
                                      6

_____ the very young and the very old, many of the victims _____ healthy
   7   8

young adults. This _____ unusual and _____ people especially afraid.
                      9   10

---

*ebook = electronic book

**the flu = the influenza virus; symptoms usually include fever, aches, tiredness, cough, and runny nose.

❑ **Exercise 20. Warm-up: listening.** (Chart 2-5)

Part I. Listen to each pair of verbs. Decide if the verb endings have the same sound or a different sound.

Example: You will hear: plays played

  You will choose: same (different)

  1. same different   3. same different

  2. same different   4. same different

Part II. Listen to the sentences. They contain past tense verbs. What sound does the **-ed** ending have: /t/, /d/, or /əd/?

Example: You will hear: Jack played a game of tennis.

  You will choose: /t/ (/d/) /əd/

  1. /t/   /d/   /əd/   3. /t/   /d/   /əd/

  2. /t/   /d/   /əd/   4. /t/   /d/   /əd/

2-5 Regular Verbs: Pronunciation of -ed Endings

(a) talked = talk/t/ stopped = stop/t/ hissed = hiss/t/ watched = watch/t/ washed = wash/t/	Final **-ed** is pronounced /t/ after voiceless sounds. You make a voiceless sound by pushing air through your mouth. No sound comes from your throat. Examples of voiceless sounds: /k/, /p/, /s/, /ch/, /sh/.
(b) called = call/d/ rained = rain/d/ lived = live/d/ robbed = rob/d/ stayed = stay/d/	Final **-ed** is pronounced /d/ after voiced sounds. You make a voiced sound from your throat. Your voice box vibrates. Examples of voiced sounds: /l/, /n/, /v/, /b/, and all vowel sounds.
(c) waited = wait/əd/ needed = need/əd/	Final **-ed** is pronounced /əd/ after "t" and "d" sounds. Adding /əd/ adds a syllable to a word.

❑ **Exercise 21. Listening.** (Chapter 1 and Chart 2-5)

Listen to each sentence and choose the verb form you hear.

Example: You will hear: I needed more help.

  You will choose: need   needs   (needed)

  1. agree   agrees   agreed   5. end   ends   ended

  2. agree   agrees   agreed   6. stop   stops   stopped

  3. arrive   arrives   arrived   7. touch   touches   touched

  4. explain   explains   explained

□ **Exercise 22. Listening.** (Chapter 1 and Chart 2-5)

Listen to each sentence and choose the correct completion.

Example: You will hear: We worked in small groups . . .

You will choose: right now.   (yesterday.)

1. every day.   yesterday.

2. right now.   last week.

3. six days a week.   yesterday.

4. now.   last weekend.

5. every day.   yesterday.

6. every day.   yesterday.

□ **Exercise 23. Listening and pronunciation.** (Chart 2-5)

Listen to the past tense pronunciation of each word. Write the **-ed** ending you hear: /t/, /d/, or /əd/. Practice pronouncing the verbs.

1. cooked /t/   5. started /   /   9. added /   /

2. served /   /   6. dropped /   /   10. passed /   /

3. wanted /   /   7. pulled /   /   11. returned /   /

4. asked /   /   8. pushed /   /   12. pointed /   /

□ **Exercise 24. Let's listen and talk.** (Charts 2-1 → 2-5)

Part I. Listen to the conversation between two friends about their weekends and answer the questions.

1. One person had a good weekend. Why?

2. His friend didn't have a good weekend. Why not?

Part II. Complete the conversation with your partner. Use past tense verbs. Practice saying it until you can do it without looking at your book. Then change roles and create a new conversation. Perform one of the conversations for the class.

A: Did you have a good weekend?

B: Yeah, I _____.

A: Really? That sounds like fun!

B: It _____ great! I _____.

How about you? How was your weekend?

A: I _____.

B: Did you have a good time?

A: Yes. / No. / Not really. _____

_____.

❏ **Exercise 25. Warm-up.** (Chart 2-6)
Match the sentences in Column A with the descriptions in Column B.

Column A

1. I looked at the limousine.
   The movie star was waving
   out the window. _____

2. I looked at the limousine.
   The movie star waved at me. _____

Column B

a. First I looked at the limousine.
   Then the movie star waved.

b. First the movie star began waving.
   Then I looked at the limousine.

2-6 Simple Past and Past Progressive

Simple Past	(a) Mary *walked* downtown yesterday.	The SIMPLE PAST is used to talk about *an activity or situation that began and ended at a particular time in the past* (e.g., *yesterday, last night, two days ago, in 2007*), as in (a) and (b).
	(b) I *slept* for eight hours last night.	
Past Progressive	(c) I sat down at the dinner table at 6:00 P.M. yesterday. Tom came to my house at 6:10 P.M. I *was eating* dinner *when Tom came*.	The PAST PROGRESSIVE expresses *an activity that was in progress (was occurring, was happening) at a point of time in the past* (e.g., *at 6:10*) or at the time of another action (e.g., *when Tom came*). In (c): eating was in progress at 6:10; eating was in progress *when Tom came*. FORM: *was/were* + *-ing*
	(d) I went to bed at 10:00. The phone rang at 11:00. I *was sleeping* when the phone rang.	

(e) *When the phone rang*, I was sleeping.	*when* = at that time
(f) The phone rang *while I was sleeping*.	*while* = during that time
	Examples (e) and (f) have the same meaning.

Forms of the Past Progressive

STATEMENT		I, She, He, It	*was working*.
		You, We, They	*were working*.
NEGATIVE		I, She, He, It	*was not* (*wasn't*) *working*.
		You, We, They	*were not* (*weren't*) *working*.
QUESTION	*Was*	I, she, he, it	*working*?
	Were	you, we, they	*working*?
SHORT ANSWER	Yes,	I, she, he, it *was*.	Yes, you, we, they *were*.
	No,	I, she, he, it *wasn't*.	No, you, we, they *weren't*.

Exercise 26. Looking at grammar. (Chart 2-6)
Complete each sentence with the simple past or past progressive form of the verb(s) in parentheses.

1. At 6:00 P.M. Robert sat down at the table and began to eat. At 6:05, Robert (*eat*)

   _____was eating_____ dinner.

2. While Robert (*eat*) _____ dinner, Ann (*come*) _____
   through the door.

3. In other words, when Ann (*come*) _____ through the door, Robert (*eat*)
   _____ dinner.

4. Robert went to bed at 10:30. At 11:00, Robert (*sleep*) _____ .

5. While Robert (*sleep*) _____ , his cell phone (*ring*) _____ .

6. In other words, when his cell phone (*ring*) _____ , Robert (*sleep*)
   _____ .

7. Robert left his house at 8:00 A.M. and (*begin*) _____ to walk to class.

8. While he (*walk*) _____ to class, he (*see*) _____
   Mr. Ito.

9. When Robert (*see*) _____ Mr. Ito, he (*stand*) _____ in his
   driveway. He (*hold*) _____ a broom.

10. Mr. Ito (*wave*) _____ to Robert when he (*see*) _____ him.

❑ **Exercise 27. Looking at grammar.** (Chart 2-6)
Complete the sentences, orally or in writing, using the information in the chart. Use the simple past for one clause and the past progressive for the other.

Activity in Progress	Beth	David	Lily
sit in a café	order a salad	pay a few bills	spill coffee on her lap
stand in an elevator	send a text message	run into an old friend	drop her glasses
swim in the ocean	avoid a shark	saw a dolphin	find a shipwreck

1. While Beth __was sitting__ in a café, she __ordered__ a salad.

2. David __paid__ a few bills while he __was sitting__ in a café.

3. Lily _____ coffee on her lap while she _____ in a café.

4. While Beth _____ in an elevator, she _____ a text message on her cell phone.

5. David _____ an old friend while he _____ in an elevator.

6. Lily _____ her glasses while she _____ in an elevator.

7. Beth _____ a shark while she _____ in the ocean.

8. While David _____ in the ocean, he _____ a dolphin.

9. While Lily _____ in the ocean, she _____ a shipwreck.

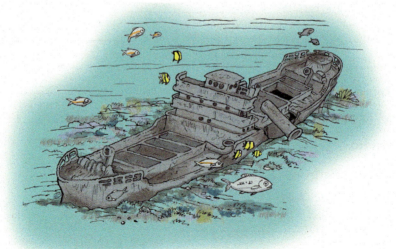

❑ **Exercise 28. Let's talk.** (Chart 2-6)

Your teacher will tell two students to perform a task. After they do, two other students will describe it. Only the teacher's book is open.

Example: To A: Write on the board.   To B: Open the door.

TO STUDENT A: Please write your name on the board. (*Student A writes on the board.*)
                 What are you doing?
STUDENT A: I'm writing on the board.
TEACHER: Good. Keep writing.

TO STUDENT B: Open the door. (*Student B opens the door.*) What did you just do?
STUDENT B: I opened the door.
TO STUDENT A: Please stop writing.

TO STUDENT C: Describe the two actions that just occurred, using *when*.
STUDENT C: When (_____) opened the door, (_____) was writing on the board.

TO STUDENT D: Now describe the actions, using *while*.
STUDENT D: While (_____) was writing on the board, (_____) opened the door.

1. To A: Write a note to (_____).   To B: Knock on the door.
2. To A: Read your book.   To B: Take (_____)'s grammar book.
3. To A: Look at me.   To B: Leave the room.
4. To A: Put your head on your desk.   To B: Drop your pencil.
5. To A: Look under your desk.   To B: Begin doing your homework.

❑ **Exercise 29. Looking at grammar.** (Chart 2-6)

Read each pair of sentences and answer the question.

1. a. Julia was eating breakfast. She heard the breaking news* report.
   b. Sara heard the breaking news report. She ate breakfast.

   QUESTION: Who heard the news report during breakfast?

2. a. Carlo was fishing at the lake. A fish was jumping out of the water.
   b. James was fishing at the lake. A fish jumped out of the water.

   QUESTION: Who saw a fish jump just one time?

3. a. When the sun came out, Paul walked home.
   b. When the sun came out, Vicky was walking home.

   QUESTION: Who walked home after the sun came out?

---

breaking news = a special news report on the TV or radio

Exercise 30. Reading. (Chart 2-6)
Read the passage and then read the statements. Circle "T" for true and "F" for false.

The First Cell Phone

The first cell phone call took place* in 1973. A man named Martin Cooper made the first call. He was working for the Motorola communications company. When Cooper placed the call, he was walking down a street in New York. People stared at him and wondered about his behavior. This was before cordless phones,** so it looked very strange.

It took another ten years before Motorola had a phone to sell to the public. That phone weighed about a pound (.45 kilogram), and it was very expensive. Now, as you know, cell phones are small enough to put in a pocket, and millions of people around the world have them.

1. A customer for Motorola made the first cell phone call.   T   F
2. Many people looked at Cooper when he was talking on the phone.   T   F
3. In the 1970s, cordless phones were very popular.   T   F
4. A few years after the first call, Motorola sold phones to the public. T   F
5. The first cell phone was very small.   T   F

❑ **Exercise 31. Listening.** (Chart 2-6)
Listen to each conversation. Then listen again and complete the sentences with the words you hear.

At a checkout stand in a grocery store

1. A: Hi. _____ what you needed?

   B: Almost everything. I _____ for sticky rice, but I _____ it.

   A: _____ on aisle 10, in the Asian food section.

2. A: This is the express lane. Ten items only. It _____ like you have more than ten. _____ count them?

   B: I _____ I _____ ten. Oh, I _____ I have more. Sorry.

   A: The checkout stand next to me is open.

3. A: _____ any coupons you wanted to use?

   B: I _____ a couple in my purse, but I can't find them now.

   A: What _____ they for? I might have some extras here.

   B: One _____ for eggs, and the other _____ for ice cream.

   A: I think I have those.

---

take place = occur, happen

**cordless phones* = phones without cords to the receiver

□ **Exercise 32. Looking at grammar.** (Charts 1-1 and 2-6)

Underline the present progressive and past progressive verbs in the following conversations. Discuss the way they are used. What are the similarities between the two tenses?

1. A: Where are Jan and Mark? Are they on vacation?
   B: Yes, they're traveling in Kenya for a few weeks.

2. A: I invited Jan and Mark to my birthday party, but they didn't come.
   B: Why not?
   A: They were on vacation. They were traveling in Kenya.

3. A: What was I talking about when the phone interrupted me? I forget!
   B: You were describing the Web site you found on the Internet yesterday.

4. A: I missed the beginning of the news report. What's the announcer talking about?
   B: She's describing damage from the earthquake in Pakistan.

□ **Exercise 33. Looking at grammar.** (Chapter 1 and Charts 2-1 → 2-6)

Complete the sentences. Use the simple present, present progressive, simple past, or past progressive form of the verbs in parentheses.

Part I.

Right now Toshi and Oscar (*sit*) ___are sitting___ in the library. Toshi (*do*)
                                   1

_____ his homework, but Oscar (*study, not*) _____. He
        2   3

(*stare*) _____ out the window. Toshi (*want*) _____ to know
              4   5

what Oscar (*look*) _____ at.
                        6

TOSHI: Oscar, what (*you, look*) _____ at?
                                        7

OSCAR: I (*watch*) _____ the skateboarder. Look at that
                       8

guy in the orange shirt. He (*turn*) _____ around
                                          9

in circles on his back wheels. He's amazing!

TOSHI: It (*be*) _____ easier than it (*look*) _____.
                    10   11

I can teach you some skateboarding basics if you'd like.

OSCAR: Great! Thanks!

Part II.

Yesterday Toshi and Oscar (*sit*) ___were sitting___ in the library. Toshi (*do*)
                                      12

_____ his homework, but Oscar (*study, not*) _____. He
        13   14

(*stare*) _____ out the window. Toshi (*want*) _____ to know
              15   16

what Oscar (*look*) _____ at. Oscar (*point*) _____ to the
                        17   18

skateboarder. He (*say*) _____ that he was amazing. Toshi (*offer*)
                              19

_____ to teach him some skateboarding basics.
        20

❑ **Exercise 34. Warm-up.** (Chart 2-7)
Check (✓) the sentences that have this meaning:
First action: We gathered our bags.
Second action: The train arrived at the station.

1. _____ We gathered our bags before the train arrived at the station.
2. _____ Before the train arrived at the station, we gathered our bags.
3. _____ After we gathered our bags, the train arrived at the station.
4. _____ As soon as the train arrived at the station, we gathered our bags.
5. _____ We didn't gather our bags until the train arrived at the station.

2-7 Expressing Past Time: Using Time Clauses

(a) time clause main clause **After I finished my work,** **I went to bed.**	**After I finished my work** = a time clause* **I went to bed** = a main clause
(b) main clause time clause **I went to bed** **after I finished my work**.	Examples (a) and (b) have the same meaning. A time clause can (1) come in front of a main clause, as in (a). (2) follow a main clause, as in (b).
(c) I went to bed **after** *I finished my work*.	These words introduce time clauses:
(d) **Before** *I went to bed,* I finished my work.	**after** **before** **until** **as soon as** } + *subject and verb* = a time clause **while** **when**
(e) I stayed up **until** *I finished my work*.	
(f) **As soon as** *I finished my work,* I went to bed.	
(g) The phone rang **while** *I was watching* TV.	
(h) **When** *the phone rang,* I was watching TV.	In (e): *until* = to that time and then no longer** In (f): *as soon as* = immediately after
	PUNCTUATION: Put a comma at the end of a time clause when the time clause comes first in a sentence (comes in front of the main clause): *time clause* + *comma* + *main clause* *main clause* + **no** *comma* + *time clause*
(i) When the phone **rang,** I **answered** it.	In a sentence with a time clause introduced by *when*, both the time clause verb and the main verb can be simple past. In this case, the action in the *when*-clause happened first. In (i): First: *The phone rang.* Then: *I answered it.*
(j) While I **was doing** my homework, my roommate **was watching** TV.	In (j): When two actions are in progress at the same time, the past progressive can be used in both parts of the sentence.

*A *clause* is a structure that has a subject and a verb.

Until can also be used to say that something does NOT happen before a particular time: *I didn't go to bed until I finished my work.*

❑ **Exercise 35. Looking at grammar.** (Chart 2-7)
Check (✓) all the clauses. Remember: a clause must have a subject and a complete verb.

1. _____ applying for a visa
2. _____ while the woman was applying for a visa
3. _____ the man took passport photos
4. _____ when the man took passport photos
5. _____ as soon as he finished
6. _____ he needed to finish
7. _____ after she sent her application
8. _____ sending her application

❑ **Exercise 36. Looking at grammar.** (Chart 2-7)
Underline the clauses. Then decide what happened first (1) and what happened second (2).

                                1   *2*

1. a. <u>After the taxi dropped me off</u>, <u>I remembered my coat in the backseat.</u>
   b. I remembered my coat in the backseat after the taxi dropped me off.

2. a. Before I got out of the taxi, I double-checked the address.
   b. Before I double-checked the address, I got out of the taxi.

3. a. As soon as I tipped the driver, he helped me with my luggage.
   b. As soon as the driver helped me with my luggage, I tipped him.

❑ **Exercise 37. Looking at grammar.** (Chart 2-7)
Combine each set of sentences into one sentence by using a time clause. Discuss correct punctuation.

1. *First:* I got home.

   Then: I ate dinner.

   After ___*I got home, I ate dinner.*___

   ___*I ate dinner*___ after ___*I got home.*___

2. *First:* I unplugged the coffee pot.

   Then: I left my apartment this morning.

   Before _____

   _____ before _____

3. *First:* I lived on a farm.

   Then: I was seven years old.

   Until _____

   _____ until _____

4. *First:* I heard the doorbell.

   Then: I opened the door.

   As soon as _____

   _____ as soon as _____

5. *First:* It began to rain.

   Then: I stood under my umbrella.

   When _____

   _____ when _____

6. *At the same time:* I was lying in bed with the flu.

   My friends were swimming at the beach.

   While _____

   _____ while _____

❑ **Exercise 38. Looking at grammar.** (Charts 2-1 → 2-7)
Complete the sentences. Use the simple past or the past progressive form of the verbs in parentheses. Use brackets to identify the time clauses.

1. My mom called me around 5:00. My husband came home a little after that. [When he

   (*get*) __got__ home,] I (*talk*) __was talking__ to my mom on the phone.

2. I (*buy*) _____ a small gift before I (*go*) _____ to the hospital

   yesterday to visit my friend.

3. Yesterday afternoon I (*go*) _____ to visit the Lopez family. When I (*get*)

   _____ there, Mrs. Lopez (*be*) _____ in the yard. She (*plant*)

   _____ flowers. Mr. Lopez (*be*) _____ in the garage.

   He (*change*) _____ the oil on his car. The kids (*play*)

   _____ in the front yard. In other words, while Mr. Lopez (*change*)

   _____ the oil in the car, the kids (*throw*) _____

   a ball in the yard.

4. I (*hit*) _____ my thumb while I (*use*) _____ the hammer.
   Ouch! That (*hurt*) _____.

5. As soon as we (*hear*) _____ about the hurricane, we (*begin*)

   _____ to get ready for the storm.

6. It was a long walk home. Mr. Chu (*get*) _____ tired and (*stop*)

   _____ after an hour. He (*rest*) _____ until he (*feel*)

   _____ strong enough to continue.

Listen to the passage with your book closed. Then listen again and complete the sentences with the words you hear.

Jennifer's Problem

Jennifer _____ for an insurance company. When people _____ help
                        1   2

with their car insurance, they _____ her. Right now it is 9:05 A.M., and Jennifer
                               3

_____ at her desk.
           4

She _____ to work on time this morning. Yesterday Jennifer _____ late
        5   6

to work because she _____ a minor auto accident. While she _____
                        7   8

to work, her cell phone _____. She _____ for it.
                          9   10

While she _____ for her phone, Jennifer _____ control of the
                  11   12

car. Her car _____ into a row of mailboxes beside the road and _____.
                13   14

Fortunately no one was hurt in the accident.

Jennifer _____ okay, but her car _____. It _____ repairs.
            15   16   17

Jennifer _____ very embarrassed now. She _____ a bad decision, especially
            18   19

since it is illegal to talk on a cell phone and drive at the same time where she lives.

❑   **Exercise 40. Warm-up.** (Chart 2-8)

Part I. Think about your experiences when you were a beginning learner of English.
Check (✓) the statements that are true for you.

When I was a beginning learner of English, . . .

1. _____ I remained quiet when someone asked me a question.

2. _____ I checked my dictionary frequently.

3. _____ I asked people to speak very, very slowly.

4. _____ I translated sentences into my language a lot.

Part II. Look at the sentences you checked. Are these statements no longer true? If the
answer is "yes," another way to express your idea is with ***used to***. Which of these sentence(s)
are true for you?

1. I used to remain quiet when someone asked me a question.

2. I used to check my dictionary frequently.

3. I used to ask people to speak very, very slowly.

4. I used to translate sentences into my language a lot.

2-8 Expressing Past Habit: *Used To*

(a) I *used to live* with my parents. Now I live in my own apartment.	*Used to* expresses a past situation or habit that no longer exists at present.
(b) Ann *used to be* afraid of dogs, but now she likes dogs.	FORM: **used to** + *the simple form of a verb*
(c) Al *used to smoke,* but he doesn't anymore.	
(d) *Did* you *used to* live in Paris? (OR *Did* you *use to* live in Paris?)	QUESTION FORM: **did** + *subject* + **used to** (OR **did** + *subject* + **use to**)*
(e) I *didn't used to* drink coffee at breakfast, but now I always have coffee in the morning. (OR I *didn't use to drink* coffee.)	NEGATIVE FORM: **didn't used to** (OR **didn't use to**)* *Didn't use(d) to* occurs infrequently. More commonly, people use *never* to express a negative idea with *used to,* as in (f).
(f) I *never used to* drink coffee at breakfast, but now I always have coffee in the morning.	

*Both forms (**used to** and **use to**) are possible in questions and negatives. English language authorities do not agree on which is preferable. This book uses both forms.

❑ **Exercise 41. Looking at grammar.** (Chart 2-8)
Make sentences with a similar meaning by using ***used to***. Some of the sentences are negative, and some of them are questions.

1. *When I was a child, I was shy. Now I'm not shy.*

   I ___used to be___ shy, but now I'm not.

2. *When I was young, I thought that people over 40 were old.*

   I _____ that people over 40 were old.

3. *Now you live in this city. Where did you live before you came here?*

   Where _____ ?

4. *Did you work for the phone company at some time in the past?*

   _____ for the phone company?

5. *When I was younger, I slept through the night. I never woke up in the middle of the night.*

   I _____ in the middle of the night, but now I do.

   I _____ through the night, but now I don't.

6. *When I was a child, I watched cartoons on TV. I don't watch cartoons anymore. Now I watch news programs.*

   I _____ cartoons on TV, but I don't anymore.

   I _____ news programs, but now I do.

7. *How about you?*

   What _____ on TV when you were little?

❑ **Exercise 42. Interview: find someone who . . . .** (Chart 2-8)

Walk around the classroom. Make a question with ***used to*** for each item. When you find a person who says *"yes,"* write down his/her name and go on to the next question. Share a few of your answers with the class.

Find someone who used to . . .

1. play in the mud. → *Did you use to play in the mud?*
2. play with dolls or toy soldiers.
3. roller skate.
4. swing on a rope swing.
5. catch frogs or snakes.
6. get into trouble at school.
7. dress up in your mother's or father's clothes.

❑ **Exercise 43. Listening.** (Chart 2-8)

Used to is often pronounced "usta." Listen to the examples. Then complete the sentences with the non-reduced words you hear.

Examples: I used to (*usta*) ride my bike to work, but now I take the bus.
I didn't used to (*usta*) be late when I rode my bike to work.
Did you use to (*usta*) ride your bike to work?

1. I ___*used to stay*___ up past midnight, but now I often go to bed at 10:00 because I have an 8:00 class.

2. What time _____ to bed when you were a child?

3. Tom _____ tennis after work every day, but now he doesn't.

4. I _____ breakfast, but now I always have something to eat in the morning because I read that students who eat breakfast do better in school.

5. I _____ grammar, but now I do.

❑ **Exercise 44. Check your knowledge.** (Chart 2-8)

Edit the sentences. Correct the errors in verb tense usage.

1. Alex used to ~~living~~ *live* in Cairo.

2. Junko used to worked for an investment company.

3. Margo was used to teach English, but now she works at a publishing company.

4. Where you used to live?

5. I didn't was used to get up early, but now I do.

6. Were you used to live in Singapore?

7. My family used to going to the beach every weekend, but now we don't.

Part I. Read the passage about a famous author. Then read the statements. Circle "T" for true and "F" for false.

J. K. Rowling

   Did you know that J. K. Rowling used to be an English language teacher before she became successful as the author of the *Harry Potter* series? She taught English to students in Portugal. She lived there from 1991 to 1994. During that time, she also worked on her first *Harry Potter* book.

   After she taught in Portugal, she went back to Scotland. By then she was a single mother with a young daughter. She didn't have much money, but she didn't want to return to teaching until she completed her book. Rowling enjoyed drinking coffee, so she did much of her writing in a café while her daughter took naps. She wrote quickly, and when her daughter was three, Rowling finished *Harry Potter and the Philosopher's Stone.*★

   Many publishers were not interested in her book. She doesn't remember how many rejection letters she got, maybe twelve. Finally a small publishing company, Bloomsbury, accepted it. Shortly after its publication, the book began to sell quickly, and Rowling soon became famous. Now there are seven *Harry Potter* books, and Rowling is one of the wealthiest and most successful women in the world.

1.	Rowling finished the first *Harry Potter* book in 1993.	T	F
2.	Rowling did a lot of writing in a café.	T	F
3.	At first, publishers loved her work.	T	F
4.	Soon after her book came out, many people bought it.	T	F
5.	Rowling still works as a teacher.	T	F

Part II. Choose a writer or a singer you are interested in. Find information about this person's life. Make a list of important or interesting events. Put the information into a paragraph. Edit your verbs carefully.

★In the United States and India, this title was changed to *Harry Potter and the Sorcerer's Stone.*

Chapter 3
Future Time

❑ **Exercise 1. Warm-up.** (Chart 3-1)
Which sentences express future meaning? Do the future sentences have the same meaning or a different meaning?

1. The train is going to leave a few minutes late today.
2. The train left a few minutes late today.
3. The train will leave a few minutes late today.

3-1 Expressing Future Time: *Be Going To* and *Will*		
Future	(a) I *am going to leave* at nine tomorrow morning. (b) I *will leave* at nine tomorrow morning.	*Be going to* and *will* are used to express future time. Examples (a) and (b) have the same meaning. Sometimes *will* and *be going to* express different meanings. The differences are discussed in Chart 3-5.
(c) Sam *is* in his office *this morning*. (d) Ann *was* in her office *this morning* at eight, but now she's at a meeting. (e) Bob *is going to be* in his office *this morning* after his dentist appointment.		*Today*, *tonight*, and *this* + *morning*, *afternoon*, *evening*, *week*, etc., can express present, past, or future time, as in (c) through (e).

NOTE: The use of *shall* (with *I* or *we*) to express future time is possible but is infrequent and quite formal; for example: *I shall leave at nine tomorrow morning*. *We shall leave at ten tomorrow morning*.

Exercise 2. Listening. (Chart 3-1)

Listen to each sentence. If it expresses future time, circle *yes*. If it does not, circle *no*.

Example: You will hear: The airport will be busy.
You will choose: (yes) no

At the airport

1. yes no	5. yes no
2. yes no	6. yes no
3. yes no	7. yes no
4. yes no	8. yes no

❑ **Exercise 3. Warm-up.** (Chart 3-2)

Complete these future sentences (*be going to*) with the correct form of *be* (+ *not*). Make true statements.

1. I _____ going to sleep in* tomorrow morning.

2. Our teacher _____ going to retire next month.

3. We _____ going to have a class party next week.

4. *To a student next to you:* You _____ going to speak English tomorrow.

3-2 Forms with *Be Going To*	
(a) We *are going to be* late.	**Be going to** is followed by the simple form of the verb, as in (a) and (b).
(b) She *'s going to come* tomorrow. INCORRECT: *She's going to comes tomorrow.*	
(c) *Am* I *Is* he, she, it } *going to be* late? *Are* they, we, you	QUESTION FORM: *be* + subject + *going to*
(d) I *am not* He, She, It *is not* } *going to be* late. They, We, You *are not*	NEGATIVE FORM: *be* + *not* + *going to*
(e) "Hurry up! We're *gonna* be late!"	**Be going to** is more common in speaking and informal writing than in formal writing. In informal speaking, it is sometimes pronounced "gonna" /gənə/. "Gonna" is not usually a written form.

---

sleep in = sleep late; not wake up early in the morning

❑ **Exercise 4. Looking at grammar.** (Charts 3-1 and 3-2)
Complete the sentences with a form of **be going to** and the words in parentheses.

1. A: What (*you, do*) ___are you going to do___ next?
   B: I (*pick*) _____ up a prescription at the pharmacy.

2. A: Where (*Alex, go*) _____ after work?
   B: He (*stop*) _____ at the post office and run
   some other errands.*

3. A: (*you, finish*) _____ the project soon?
   B: Yes, (*finish*) _____ it by noon today.

4. A: What (*Dr. Ahmad, talk*) _____ about in her
   lecture tonight?
   B: She (*discuss*) _____ how to reduce health-care costs.

5. A: When (*you, call*) _____ your sister?
   B: I (*call, not*) _____ her. I (*text*) _____
   _____ her.

❑ **Exercise 5. Let's talk: pairwork.** (Charts 3-1 and 3-2)
Work with a partner. Take turns asking and answering questions with **be going to.**

Example: what \ you \ do \ after class?
SPEAKER A: What are you going to do after class?
SPEAKER B: I'm going to get a bite to eat** after class.

Example: you \ watch TV \ tonight?
SPEAKER A: Are you going to watch TV tonight?
SPEAKER B: Yes, I'm going to watch TV tonight. OR No, I'm not going to watch TV tonight.

1. where \ you \ go \ after your last class \ today?
2. what time \ you \ wake up \ tomorrow?
3. what \ you \ have \ for breakfast \ tomorrow?
4. you \ be \ home \ this evening?
5. where \ you \ be \ next year?
6. you \ become \ famous \ some day?
7. you \ take \ a trip \ sometime next year?
8. you \ do \ something unusual \ in the near future?

---

*run errands = go somewhere to pick up or deliver something

**get a bite to eat = get something to eat

Part I. Listen to the pronunciation of the reduced forms of *going to* in the conversation.

Looking for an apartment

A: We're going to look for an apartment to rent this weekend.

B: Are you going to look in this area?

A: No, we're going to search in an area closer to our jobs.

B: Is the rent going to be cheaper in that area?

A: Yes, apartment rents are definitely going to be cheaper.

B: Are you going to need to pay a deposit?

A: I'm sure we're going to need to pay the first and last month's rent.

Part II. Listen to the conversation and write the non-reduced form of the words you hear.

A: Where ___*are you going to*___ move to?
         ₁

B: We _____ look for something outside the city. We
              ₂

_____ spend the weekend apartment-hunting.*
       ₃

A: What fees _____ need to pay?
                    ₄

B: I think we _____ need to pay the first and last month's rent.
                    ₅

A: _____ there _____ be other fees?
       ₆   ₇

B: There _____ probably _____ be an application fee and a
              ₈   ₉

cleaning fee. Also, the landlord _____ probably _____ run a
                                        ₁₀   ₁₁

credit check,** so we _____ need to pay for that.
                           ₁₂

❏ **Exercise 7. Let's talk: interview.** (Chapters 1 and 2; Charts 3-1 and 3-2)
Walk around the room. Ask and answer questions using **what** + **do** + the given time
expression. Share some of your classmates' answers with the class.

Example: this evening
SPEAKER A: What are you going to do this evening?
SPEAKER B: I'm going to get on the Internet for a while.

1. yesterday
2. tomorrow
3. right now
4. every day
5. a week from now

6. the day before yesterday
7. the day after tomorrow
8. last week
9. every week
10. this weekend

---

*apartment-hunting = looking for an apartment

**run a credit check = get information about a person's financial history including the employer's name, one's income, the
amount of money in the bank, and a history of late or unpaid bills

❑ **Exercise 8. Let's talk: pairwork.** (Chapters 1 and 2; Charts 3-1 and 3-2)
Work with a partner. Complete the conversation with your own words. Be creative! The conversation reviews the forms (statement, negative, question, short answer) of the simple present, simple past, and **be going to**.

Example:
SPEAKER A: I rode a skateboard to school yesterday.
SPEAKER B: Really? Wow! Do you ride a skateboard to school often?
SPEAKER A: Yes, I do. I ride a skateboard to school almost every day.
             Did you ride a skateboard to school yesterday?
SPEAKER B: No, I didn't. I came by helicopter.
SPEAKER A: Are you going to come to school by helicopter tomorrow?
SPEAKER B: No, I'm not. I'm going to ride a motorcycle to school tomorrow.

A: I _____ yesterday.

B: Really? Wow! _____ you _____ often?

A: Yes, I _____ . I _____ almost every day.

    _____ you _____ yesterday?

B: No, I _____ . I _____ .

A: Are you _____ tomorrow?

B: No, I _____ . I _____ tomorrow.

❑ **Exercise 9. Warm-up.** (Chart 3-3)
Complete the sentences with **will** or **won't**.

1. It _____ rain tomorrow.

2. We _____ study Chart 3-3 next.

3. I _____ teach the class next week.

4. *To your teacher:* You _____ need to assign homework for tonight.

3-3 Forms with *Will*

STATEMENT	I, You, She, He, It, We, They **will come** tomorrow.	
NEGATIVE	I, You, She, He, It, We, They **will not** (**won't**) **come** tomorrow.	
QUESTION	**Will** I, you, she, he, it, we, they **come** tomorrow?	
SHORT ANSWER	Yes, } No, } I, you, she, he, it, we, they { **will**.* { **won't**.	
CONTRACTIONS	I **'ll** she **'ll** we **'ll** you **'ll** he **'ll** they **'ll** it **'ll**	**Will** is usually contracted with pronouns in both speech and informal writing.
	Bob + **will** = "Bob **'ll**" the teacher + **will** = "the teacher **'ll**"	**Will** is often contracted with nouns in speech, but usually not in writing.

*Pronouns are NOT contracted with helping verbs in short answers.
 CORRECT: *Yes, I will.*
 INCORRECT: *Yes, I'll.*

☐ **Exercise 10. Listening.** (Chart 3-3)

Part I. Listen to the pronunciation of contractions with *will* in these sentences.

1. I'll be ready to leave soon.
2. You'll need to come.
3. He'll drive us.
4. She'll come later.
5. We'll get there a little late.
6. They'll wait for us.

Part II. Listen to the sentences and write the contractions you hear.

1. Don't wait up for me tonight. ___*I'll*___ be home late.

2. I paid the bill this morning. _____ get my check in the next day or two.

3. We have the better team. _____ probably win the game.

4. Henry twisted his ankle while running down a hill. _____ probably take a break from running this week.

5. We can go to the beach tomorrow, but _____ probably be too cold to go swimming.

6. I invited some guests for dinner. _____ probably get here around seven.

7. Karen is doing volunteer work for a community health-care clinic this week. _____ be gone a lot in the evenings.

Part I. Listen to the sentences. Notice the pronunciation of contractions with nouns + *will*.

At the doctor's office

1. The doctor'll be with you in a few minutes.
2. Your appointment'll take about an hour.
3. Your fever'll be gone in a few days.
4. Your stitches'll disappear over the next two weeks.
5. The nurse'll schedule your tests.
6. The lab'll have the results next week.
7. The receptionist at the front desk'll set up* your next appointment.

Part II. Listen to the sentences and write the words you hear. Write the full form of the contractions.

At the pharmacy

1. Your prescription ___will be___ ready in ten minutes.

2. The medicine _____ you feel a little tired.

3. The pharmacist _____ your doctor's office.

4. This cough syrup _____ your cough.

5. Two aspirin _____ enough.

6. The generic** drug _____ less.

7. This information _____ all the side effects*** for this medicine.

❏ **Exercise 12. Warm-up.** (Chart 3-4)

How certain is the speaker in each sentence? Write the percentage next to each sentence: 100%, 90%, or 50%.

What is going to happen to gasoline prices?

1. _____ Gas prices may rise.
2. _____ Maybe gas prices will rise.
3. _____ Gas prices will rise.
4. _____ Gas prices will probably rise.
5. _____ Gas prices are going to rise.
6. _____ Gas prices won't rise.

___

**set up = schedule

**generic = medicine with no brand name

***side effects = reactions, often negative, that a patient can have from a medicine*

3-4 Certainty About the Future

100% sure	(a) I *will be* in class tomorrow. OR I *am going to be* in class tomorrow.	In (a): The speaker uses *will* or *be going to* because he feels sure about his future activity. He is stating a fact about the future.
90% sure	(b) Po *will probably be* in class tomorrow. OR Po *is probably going to be* in class tomorrow.	In (b): The speaker uses *probably* to say that he expects Po to be in class tomorrow, but he is not 100% sure. He's almost sure, but not completely sure.
	(c) Anna *probably won't be* in class tomorrow. OR Anna *probably isn't going to be* in class tomorrow.	Word order with *probably:** (1) in a statement, as in (b): *helping verb* + *probably* (2) with a negative verb, as in (c): *probably* + *helping verb*
50% sure	(d) Ali *may come* to class tomorrow. OR Ali *may not come* to class tomorrow. I don't know what he's going to do.	*May* expresses a future possibility: maybe something will happen, and maybe it won't happen.** In (d): The speaker is saying that maybe Ali will come to class, or maybe he won't come to class. The speaker is guessing.
	(e) *Maybe* Ali *will come* to class, and *maybe* he *won't*. OR *Maybe* Ali *is going to come* to class, and *maybe* he *isn't*.	*Maybe* + *will/be going to* gives the same meaning as *may*. Examples (d) and (e) have the same meaning. *Maybe* comes at the beginning of a sentence.

*Probably is a midsentence adverb. See Chart 1-3, p. 10, for more information about the placement of midsentence adverbs.
**See Chart 7-3, p. 182, for more information about *may*.

□ **Exercise 13. Listening.** (Chart 3-4)
Listen to the sentences. Decide how certain the speaker is in each one: 100%, 90%, or 50%.

Example: You will hear: The bank will be open tomorrow.
You will write: __100%__

My day tomorrow

1. _____
2. _____
3. _____
4. _____
5. _____
6. _____

□ Exercise 14. Looking at grammar. (Chart 3-4)

For each situation, predict what probably will happen and what probably won't happen. Use either **will** or **be going to**. Include **probably** in your prediction.

1. Antonio is late to class almost every day.
   (be on time tomorrow? be late again?)
   → *Antonio probably won't be on time tomorrow. He'll probably be late again.*

2. Rosa has a terrible cold. She feels miserable.
   (go to work tomorrow? stay home and rest?)

3. Sami didn't sleep at all last night.
   (go to bed early tonight? stay up all night again tonight?)

4. Gina loves to run, but right now she has sore knees and a sore ankle.
   (run in the marathon race this week? skip the race?)

□ Exercise 15. Looking at grammar. (Chart 3-4)

Rewrite the sentences using the words in parentheses.

1. I may be late. (*maybe*)

   Maybe I will be late.

2. Lisa may not get here. (*maybe*)

   _____

3. Maybe you will win the contest. (*may*)

   _____

4. The plane may land early. (*maybe*)

   _____

5. Maybe Sergio won't pass the class. (*may*)

   _____

□ Exercise 16. Let's talk: interview. (Chart 3-4)

Walk around the room. Ask and answer questions. Ask two classmates each question. Answer the questions using **will, be going to,** or **may**. Include **probably** or **maybe** as appropriate. Share some of your classmates' answers with the class.

Example: What will you do after class tomorrow?
   → *I'll probably go back to my apartment.* OR *I'm not sure. I may go to the bookstore.*

1. What will the weather be like tomorrow?
2. Where will you be tomorrow afternoon?
3. What are you going to do on your next vacation?
4. Who will be the most famous celebrity next year?
5. What will a phone look like ten years from now?
6. Think about forms of communication (like email, social websites, phone, texting, etc.).
   What do you think will be the most common form ten years from now?
7. When do you think scientists will discover a cure for cancer?

❑ **Exercise 17. Listening.** (Chart 3-4)

Think about life 100 years from now. What will it be like? Listen to each sentence. Do you agree or disagree? Circle *yes* or *no*. Discuss your answers.

Predictions about the future

1.	yes	no	6.	yes	no
2.	yes	no	7.	yes	no
3.	yes	no	8.	yes	no
4.	yes	no	9.	yes	no
5.	yes	no	10.	yes	no

❑ **Exercise 18. Reading, grammar, and speaking.** (Chart 3-4)

Part I. Read the passage.

An Old Apartment

Ted and Amy live in an old, run-down apartment and want to move. The building is old and has a lot of problems. The ceiling leaks when it rains. The faucets drip. The toilet doesn't always flush properly. The windows don't close tightly, and heat escapes from the rooms in the winter. In the summer, it is very hot because there is no air conditioner.

Their apartment is in a dangerous part of town. Ted and Amy both take the bus to work and have to walk a long distance to the bus stop. Their apartment building doesn't have laundry facilities, so they also have to walk to a laundromat to wash their clothes. They are planning to have children in the near future, so they want a park or play area nearby for their children. A safe neighborhood is very important.

Part II. Ted and Amy are thinking about their next apartment and are making a list of what they want and don't want. Complete the sentences with **will** or **won't**.

Our next apartment

1. It ___won't___ have leaky faucets.

2. The toilet _____ flush properly.

3. It _____ have windows that close tightly.

4. There _____ be air-conditioning for hot days.

5. It _____ be in a dangerous part of town.

6. It _____ be near a bus stop.

7. There _____ be laundry facilities in the building.

8. We _____ need to walk to a laundromat.

9. A play area _____ be nearby.

Part III. Imagine you are moving to a new home. Decide the six most important things you want your home to have (*It will have . . .*). You can brainstorm ideas in small groups and then discuss your ideas with the class.

❑ **Exercise 19. Warm-up.** (Chart 3-5)
In which conversation does Speaker B have a prior plan (a plan made before the moment of speaking)?

1. A: Oh, are you leaving?
   B: Yes. I'm going to pick up my children at school. They have dentist appointments.

2. A: Excuse me, Mrs. Jones. The nurse from your son's school is on the phone. He's got a fever and needs to go home.
   B: Okay. Please let them know I'll be there in 20 minutes.

3-5 *Be Going To vs. Will*	
(a) She *is going to succeed* because she works hard.	*Be going to* and *will* mean the same when they are used to make predictions about the future.
(b) She *will succeed* because she works hard.	Examples (a) and (b) have the same meaning.
(c) I bought some wood because I *am going to build* a bookcase for my apartment.	*Be going to* (but not *will*) is used to express a prior plan (i.e., a plan made before the moment of speaking).
	In (c): The speaker plans to build a bookcase.
(d) This chair is too heavy for you to carry alone. I *'ll help* you.	*Will* (but not *be going to*) is used to express a decision the speaker makes at the moment of speaking.
	In (d): The speaker decides or volunteers to help at the immediate present moment; he did not have a prior plan or intention to help.

❑ **Exercise 20. Looking at grammar.** (Charts 3-1 → 3-5)

Discuss the *italicized* verb(s). Is the speaker expressing plans made before the moment of speaking (prior plans)? If so, circle *yes*. If not, circle *no*.

PRIOR PLAN?

1. A: Did you return Carmen's phone call?
   B: No, I forgot. Thanks for reminding me. *I'll call* her right away.   yes   no

2. A: *I'm going to call* Martha later this evening. Do you want to talk to her too?
   B: No, I don't think so.   yes   no

3. A: Jakob is in town for a few days.
   B: Really? Great! *I'll give* him a call. Is he staying at his Aunt Lara's?   yes   no

4. A: Alex is in town for a few days.
   B: I know. He called me yesterday. *We're going to get* together for dinner after I get off work tonight.   yes   no

5. A: I need some fresh air. I'm going for a short walk.
   B: *I'll come* with you.   yes   no

6. A: *I'm going to take* Hamid to the airport tomorrow morning. Do you want to come along?
   B: Sure.   yes   no

7. A: *We're going to go* to Uncle Scott's over the break. Are you interested in coming with us?   yes   no
   B: Gee, I don't know. *I'll think* about it. When do you need to know?   yes   no

❑ **Exercise 21. Looking at grammar.** (Charts 3-1 → 3-5)

Restate the sentences orally or in writing. Use **be going to**.

My trip to Thailand

1. I'm planning to be away for three weeks.
2. My husband and I are planning to stay in small towns and camp on the beach.
3. We're planning to bring a tent.
4. We're planning to celebrate our wedding anniversary there.
5. My father, who was born in Thailand, is planning to join us, but he's planning to stay in a hotel.

❑ **Exercise 22. Looking at grammar.** (Charts 3-1 → 3-5)

Complete the sentences with **be going to** or **will**. Use **be going to** to express a prior plan.

1. A: Are you going by the post office today? I need to mail this letter.
   B: Yeah, I _'ll_____ mail it for you.
   A: Thanks.

2. A: Why are you carrying that package?

   B: It's for my sister. I _'m going to_ mail it to her.

3. A: Why did you buy so many eggs?

   B: I _____ make a special dessert.

4. A: I have a book for Joe from Rachel. I'm not going to see him today.

   B: Let me have it. I _____ give it to him. He's in my algebra class.

5. A: Did you apply for the job you told me about?

   B: No, I _____ take a few more classes and get more experience.

6. A: Did you know that I found an apartment on 45th Street? I'm planning to move soon.

   B: That's a nice area. I _____ help you move if you like.

   A: Great! I'd really appreciate that.

7. A: Why can't you come to the party?

   B: We _____ be with my husband's family that weekend.

8. A: I have to leave. I don't have time to finish the dishes.

   B: No problem. I _____ do them for you.

9. A: Do you want to go to the meeting together?

   B: Sure. I _____ meet you by the elevator in ten minutes.

❏ **Exercise 23. Listening.** (Chart 3-1 → 3-5)

Listen to each question and circle the <u>expected</u> response (a. or b.).

1. a. Sure, I'll do it.
   b. Sure, I'm going to do it.

2. a. Yes. I'll look at laptop computers.
   b. Yes. I'm going to look at laptop computers.

3. a. Yeah, but I'll sell it. I don't need it now that I live in the city.
   b. Yeah, but I'm going to sell it. I don't need it now that I live in the city.

4. a. Uh, I'll get your coat and we can go.
   b. Uh, I'm going to get your coat and we can go.

❏ **Exercise 24. Warm-up.** (Chart 3-6)

Complete the sentences with your own words. What do you notice about the verb tenses and the words in **boldface**?

1. **After** I leave school today, I'm going to _____.

2. **Before** I come to school tomorrow, I will _____.

3. **If** I have time this weekend, I will _____.

3-6 Expressing the Future in Time Clauses and *If*-Clauses

(a) time clause **Before I go** to class tomorrow, I'm going to eat breakfast.	In (a) and (b): *before I go to class tomorrow* is a future time clause.
(b) I'm going to eat breakfast time clause **before I go** to class tomorrow.	**before** **after** **when** ⎫ **as soon as** ⎬ + *subject and verb* = a time clause **until** ⎭ **while**
(c) *Before I go* home tonight, I'm going to stop at the market. (d) I'm going to eat dinner at 6:00 tonight. *After I eat dinner,* I'm going to study in my room. (e) I'll give Rita your message *when I see her.* (f) It's raining right now. *As soon as the rain stops,* I'm going to walk downtown. (g) I'll stay home *until the rain stops.* (h) *While you're at school tomorrow,* I'll be at work.	The simple present is used in a future time clause. **Will** and **be going to** are NOT used in a future time clause. INCORRECT: *Before I will go to class, I'm going to eat breakfast.* INCORRECT: *Before I am going to go to class tomorrow, I'm going to eat breakfast.* All of the example sentences (c) through (h) contain future time clauses.
(i) Maybe it will rain tomorrow. *If it rains* tomorrow, I'm going to stay home.	In (i): *If it rains tomorrow* is an *if*-clause. *if* + *subject and verb* = an *if*-clause When the meaning is future, the simple present (not **will** or **be going to**) is used in an *if*-clause.

❏ **Exercise 25. Looking at grammar.** (Chart 3-6)
Choose the correct verbs.

1. Before   *I'm going to return,* (*I return*)   to my country next year, I'm going to finish my graduate degree in computer science.

2. The boss will review your work after she   *will return, returns*   from vacation next week.

3. I'll give you a call on my cell phone as soon as my plane   *will land, lands.*

4. I don't especially like my current job, but I'm going to stay with this company until I *find, will find*   something better.

5. When you   *will be, are*   in Australia next month, are you going to go snorkeling at the Great Barrier Reef?

6. I need to know what time the meeting starts. Please be sure to call me as soon as you   *find out, will find out* anything about it.

7. If it   *won't be, isn't*   cold tomorrow, we'll go to the beach.
   If it   *is, will be*   cold tomorrow, we'll go to a movie.

Exercise 26. Looking at grammar. (Chart 3-6)
Use the given verbs to complete the sentences. Use **be going to** for the future.

1. *take, read*

   I _'m going to read_ the textbook **before** I __take__ the final exam next month.

2. *return, call*

   Mr. Lee _____ his wife **as soon as** he _____

   to the hotel tonight.

3. *make, go*

   Before I _____ to my job interview tomorrow, I _____

   a list of questions I want to ask about the company.

4. *visit, take*

   We _____ Sabrina to our favorite seafood restaurant **when** she

   _____ us this weekend.

5. *keep, call*

   I _____ my cell* on **until** Lena _____.**

6. *miss, understand not*

   If Adam _____ the meeting, he _____ the next project.

7. *get, eat*

   If Eva _____ home early, we _____ dinner at 6:30.

❑ **Exercise 27. Let's talk: pairwork.** (Chart 3-6)
Work with a partner. Read each sentence and make a follow-up sentence using **if**. Pay special attention to the verb in the **if**-clause. Share some of your partner's answers with the class.

Example: Maybe you'll go downtown tomorrow.
PARTNER A: If I **go** downtown tomorrow, I'm going to buy some new clothes.
PARTNER B: If I **go** downtown tomorrow, I'm going to look at laptop computers.

1. Maybe you'll have some free time tomorrow.
2. Maybe it'll rain tomorrow.
3. Maybe it won't rain tomorrow.
4. Maybe the teacher will be absent next week.

---

*cell = cell phone

Time clauses beginning with **until usually <u>follow</u> the main clause.
    Usual: I'm going to keep my cell on **until Lena calls**.
    Possible but less usual: **Until Lena calls**, I'm going to keep my cell on.

Change roles.
5. Maybe you'll be tired tonight.
6. Maybe you won't be tired tonight.
7. Maybe it'll be nice tomorrow.
8. Maybe we won't have class on Monday.

❑ **Exercise 28. Looking at grammar.** (Chart 3-6)
Look at Sue's day planner. She has a busy morning. Make sentences using the word in parentheses and the given information. Use *be going to* for the future.

1. (after)   go to the dentist \ pick up groceries
   → *After Sue goes to the dentist, she is going to pick up groceries.*
2. (before)   go to the dentist \ pick up groceries
3. (before)   have lunch with Hiro \ pick up groceries
4. (after)   have lunch with Hiro \ pick up groceries
5. (before)   have lunch with Hiro \ take her father to his doctor's appointment

❑ **Exercise 29. Reading, grammar, and writing.** (Chart 3-6)
Part I. Read the passage.

The Home of the Future

What will the home of the future look like? Imagine life 50 years from now. What kinds of homes will people have? Here are some interesting possibilities.

The living room walls will have big plasma screens. Instead of pictures on the wall, the screens will show changing scenery. If walls have different scenes, people may not even want many windows. As you know, fewer windows will make it easier to heat a house.

The house will have special electronic features, and people will control them with a remote control. For example, a person can lie in bed at night and lock all the doors in his or her house with one push of a button. Before someone arrives home from work, the remote will turn on the lights, preheat the oven, and even turn on favorite music. The bathroom faucets will have a memory. They will remember the temperature a person likes, and when he or she turns on the water in the tub or shower, it will be at the correct temperature. Maybe bedroom closets will have racks that move automatically at the touch of a button. When the weather is cold, the racks will deliver clothes that keep a person warm, and on warm days, the racks will deliver clothes that keep a person cool.

Finally, homes will be more energy-efficient. Most of the heat will probably come from the sun. Of course, solar heat will be popular because it will be inexpensive.

Which ideas do you like? Which ones do you think you may see in your lifetime?

Part II. Complete the sentences with information from the passage. More than one answer may be possible.

1. When people look at the living room walls, they _____.

2. When a person is coming home from work, the remote _____.

3. As soon as a person gets home, _____.

4. If the bathroom faucets have a memory, they _____.

5. Before a person goes to sleep, _____.

6. When a person pushes a button, the closet racks _____.

7. When the weather is cold, the closet racks _____.

8. If a home has solar heat, the cost of heating the home _____.

Part III. Imagine you can build your dream house — 50 years from now. It can be any type of house you want. Think about the style, size, kinds of rooms, location, etc. Write a paragraph about this house. Begin with this topic sentence: *My dream house will have . . . .*

❏ **Exercise 30. Looking at grammar.** (Chapters 1, 2 and Charts 3-1 → 3-6)
Complete each sentence with a form of the words in parentheses. Read carefully for time expressions.

1. Before Tim (*go*) __goes__ to bed, he always (*brush*) __brushes__ his teeth.

2. Before Tim (*go*) _____ to bed later tonight, he (*email*) _____ his girlfriend.

3. Before Tim (*go*) _____ to bed last night, he (*take*) _____ a shower.

4. While Tim (*take*) _____ a shower last night, the phone (*ring*) _____.

5. As soon as the phone (*ring*) _____ last night, Tim (*jump*) _____ out of the shower to answer it.

6. As soon as Tim (*get*) _____ up tomorrow morning, he (*brush*) _____ his teeth.

7. Tim always (*brush*) _____ his teeth as soon as he (*get*) _____ up.

❏ **Exercise 31. Warm-up.** (Chart 3-7)
Which sentences express future time?

1. I'm catching a train tonight.
2. I'm going to take the express train.
3. The trip will only take an hour.

3-7 Using the Present Progressive to Express Future Time

(a) Tim *is going to come* to the party tomorrow. (b) Tim *is coming* to the party tomorrow. (c) We *'re going to go* to a movie tonight. (d) We *'re going* to a movie tonight. (e) I *'m going to stay* home this evening. (f) I *'m staying* home this evening. (g) Ann *is going to fly* to Chicago next week. (h) Ann *is flying* to Chicago next week.	The present progressive can be used to express future time. Each pair of example sentences has the same meaning. The present progressive describes *definite plans for the future, plans that were made before the moment of speaking.* A future meaning for the present progressive is indicated either by future time words (e.g., *tomorrow*) or by the situation.*
(i) You *'re going to laugh* when you hear this joke. (j) INCORRECT: *You're laughing when you hear this joke.*	The present progressive is NOT used for predictions about the future. In (i): The speaker is predicting a future event. In (j): The present progressive is not possible; laughing is a prediction, not a planned future event.

*COMPARE: Present situation: *Look! Mary's coming. Do you see her?*
Future situation: *Are you planning to come to the party? Mary's coming. So is Alex.*

❑ **Exercise 32. Looking at grammar.** (Chart 3-7)
Complete the conversations with the correct form of the given verbs. Use the present progressive if possible. Discuss whether the present progressive expresses present or future time.

1. A: What (*you, do*) __are you doing__ tomorrow afternoon?

   B: I (*go*) __am going__ to the mall. How about you? What (*you, do*)

   _____ tomorrow afternoon?

   A: I (*go*) _____ to a movie with Dan. After the movie, we (*go*)

   _____ out to dinner. Would you like to meet us for dinner?

   B: No, thanks. I can't. I (*meet*) _____ my son for dinner.

2. A: What (*you, major*) _____ in?

   B: I (*major*) _____ in engineering.

   A: What courses (*you, take*) _____ next semester?

   B: I (*take*) _____ English, math, and physics.

3. A: Stop! Paula! What (*you, do*) _____?

   B: I (*cut*) _____ my hair, Mom.

   A: Oh dear!

Exercise 33. Listening. (Chart 3-7)

Listen to the conversation and write the words you hear.

Going on vacation

A: I _____ on vacation tomorrow.

B: Where _____ you _____?

A: To San Francisco.

B: How are you getting there? _____ you _____ or _____ your car?

A: I _____. I have to be at the airport by seven tomorrow morning.

B: Do you need a ride to the airport?

A: No, thanks. I _____ a taxi.

What about you? Are you planning to go somewhere over vacation?

B: No. I _____ here.

Exercise 34. Let's talk: pairwork. (Chart 3-7)

Work with a partner. Tell each other your plans. Use the present progressive.

Example: What are your plans for this evening?
SPEAKER A: I'm staying home. How about you?
SPEAKER B: I'm going to a coffee shop to work on my paper for a while. Then I'm meeting some friends for a movie.

What are your plans . . .
1. for the rest of today?
2. for tomorrow?
3. for this coming weekend?
4. for next month?

Exercise 35. Let's write. (Chart 3-7)

Imagine you have a week's vacation. You can go anywhere you want. Think of a place you would like to visit. Write a paragraph in which you describe your trip. Use the present progressive where appropriate.

Example: My friend Sara and I are taking a trip to Nashville, Tennessee. Nashville is the home of country music, and Sara loves country music. She wants to go to lots of shows. I don't know anything about country music, but I'm looking forward to going to Nashville. We're leaving Friday afternoon as soon as Sara gets off work. (Etc.)

Possible questions to answer in your paragraph:
1. Where are you going?
2. When are you leaving?
3. Who are you going with, or are you traveling alone?
4. How are you getting there?
5. Where are you staying?
6. Are you visiting anyone? Who?
7. How long are you staying there?
8. When are you getting back?

❑ **Exercise 36. Warm-up.** (Chart 3-8)
Circle all the possible completions.

1. Soccer season begins _____ .
   a. today   b. next week   c. yesterday

2. The mall opens _____ .
   a. next Monday   b. tomorrow   c. today

3. There is a party _____ .
   a. last week   b. tonight   c. next weekend

4. The baby cries _____ .
   a. every night   b. tomorrow night   c. in the evenings

3-8 Using the Simple Present to Express Future Time

(a) My plane *arrives* at 7:35 *tomorrow evening*. (b) Tim's new job *starts* next week. (c) The semester *ends* in two more weeks. (d) There *is* a meeting at ten *tomorrow morning*.	The simple present can express future time when events are on a definite schedule or timetable. Only a few verbs are used in the simple present to express future time. The most common are *arrive*, *leave*, *start*, *begin*, *end*, *finish*, *open*, *close*, *be*.
(e) INCORRECT: *I wear my new suit to the wedding next week.* CORRECT: *I am wearing/am going to wear* my new suit to the wedding next week.	Most verbs CANNOT be used in the simple present to express future time. For example, in (e): The verb *wear* does not express an event on a schedule or timetable. It cannot be used in the simple present to express future time.

❑ **Exercise 37. Looking at grammar.** (Charts 3-7 and 3-8)
Circle all the possible completions.

1. The concert _____ at eight tonight.
   a. begins   b. is beginning   c. is going to begin

2. I _____ seafood pasta for dinner tonight.
   a. make   b. am making   c. am going to make

3. I _____ to school tomorrow morning. I need the exercise.
   a. walk   b. am walking   c. am going to walk

4. The bus _____ at 8:15 tomorrow morning.
   a. leaves   b. is leaving   c. is going to leave

5. I _____ the championship game on TV at Jonah's house tomorrow.
   a. watch   b. am watching   c. am going to watch

6. The game _____ at 1:00 tomorrow afternoon.
   a. starts   b. is starting   c. is going to start

7. Alexa's plane _____ at 10:14 tomorrow morning.
   a. arrives   b. is arriving   c. is going to arrive

8. I can't pick her up tomorrow, so she _____ the airport bus into the city.
   a. takes   b. is taking   c. is going to take

9. Jonas _____ to several companies. He hopes to get a full-time job soon.
   a. applies   b. is applying   c. is going to apply

10. School _____ next Wednesday. I'm excited for vacation to begin.
    a. ends   b. is ending   c. is going to end

☐ **Exercise 38. Warm-up.** (Chart 3-9)
Choose the picture that best describes this sentence: Joanne is about to leave for work.

Picture A

Picture B

3-9 Immediate Future: Using *Be About To*	
(a) Ann's bags are packed, and she is wearing her coat. She ***is about to leave*** for the airport. (b) Shhh. The movie ***is about to begin***.	The idiom ***be about to do something*** expresses an activity that will happen *in the immediate future,* usually within minutes or seconds. In (a): Ann is going to leave sometime in the next few minutes. In (b): The movie is going to start in the next few minutes.

Exercise 39. Let's talk. (Chart 3-9)
Describe the action that is about to happen in each picture. Use **be about to**. Work in pairs, in small groups, or as a class.

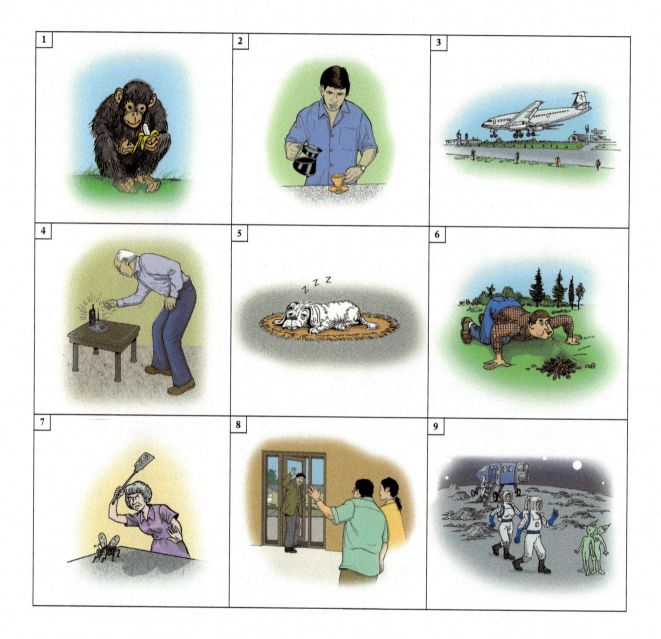

Exercise 40. Game. (Chart 3-9)

Think of an action to perform. Don't tell what it is. Get ready to do it, but just before you perform the action, ask the class to describe what you are about to do. Perform with a partner if you wish. Use your own ideas or suggestions from the list.

Example: (Students A and B hold out their hands to each other.)
Possible guess: They are about to shake hands.

Suggestions:

stand up	sneeze	pick up a pen	erase a word
open the door	fall down	close your book	look up a word
close the window	cry	write on the board	get out your wallet

❑ **Exercise 41. Warm-up.** (Chart 3-10)

Circle all the possible completions for each sentence.

1. Fifteen years from now, my wife and I will retire and _____ all over the world.
   - a. will travel
   - b. travel
   - c. traveling
   - d. going to travel
   - e. are traveling
   - f. traveled

2. I opened the door and _____ my friend to come in.
   - a. will invite
   - b. invite
   - c. inviting
   - d. am going to invite
   - e. am inviting
   - f. invited

3-10 Parallel Verbs

(a) Jim **makes** his bed *and* **cleans** up his room every morning. (b) Anita **called** *and* **told** me about her new job.	Often a subject has two verbs that are connected by **and**. We say that the two verbs are parallel: V + **and** + V *makes and cleans* = parallel verbs
(c) Ann **is cooking** dinner *and (is)* **talking** on the phone at the same time. (d) I **will stay** home *and (will)* **study** tonight. (e) I **am going to stay** home *and (am going to)* **study** tonight.	It is not necessary to repeat a helping verb (an auxiliary verb) when two verbs are the same tense and are connected by **and**.

❑ **Exercise 42. Looking at grammar.** (Chart 3-10)

Complete each sentence with the correct form of the verbs in parentheses.

1. When I (*walk*) __walked__ into the living room yesterday, Grandpa (*read*)

   _____ a newspaper and (*listen*) _____ to music.

2. Helen will graduate soon. She (*move*) _____ to New York and (*look*)

   _____ for a job after she (*graduate*) _____.

3. Every day my neighbor (call) _____ me on the phone and (complain) _____ about the weather.

4. Look at Erin. She (cry) _____ and (laugh) _____ at the same time! I wonder if she is happy or sad?

5. I'm beat.* I can't wait to get home. After I (get) _____ home, I (take) _____ a hot bath and (go) _____ to bed.

6. While Paul (carry) _____ brushes and paint and (climb) _____ a ladder, a bee (land) _____ on his arm and (sting) _____ him. Paul (drop) _____ the paint and (spill) _____ it all over the ground.

❏ **Exercise 43. Looking at grammar.** (Chapters 1 → 3)
Complete each sentence with the correct form of the words in parentheses.

1. I usually (ride) ___ride___ my bike to work in the morning, but it (rain) _____ when I left my house early this morning, so I (take) _____ the bus. After I (get) _____ to work, I (find) _____ out** that I had left my briefcase on the bus.

2. A: Are you going to take the kids to the amusement park tomorrow morning?
   B: Yes. It (open) _____ at 10:00. If we (leave) _____ here at 9:30, we'll get there at 9:55. The kids can be the first ones in the park.

3. A: Ouch! I (cut) _____ my finger. It (bleed) _____!
   B: Put pressure on it. I (get) _____ some antibiotics and a bandage.
   A: Thanks.

4. A: Your phone (ring) _____.
   B: I (know) _____.
   A: (you, want) _____ me to get it?
   B: No.
   A: Why don't you want to answer your phone?
   B: I (answer, not) _____ during dinner.

---

*be beat = be very, very tired; be exhausted

**find out = discover; learn

5. A: Look! There (be) _____ a police car behind us. Its lights (flash)

   _____.

   B: I (know) _____. I (know) _____. I (see) _____ it.

   A: What (go) _____ on? (you, speed) _____?

   B: No, I'm not. I (drive) _____ the speed limit.

   A: Oh, look. The police car (pass) _____ us.

   B: Whew!

❑ **Exercise 44. Listening.** (Chapters 1 → 3)

Part I. Complete the sentences with the words you hear.

At a Chinese restaurant

   A: Okay, let's all open our fortune cookies.

   B: What _____ yours _____?

   A: Mine says, "You _____ an unexpected gift." Great! Are you

   planning to give me a gift soon?

   B: Not that I know of. Mine says, "Your life _____ long and happy."

   Good. I _____ a long life.

   C: Mine says, "A smile _____ all communication problems." Well,

   that's good! After this, when I _____ someone,

   _____ just _____ at them.

   D: My fortune is this: "If you _____ hard, you _____ successful."

   A: Well, it _____ like all of us _____ good luck in the future!

Part II. Work in small groups. Together, write a fortune for each person in your group.

❑ **Exercise 45. Check your knowledge.** (Chapters 1 → 3)

Edit the paragraph. Correct errors in verb tense usage.

My Cousin Pablo

                  is
I want to tell you about Pablo. He ⌃ my cousin. He comes here four years ago. Before he

came here, he study statistics in Chile. He leaves Chile and move here. He went to New York

and stay there for three years. He graduated from New York University. Now he study at this

school. After he finish his master's degree, he return to Chile.

Pretend that you have the ability to see into the future. Choose a person you know (classmate, teacher, family member, friend) and tell this person in writing about his/her future life. Give some interesting or unusual details.

Example:

My Son's Future

My son is 15 years old now. In the future, he will have a happy and successful life. After he finishes high school, he will go to college. He really loves to study math. He also loves to build bridges out of toothpicks. He will study engineering, and he will specialize in bridge building. He likes to travel, so he will get a job with an international company and build bridges around the world. He will also work in poor villages, and his bridges will connect rural areas. This will make people's lives better. I will be very proud of him.

❑ **Exercise 1. Warm-up.** (Chart 4-1)

Do you know the past participle form of these verbs? Complete the chart. What is the difference between the past participle forms in items 1–4 and 5–8?

Simple Form	Simple Past	Past Participle
1. stay	stayed	_stayed_
2. work	worked	_worked_
3. help	helped	_____
4. visit	visited	_____
5. go	went	_gone_
6. begin	began	_begun_
7. write	wrote	_____
8. see	saw	_____

4-1	Past Participle			
	Simple Form	**Simple Past**	**Past Participle**	The **past participle** is one of the principal parts of a verb. (See Chart 2-3, p. 31.)
REGULAR VERBS	finish stop wait	finished stopped waited	**finished** **stopped** **waited**	The past participle is used in the PRESENT PERFECT tense and the PAST PERFECT tense.* The past participle of regular verbs is the same as the simple past form: both end in **-ed**.
IRREGULAR VERBS	see make put	saw made put	**seen** **made** **put**	See Chart 2-4, p. 32, or the inside back cover for a list of irregular verbs.

*The past participle is also used in the passive. See Chapter 10.

Exercise 2. Listening. (Charts 2-3, 2-4, and 4-1)

Write the words you hear.

Example: You will hear: go   went   gone

You will write: go   went   _gone_

Simple Form	Simple Past	Past Participle		Simple Form	Simple Past	Past Participle
1. call	called	_____	6. come	came	_____
2. speak	spoke	_____	7. eat	ate	_____
3. do	did	_____	8. cut	cut	_____
4. know	knew	_____	9. read	read	_____
5. meet	met	_____	10. be	was/were	_____

Exercise 3. Looking at grammar. (Charts 2-3, 2-4, and 4-1)

Make your own chart. Write the past participles.

Simple Form	Simple Past	Past Participle		Simple Form	Simple Past	Past Participle
1. finish	finished	_finished_	6. hear	heard	_____
2. have	had	_____	7. study	studied	_____
3. think	thought	_____	8. die	died	_____
4. teach	taught	_____	9. buy	bought	_____
5. live	lived	_____	10. start	started	_____

Exercise 4. Warm-up. (Chart 4-2)

Decide which sentence (a. or b.) is correct for each situation.

1. It's 10:00 A.M. Layla has been at the bus stop since 9:50.
   a. She is still there.
   b. The bus picked her up.

2. Toshi has lived in the same apartment for 30 years.
   a. After 30 years, he moved somewhere else.
   b. He still lives there.

4-2 Present Perfect with *Since* and *For*

	(a) I **'ve been** in class **since** *ten o'clock this morning*. (b) We **have known** Ben **for** *ten years*. We met him ten years ago. We still know him today. We are friends.	The present perfect tense is used in sentences with **since** and **for** to express situations that began in the past and continue to the present. In (a): Class started at ten. I am still in class now, at the moment of speaking. *INCORRECT: I am in class since ten o'clock this morning.*

(c)   I *have*
    You *have*
   She, He, It *has*   } *been* here for one hour.
    We *have*
    They *have*
		FORM: **have/has** + *past participle*
		
		CONTRACTED FORMS: *I've, You've, He's, She's, It's, We've, They've.*

Since

(d) I *have been* here {	**since** eight o'clock. **since** Tuesday. **since** 2009 **since** yesterday. **since** last month.	**Since** is followed by the mention of a *specific point in time:* an hour, a day, a month, a year, etc. **Since** expresses the idea that something began at a specific time in the past and continues to the present.
(e) CORRECT: I *have lived* here since May.* CORRECT: I *have been* here since May. (f) INCORRECT: I *am living* here since May. (g) INCORRECT: I *live* here since May. (h) INCORRECT: I *lived* here since May. (i) INCORRECT: I *was* here since May.		Notice the incorrect sentences: In (f): The present progressive is NOT used. In (g): The simple present is NOT used. In (h) and (i): The simple past is NOT used.
MAIN CLAUSE *SINCE*-CLAUSE (present perfect) (simple past) (j) I *have lived* here since I *was* a child. (k) Al *has met* many people since he *came* here.		**Since** may also introduce a time clause (i.e., a subject and verb may follow **since**). Notice in the examples: The present perfect is used in the main clause; the simple past is used in the *since*-clause.

For

(l) I *have been* here {	**for** ten minutes. **for** two hours. **for** five days. **for** about three weeks. **for** almost six months. **for** many years. **for** a long time.	**For** is followed by the mention of a *length of time:* two minutes, three hours, four days, five weeks, etc.). NOTE: If the noun ends in *-s* (*hours, days, weeks, etc.*), use **for** in the time expression, not **since**.

*Also correct: *I have been living* here since May.* See Chart 4-6 for a discussion of the present perfect progressive.

❑ Exercise 5. Looking at grammar. (Chart 4-2)
Complete the sentences with *since* or *for*.

Amy has been here . . .

1. _____for_____ two months.
2. _____since_____ September.
3. _____ yesterday.
4. _____ the term started.
5. _____ a couple of hours.
6. _____ fifteen minutes.

Ms. Ellis has worked as a substitute teacher . . .

11. _____ school began.
12. _____ last year.
13. _____ 2008.
14. _____ about a year.
15. _____ September.
16. _____ a long time.

The Smiths have been married . . .

7. _____ two years.
8. _____ last May.
9. _____ five days.
10. _____ a long time.

I've known about Sonia's engagement . . .

17. _____ almost four months.
18. _____ the beginning of the year.
19. _____ the first of January.
20. _____ yesterday.

❑ Exercise 6. Looking at grammar. (Chart 4-2)
Complete the sentences with information about yourself.

1. I've been in this building . . . . { since _____nine o'clock this morning_____.
      for _____27 minutes_____.

2. We've been in class . . . . { since _____.
      for _____.

3. I've been in this city . . . . { since _____.
      for _____.

4. I've had an ID★ card . . . . { since _____.
      for _____.

5. I've had this book . . . . { since _____.
      for _____.

★ID = identification

Exercise 7. Looking at grammar. (Chart 4-2)

Complete each sentence with the present perfect form of the given verb.

Since 1995, Theresa, a talk-show host, . . .

1. work _____ *has worked* _____ for a TV station in London.

2. interview _____ hundreds of guests.

3. meet _____ many famous people.

4. find _____ out about their lives.

5. make _____ friends with celebrities.

6. became _____ a celebrity herself.

7. sign _____ lots of autographs.

8. shake _____ hands with thousands of people.

9. write _____ two books about how to interview people.

10. think _____ a lot about the best ways to help people feel

comfortable on her show.

□

Exercise 8. Let's talk. (Chart 4-2)

Your teacher will ask a question. Two students will answer. Speaker A will answer with **since**. Speaker B will use Speaker A's information and answer with **for**. Only the teacher's book is open.

Example:
To SPEAKER A: How long have you been in this room?
    SPEAKER A: I've been in this room **since** (10:00).
To SPEAKER B: How long has (*Student A*) been in this room?
    SPEAKER B: She/He has been in this room **for** (15 minutes).

1. How long have you known me?
2. How long have you been up* today?
3. Where do you live? How long have you lived there?
4. Who has a cell phone? How long have you had your phone?
5. Who has a bike? How long have you had it?
6. How long have you been in this building today?
7. Who is wearing something new? What is new? How long have you had it/them?
8. Who is married? How long have you been married?

---

be up = be awake and out of bed

❏ **Exercise 9. Looking at grammar.** (Chart 4-2)
Complete the sentences with the correct form of the words in parentheses. Put brackets around the *since*-clauses.

1. I (*know*) ___have known___ Mark Miller [ever since* we (*be*) ___were___ in college.]

2. Pedro (*change*) _____ his major three times since he (*start*) _____ school.

3. Ever since I (*be*) _____ a child, I (*be*) _____ afraid of snakes.

4. I can't wait to get home to my own bed. I (*sleep, not*) _____ well since I (*leave*) _____ home three days ago.

5. Ever since Pete (*meet*) _____ Nicole, he (*think, not*) _____ about anything or anyone else. He's in love.

6. Otto (*have*) _____ a lot of problems with his car ever since he (*buy*) _____ it. It's a lemon.**

7. A: What (*you, eat*) _____ since you (*get*) _____ up this morning?

   B: So far, I (*eat*) _____ a banana and some yogurt.***

❏ **Exercise 10. Warm-up: pairwork.** (Chart 4-3)
Work with a partner. Partner A makes a true statement with a phrase from the list and then changes it to a question. Partner B gives a true answer.

climbed a tree	heard bedtime stories	ridden a tricycle
flown a kite	played in the dirt	slept with a stuffed animal

PARTNER A: Since my childhood, I haven't _____.
                   Since your childhood, have you _____?

PARTNER B: Yes, I have. OR No, I haven't.

---

*Ever since has the same meaning as *since*.

**a lemon = a car with a lot of problems

***So far + present perfect expresses situations that began in the past and continue to the present.

4-3 Negative, Question, and Short-Answer Forms

Negative

(a) I **have not** (**haven't**) **seen** Tom since lunch.	NEGATIVE: **have/has** + **not** + past participle
(b) Ann **has not** (**hasn't**) **eaten** for several hours.	NEGATIVE CONTRACTIONS: **have** + **not** = **haven't** **has** + **not** = **hasn't**

Question

(c) **Have you seen Tom?**	QUESTION: **have/has** + subject + past participle
(d) **Has Ann eaten?**	
(e) How long **have you lived** here?	
(f) — Have you **ever** met a famous person? — No, I've **never** met a famous person.	In (f): **ever** = in your lifetime; from the time you were born to the present moment. Questions with **ever** frequently use the present perfect. When answering questions with **ever**, speakers often use **never**. **Never** is frequently used with the present perfect. In the answer to (f), the speaker is saying: "No, I haven't met a famous person from the time I was born to the present moment."

Short Answer

(g) — Have you seen Tom? — Yes, I **have**. OR No, I **haven't**.	SHORT ANSWER: **have/haven't** or **has/hasn't** NOTE: The helping verb in the short answer is not contracted with the pronoun. INCORRECT: Yes, I've. OR Yes, he's.
(h) — Has Ann eaten lunch? — Yes, she **has**. OR No, she **hasn't**.	

❑ **Exercise 11. Looking at grammar.** (Chart 4-3)
Complete the conversations. Use the present perfect form of the verbs in parentheses.

1. A: (*you, eat, ever*) ___Have you ever eaten___ an insect?

   B: No, I ___haven't___. I (*eat, never*) ___have never___ eaten an insect.

2. A: (*you, stay, ever*) _____ in a room on the top

   floor of a hotel?

   B: Yes, I _____. I (*stay*) _____ in a room on the

   top floor of a hotel a few times.

3. A: (*you, meet, ever*) _____ a movie star?

   B: No, I _____. I (*meet, never*) _____ a movie star.

4. A: (*Ted, travel, ever*) _____ overseas?

   B: Yes, he _____. He (*travel*) _____ to several

   countries on business.

5. A: (*Lara, be, ever*) _____ in Mexico?

   B: No, she _____. She (*be, never*) _____ in any

   Spanish-speaking countries.

Listen to each sentence and then the beginning of a question. Complete the question with the
past participle of the verb you heard in the first sentence. Have you ever done these things?
Circle *yes* or *no*.

Example: You will hear: I saw a two-headed frog once. Have you ever . . . ?
You will write: Have you ever ___*seen*___ a two-headed frog?   yes   (no)

1. Have you ever _____ a two-headed snake?   yes   no

2. Have you ever _____ in a small plane?   yes   no

3. Have you ever _____ in a limousine?   yes   no

4. Have you ever _____ volunteer work?   yes   no

5. Have you ever _____ a shirt?   yes   no

6. Have you ever _____ a scary experience on an airplane?   yes   no

7. Have you ever _____ out of a boat?   yes   no

8. Have you ever _____ so embarrassed that your face got hot?   yes   no

9. Have you ever _____ to a famous person?   yes   no

10. Have you ever _____ to be famous?   yes   no

❑ **Exercise 13. Let's talk: interview.** (Charts 2-4 and 4-3)
Interview your classmates. Make questions using the present perfect form of the given verbs.

1. you \ ever \ cut \ your own hair
2. you \ ever \ catch \ a big fish
3. you \ ever \ take care of \ an injured animal
4. you \ ever \ lose \ something very important
5. you \ ever \ sit \ on a bee
6. you \ ever \ fly \ in a private plane
7. you \ ever \ break \ your arm or your leg
8. you \ ever \ find \ something very valuable
9. you \ ever \ swim \ near a shark
10. you \ ever \ throw \ a ball \ and \ break \ a window

Exercise 14. Let's talk and write: interview. (Charts 2-3, 2-4, 4-2, and 4-3)

Part I. Work with a partner. Take turns asking and answering questions. Begin your questions with *How long have you* and the present perfect. Answer questions with *since, for,* or *never* and the present perfect.

Example: have a pet
PARTNER A: How long have you had a pet?
PARTNER B: I've had (*a cat, a dog, a bird, etc.*) for two years.   OR
I've had (*a cat, a dog, a bird, etc.*) since my 18th birthday.   OR
I've never had a pet.

1. live in (*this area*)
2. study English
3. be in this class / at this school
4. have long hair / short hair
5. have a beard / a mustache
6. wear glasses / contact lenses
7. have a roommate / a pet
8. be interested in (*a particular subject*)
9. be married

Part II. Use the information from your interview to write a paragraph about your partner. You can add some information to make it more interesting. Use the following paragraph as an example. Notice the present perfect phrases in green.

Example:

Ellie

I'd like to tell you a little about Ellie. She has lived in Vancouver, Canada, for six months. She has studied English for five years. She has been at this school since September. She likes it here.

She has short hair. She has worn short hair for a few years. Of course, she doesn't have a mustache! She has never worn glasses, except sunglasses.

Ellie doesn't have a roommate, but she has a pet bird. She has had her bird for one month. Its name is Howie, and he likes to sing.

She is interested in biology. She has been interested in biology since she was a child. She has never been married. She wants to be a doctor. She wants to become a doctor before she has a family.

❑ **Exercise 15. Warm-up.** (Chart 4-4)
Circle the correct completion (a. or b.) for each sentence.

1. Tyler has rented a house _____ .
   a. last week.   b. already.

2. I have seen it _____ .
   a. recently.   b. two days ago.

3. His parents haven't seen it _____ .
   a. yesterday.   b. yet.

4. I have been there _____ .
   a. two times.   b. yesterday.

4-4 Present Perfect with Unspecified Time

Toshi has already eaten lunch.

Eva hasn't eaten lunch yet.

before now time?	(a) Toshi *has **just** eaten* lunch. (b) Jim *has **recently** changed* jobs.	The PRESENT PERFECT expresses an activity or situation that occurred (or did not occur) *before now, at some unspecified or unknown time in the past.* Common time words that express this idea are *just, recently, already, yet, ever, never.* In (a): Toshi's lunch occurred before the present time. The *exact* time is not mentioned; it is unimportant or unknown.
before now	(c) Pete *has eaten* at that restaurant ***many times**.* (d) I *have eaten* there ***twice**.*	An activity may be repeated two, several, or more times *before now,* at *unspecified times in the past,* as in (c) and (d).
	(e) Pete *has **already** left*. OR Pete *has left **already***.	In (e): ***Already*** is used in affirmative statements. It can come after the helping verb or at the end of the sentence. Idea of ***already**:* Something happened before now, before this time.
	(f) Min *hasn't left **yet***.	In (f): ***Yet*** is used in negative statements and comes at the end of the sentence. Idea of ***yet**:* Something did not happen before now (up to this time), but it may happen in the future.
	(g) *Have you **already** left?* *Have you left **already**?* *Have you left **yet**?*	In (g): Both ***yet*** and ***already*** can be used in questions.

Exercise 16. Looking at grammar. (Chart 4-4)

Circle all the possible answers for each question. Work in small groups and then discuss your answers as a class.

SITUATION 1:
Sara is at home. At 12:00 P.M., the phone rang. It was Sara's friend from high school. They had a long conversation, and Sara hung up the phone at 12:59. It is now 1:00. Which sentences describe the situation?

   a. Sara has just hung up the phone.
   b. She has hung up the phone already.
   c. The phone has just rung.
   d. Sara hasn't finished her conversation yet.
   e. Sara has been on the phone since 12:00 P.M.

SITUATION 2:
Mr. Peters is in bed. He became sick with the flu eight days ago. Mr. Peters isn't sick very often. The last time he had the flu was one year ago. Which sentences describe the situation?

   a. Mr. Peters has been sick for a year.
   b. He hasn't gotten well yet.
   c. He has just gotten sick.
   d. He has already had the flu.
   e. He hasn't had the flu before.

SITUATION 3:
Rob is at work. His boss, Rosa, needs a report. She sees Rob working on it at his desk. She's in a hurry, and she's asking Rob questions. What questions is she going to ask him?

   a. Have you finished?
   b. Have you finished yet?
   c. Have you finished already?

❑
Exercise 17. Listening. (Charts 2-4 and 4-4)

Richard and Lori are new parents. Their baby was born a week ago. Listen to each sentence and complete the question with the past participle of the verb you hear.

1. Has Richard ___*held*___ the baby a lot yet?

2. Has Lori _____ the baby a bath yet?

3. Has Richard _____ a diaper yet?

4. Has Lori _____ some pictures of the baby yet?

5. Has Richard _____ up when the baby cries yet?

6. Has Lori _____ some of the household chores yet?

7. Has Richard _____ tired during the day yet?

Exercise 18. Looking at grammar. (Chart 4-4)
Look at Andy's day planner. Write answers to the questions. Make complete sentences with *yet* and *already*.

```
MAY
Wednesday 17
 9:00 | dentist appointment        1:00 | finish errands
10:00 | take car for an oil change  2:00 | pick up kids at school
11:00 | shop for groceries          3:00 |
12:00 | have lunch with Michael     4:00 |
```

It is 11:55 A.M. right now.

1. Has Andy had his dentist appointment yet?   *Yes, he has had his dentist*
   appointment already.

2. Has Andy picked up his kids at school yet? _____
   _____

3. Has Andy taken his car for an oil change already? _____
   _____

4. Has Andy finished his errands yet? _____
   _____

5. Has Andy shopped for groceries already? _____
   _____

6. Has Andy had lunch with Michael yet? _____
   _____

□ **Exercise 19. Listening.** (Charts 4-2 → 4-4)
Both *is* and *has* can be contracted to *'s*. Listen to each sentence. Decide if the contracted verb is *is* or *has*. Before you begin, you may want to check your understanding of these words: *order, waiter*.

Examples: You will hear: I have to leave. My order's taking too long.
            You will choose: ⓘ has

            You will hear: I have to leave. My order's taken too long.
            You will choose: is (has)

At a restaurant

1. is   has   3. is   has   5. is   has

2. is   has   4. is   has   6. is   has

Answer the questions and then listen to the job interview. Listen again and complete the sentences with the words you hear. Before you begin, you may want to check your understanding of these words: *clinic, prison, volunteer, low-income, patient, challenge.*

What types of jobs can nurses have?
Which ones could be very exciting?

A job interview

Mika is a nurse. She is interviewing for a job with the manager of a hospital emergency room. He is looking at her résumé and asking her some general questions.

INTERVIEWER: It looks like _____ a lot of things since you became a
1

nurse.

MIKA: Yes, _____ for a medical clinic. _____
2   3

in a prison. _____ in several area hospitals. And
4

_____ volunteer work at a community health center for
5

low-income patients.

INTERVIEWER: Very good. But, let me ask you, why _____
6

jobs so often?

MIKA: Well, I like having new challenges and different experiences.

INTERVIEWER: Why _____ for this job?
7

MIKA: Well, I'm looking for something more fast-paced,* and _____
8

interested in working in an E.R.** for a long time. _____
9

that this hospital provides great training for its staff, and it offers excellent

patient care.

INTERVIEWER: Thank you for coming in. I'll call you next week with our decision.

MIKA: It was good to meet you. Thank you for your time.

---

more fast-paced = at a faster speed

**E.R.* = emergency room

□ **Exercise 21. Warm-up.** (Chart 4-5)
Read the short conversation. Who is more likely to say the last sentence, Pamela or Jenna?

PAMELA: I've traveled around the world several times.
JENNA: I traveled around the world once.

_____: I'm looking forward to my next trip.

4-5 Simple Past vs. Present Perfect

SIMPLE PAST (a) I **finished** my work *two hours ago*. PRESENT PERFECT (b) I **have** already **finished** my work.	In (a): I finished my work at a specific time in the past (*two hours ago*). In (b): I finished my work at an unspecified time in the past (*sometime before now*).
SIMPLE PAST (c) I **was** in Europe *last year / three years ago / in 2006 / in 2008 and 2010 / when I was ten years old*. PRESENT PERFECT (d) I **have been** in Europe *many times / several times / a couple of times / once / (no mention of time)*.	The SIMPLE PAST expresses an activity that occurred at a specific time (or times) in the past, as in (a) and (c). The PRESENT PERFECT expresses an activity that occurred at an unspecified time (or times) in the past, as in (b) and (d).
SIMPLE PAST (e) Ann **was** in Miami *for two weeks*. PRESENT PERFECT (f) Bob **has been in** Miami for *two weeks / since May 1st*.	In (e): In sentences where **for** is used in a time expression, the simple past expresses an activity that began and ended in the past. In (f): In sentences with **for** or **since**, the present perfect expresses an activity that began in the past and continues to the present.

□ **Exercise 22. Looking at grammar.** (Chart 4-5)
Answer each question and discuss the meanings of the verb tenses in *italics*.

1. All of these verbs talk about past time, but the verb in (a) is different from the other three verbs. What is the difference?
   (a) I *have had* several bicycles in my lifetime.
   (b) I *had* a red bicycle when I was in elementary school.
   (c) I *had* a blue bicycle when I was a teenager.
   (d) I *had* a green bicycle when I lived and worked in Hong Kong.

2. What are the differences in the ideas the verb tenses express?
   (e) I *had* a wonderful bicycle last year.
   (f) I *'ve had* many wonderful bicycles.

3. What are the differences in the ideas the verb tenses express?
   (g) Ann *had* a red bike for two years.
   (h) Sue *has had* a red bike for two years.

4. Who is still alive, and who is dead?
   (i) In his lifetime, Uncle Alex *had* several red bicycles.
   (j) In his lifetime, Grandpa *has had* several red bicycles.

□ **Exercise 23. Looking at grammar.** (Chart 4-5)

Look at each verb in *italics*. Is it simple past or present perfect? Check (✓) the box that describes whether the verb expresses something that happened at a specified or unspecified time in the past.

	SPECIFIED TIME IN THE PAST	UNSPECIFIED TIME IN THE PAST
1. Ms. Parker *has been* in Tokyo many times. → *present perfect*	□	☑
2. Ms. Parker *was* in Tokyo last week. → *simple past*	☑	□
3. I*'ve met* Kaye's husband. He's a nice guy.	□	□
4. I *met* Kaye's husband at a party last week.	□	□
5. Mr. White *was* in the hospital three times last month.	□	□
6. Mr. White *has been* in the hospital many times.	□	□
7. I like to travel. I*'ve been* to more than 30 foreign countries.	□	□
8. I *was* in Morocco in 2008.	□	□
9. Venita *has never been* to Morocco.	□	□
10. Venita *wasn't* in Morocco when I was there in 2008.	□	□

□ **Exercise 24. Looking at grammar.** (Chart 4-5)

Complete the sentences. Use the present perfect or the simple past form of the verbs in parentheses.

1. A: Have you ever been to Singapore?

   B: Yes, I (be) ___have___. I (be) ___have been___ to Singapore several times. In fact,

   I (be) ___was___ in Singapore last year.

2. A: Are you going to finish your work before you go to bed?

   B: I (*finish, already**) ___have already finished___ it. I (*finish*) ___finished___ my work

   two hours ago.

3. A: Have you ever eaten at the Sunset Beach Café?

   B: Yes, I _____. I (*eat*) _____ there many times. In

   fact, my wife and I (*eat*) _____ lunch there yesterday.

---

*In informal spoken English, the simple past is sometimes used with *already*. Practice using the present perfect with *already* in this exercise.

4. A: Do you and Erica want to go to the movie at the Galaxy Theater with us tonight?

   B: No thanks. We (*see, already*) _____ it. We (*see*)

   _____ it last week.

5. A: When are you going to write your report for Mr. Berg?

   B: I (*write, already*) _____ it. I (*write*)

   _____ it two days ago and gave it to him.

6. A: (*Antonio, have, ever*) _____ a job?

   B: Yes, he _____. He (*have*) _____ lots of part-time

   jobs. Last summer he (*have*) a _____ a job at his uncle's auto shop.

7. A: This is a good book. Would you like to read it when I'm finished?

   B: Thanks, but I (*read, already*) _____ it. I (*read*)

   _____ it a couple of months ago.

8. A: What African countries (*you, visit*) _____?

   B: I (*visit*) _____ Kenya and Ethiopia. I (*visit*)

   _____ Kenya in 2002. I (*be*) _____ in

   Ethiopia last year.

❑ **Exercise 25. Let's talk: pairwork.** (Chart 4-5)
Work with a partner. Take turns asking and answering the questions. Use the present perfect
and the simple past. Share a few of your partner's answers with the class.

Example:
PARTNER A: What countries have you been to?
PARTNER B: I've been to Norway and Finland.
PARTNER A: When were you in Norway?
PARTNER B: I was in Norway three years ago. How about you? What countries have you been to?
PARTNER A: I've never been to Norway or Finland, but I've been to . . . .

1. What countries have you been to?
   When were you in . . . ?

2. Where are some interesting places you have lived?
   When did you live in . . . ?

3. What are some interesting / unusual / scary things you have done in your lifetime?
   When did you . . . ?

4. What are some helpful things (for a friend / your family / your community) you have done
   in your lifetime?
   When did you . . . ?

Exercise 26. Listening. (Charts 2-4 and 4-5)

For each item, you will hear two complete sentences and then the beginning of a third sentence. Complete the third sentence with the past participle of the verb you heard in the first two sentences.

Example: You will hear: I eat vegetables every day. I ate vegetables for dinner last night. I have . . .

You will write: I have ___eaten___ vegetables every day for a long time.

1. Since Friday, I have _____ a lot of money.

2. All week, I have _____ big breakfasts.

3. Today, I have already _____ several emails.

4. I just finished dinner, and I have _____ a nice tip.

5. Since I was a teenager, I have _____ in late on weekends.

6. All my life, I have _____ very carefully.

7. Since I was little, I have _____ in the shower.

□
Exercise 27. Game. (Charts 2-4 and 4-5)

Work in groups.

    (1) On a piece of paper, write down two statements about yourself, one in the simple past tense and one in the present perfect tense.
    (2) Make one statement true and one statement false.
    (3) The other members of your group will try to guess which one is true.
    (4) Tell the group the correct answers when everyone has finished guessing.

The person with the most correct guesses at the end of the game is the winner.

Example:

STUDENT A: I've never cooked dinner.
              I saw a famous person last year.

STUDENT B: *You've never cooked dinner is true.*
              You saw a famous person last year is false.

□
Exercise 28. Warm-up. (Chart 4-6)

Complete the sentences with time information.

1. I am sitting at my desk right now. I have been sitting at my desk since _____.

2. I am looking at my book. I have been looking at my book for _____.

Al and Ann are in their car right now. They are driving home. It is now four o'clock.	The PRESENT PERFECT PROGRESSIVE talks about *how long* an activity has been in progress before now.
(a) They **have been driving** since two o'clock.	NOTE: Time expressions with **since**, as in (a), and **for**, as in (b), are frequently used with this tense.
(b) They **have been driving** for two hours. They will be home soon.	STATEMENT: **have/has** + **been** + **-ing**
(c) How long **have** they **been driving**?	QUESTION: **have/has** + subject + **been** + **-ing**

Present Progressive vs. Present Perfect Progressive

Present Progressive	(d) Po **is sitting** in class right now.	The PRESENT PROGRESSIVE describes an activity that is in progress right now, as in (d). It does not discuss duration (length of time).
		INCORRECT: *Po has been sitting in class right now.*
Present Perfect Progressive 	Po is sitting at his desk in class. He sat down at nine o'clock. It is now nine-thirty. (e) Po **has been sitting** in class since nine o'clock. (f) Po **has been sitting** in class for thirty minutes.	The PRESENT PERFECT PROGRESSIVE expresses the **duration** (length of time) of an activity that began in the past and is in progress right now. INCORRECT: *Po is sitting in class since nine o'clock.*

(g) CORRECT: I **know** Yoko. (h) INCORRECT: I am knowing Yoko. (i) CORRECT: I **have known** Yoko **for** two years. (j) INCORRECT: I have been knowing Yoko for two years.	NOTE: Non-action verbs (e.g., *know, like, own, belong*) are generally not used in the progressive tenses.* In (i): With non-action verbs, the present perfect is used with **since** or **for** to express the duration of a situation that began in the past and continues to the present.

*See Chart 1-6, Non-Action Verbs, p. 17.

Exercise 29. Looking at grammar. (Chart 4-6)
Complete the sentences. Use the present progressive or the present perfect progressive form of the verbs in parentheses.

1. I (*sit*) ___am sitting___ in the cafeteria right now. I (*sit*) ___have been sitting___

   here since twelve o'clock.

2. Kate is standing at the corner. She (*wait*) _____ for the bus. She

   (*wait*) _____ for the bus for twenty minutes.

3. Scott and Rebecca (*talk*) _____ on the phone right now. They

   _____ (*talk*) on the phone for over an hour.

4. Right now we're in class. We (*do*) _____ an exercise. We (*do*)

   _____ this exercise for a couple of minutes.

5. A: You look busy right now. What (*you, do*) _____?

   B: I (*work*) _____ on my physics experiment. It's a difficult

      experiment.

   A: How long (*you, work*) _____ on it?

   B: I started planning it last January. I (*work*) _____

      on it since then.

❑ **Exercise 30. Let's talk.** (Chart 4-6)
Answer the questions your teacher asks. Your book is closed.

Example:
TEACHER: Where are you living?
STUDENT A: I'm living in an apartment on Fourth Avenue.
TEACHER: How long have you been living there?
STUDENT A: I've been living there since last September.

1. Right now you are sitting in class. How long have you been sitting here?
2. When did you first begin to study English? How long have you been studying English?
3. I began to teach English in (*year*). How long have I been teaching English?
4. I began to work at this school in (*month or year*). How long have I been working here?
5. What are we doing right now? How long have we been doing it?
6. (*Student's name*), I see that you wear glasses. How long have you been wearing glasses?
7. Who drives? When did you first drive a car? How long have you been driving?
8. Who drinks coffee? How old were you when you started to drink coffee? How long have you been drinking coffee?

Exercise 31. Listening. (Charts 4-2 → 4-6)

Part I. When speakers use the present perfect in everyday speech, they often contract *have* and *has* with nouns. Listen to the sentences and notice the contractions.

1. Jane has been out of town for two days.
2. My parents have been active in politics for 40 years.
3. My friends have moved into a new apartment.
4. I'm sorry. Your credit card has expired.
5. Bob has been traveling in Montreal since last Tuesday.
6. You're the first one here. No one else* has come yet.

Part II. Listen to the sentences. Complete them with the words you hear: *noun + have/has*.

1. The ___*weather has*___ been warm since the beginning of April.

2. This _____ been unusually warm.

3. My _____ been living in the same house for 25 years.

4. My _____ lived in the same town all their lives.

5. You slept late. Your _____ already gotten up and made breakfast.

6. My _____ planned a going-away party for me. I'm moving back to my hometown.

7. I'm afraid your _____ been getting a little sloppy.**

8. My _____ traveled a lot. She's visited many different countries.

□ **Exercise 32. Warm-up.** (Chart 4-7)

Read the situations and answer the questions.

SITUATION 1:
Roger is having trouble with math. I am helping him with his homework tonight. I **have been helping** him since 6:00.

SITUATION 2:
Roger is moving to a new apartment. I **have helped** him move furniture several times this week.

SITUATION 3:
I sure was busy last week. I **helped** Roger with his homework, and I **helped** him move to a new apartment.

a. In which situation does the speaker emphasize the duration or the time that something continues?
b. In which situation(s) is the speaker finished with the activity?
c. Do you think the activity in situation 1 or 2 is more recent? Why?

---

*else is an adverb and is frequently contracted with *have* and *has* in phrases such as *no one else, someone else, anyone else*, etc.

**sloppy = careless or messy

4-7 Present Perfect Progressive vs. Present Perfect

Present Perfect Progressive

(a) Gina and Tarik are talking on the phone. They *have been talking* on the phone for 20 minutes.	The PRESENT PERFECT PROGRESSIVE expresses the **duration of present *activities***, using action verbs, as in (a). The activity began in the past and is still in progress.

Present Perfect

(b) Gina *has talked* to Tarik on the phone many times (before now).	The PRESENT PERFECT expresses
(c) *INCORRECT: Gina has been talking to Tarik on the phone many times.*	(1) repeated activities that occur at **unspecified times in the past**, as in (b), OR
(d) Gina *has known* Tarik for two years.	(2) the **duration of present *situations***, as in (d), using non-action verbs.
(e) *INCORRECT: Gina has been knowing Tarik for two years.*	

Present Perfect Progressive and Present Perfect

(f) I *have been living* here for six months. OR	For some (not all) verbs, duration can be expressed by either the present perfect or the present perfect progressive.
(g) I *have lived* here for six months.	
(h) Ed *has been wearing* glasses since he was ten. OR Ed *has worn* glasses since he was ten.	Examples (f) and (g) have essentially the same meaning, and both are correct.
(i) I *'ve been going* to school ever since I was five years old. OR I *'ve gone* to school ever since I was five years old.	Often either tense can be used with verbs that express the **duration of usual or habitual activities/situations** (things that happen daily or regularly), e.g., *live, work, teach, smoke, wear glasses, play chess, go to school, read the same newspaper every morning, etc.*

Complete the sentences. Use the present perfect or the present perfect progressive form of the verbs in parentheses. In some sentences, either form is possible.

1. A: I'm tired. We (hike) ___have been hiking___ for more than an hour.
   B: Well, let's stop and rest for a while.

2. A: Is the hike to Glacier Lake difficult?
   B: No, not at all. I (hike) ___have hiked___ it many times with my kids.

3. A: Do you like it here?
   B: I (live) ___have been living / have lived___ here for only a short while. I don't know yet.

4. A: My eyes are getting tired. I (read) _____ for two hours.
      I think I'll take a break.
   B: Good idea.

5. A: I (read) _____ this same page in my chemistry book three times,
      and I still don't understand it.
   B: Maybe I can help.

6. A: Do you like the Edgewater Inn?
   B: Very much. I (stay) _____ there at least a dozen times. It's
      my favorite hotel.

7. A: The baby's crying. Shouldn't we do something? He (cry) _____
      for several minutes.
   B: I'll go check.

8. A: Who's your daughter's teacher for next year?
   B: I think her name is Mrs. Jackson.
   A: She's one of the best teachers at the elementary school. She (teach) _____
      _____ kindergarten for twenty years.

9. A: Ed (play) _____ tennis for ten years, but he still doesn't have
      a good serve.
   B: Neither do I, and I (play) _____ tennis for twenty years.

10. A: Where does Mrs. Alvarez work?
    B: At the power company. She (work) _____ there for fifteen
       years. She likes her job.
    A: What about her husband?
    B: He's currently unemployed, but he'll find a new job soon.
    A: What kind of experience does he have?
    B: He (work) _____ for two different accounting firms and at
       one of the bigger software companies. With his work experience, he won't have any
       trouble finding another job.

Exercise 34. Listening. (Chart 4-7)

Listen to the weather report. Then listen again and complete the sentences with the words you hear. Before you begin, you may want to check your understanding of these words: *hail, weather system, rough.*

Today's Weather

The weather _____ certainly _____ today. Boy,
                          1   2

what a day! _____ already _____ rain, wind, hail, and sun. So, what's
                 3   4

in store* for tonight? As you _____ probably _____, dark clouds
                          5   6

_____. We have a weather system moving in that is going to
              7

bring colder temperatures and high winds. _____ all week that
                                8

this system is coming, and it looks like tonight is it! _____ even
                                        9

_____ snow down south of us, and we could get some snow here too. So hang
          10

onto your hats! We may have a rough night ahead of us.

❑ **Exercise 35. Looking at grammar.** (Chapters 1, 2, and 4)

Look at each pair of sentences. Compare the meanings of the verb tenses in *italics*. Check (✓) the sentences that express duration.

1. a. _____ Rachel *is taking* English classes.

   b. _____ Nadia *has been taking* English classes for two months.

2. a. _____ Ayako *has been living* in Jerusalem for two years. She likes it there.

   b. _____ Beatriz *has lived* in Jerusalem. She's also lived in Paris. She's lived in New York and Tokyo. She's lived in lots of cities.

3. a. _____ Jack *has visited* his aunt and uncle many times.

   b. _____ Matt *has been visiting* his aunt and uncle for the last three days.

4. a. _____ Cyril *is talking* on the phone.

   b. _____ Cyril *talks* on the phone a lot.

   c. _____ Cyril *has been talking* to his boss on the phone for half an hour.

   d. _____ Cyril *has talked* to his boss on the phone lots of times.

5. a. _____ Mr. Woods *walks* his dog in Forest Park every day.

   b. _____ Mr. Woods *has walked* his dog in Forest Park many times.

   c. _____ Mr. Woods *walked* his dog in Forest Park five times last week.

   d. _____ Mr. Woods *is walking* his dog in Forest Park right now.

   e. _____ Mr. Woods *has been walking* his dog in Forest Park since two o'clock.

---

what's in store = what to expect or what is coming in the future

Exercise 36. Listening. (Charts 4-1 → 4-7)

Listen to each conversation and choose the sentence (a. or b.) that best describes it.

Example: You will hear: A: This movie is silly.
                                            B: I agree. It's really dumb.

   You will choose: (a.) The couple has been watching a movie.
                                      b. The couple finished watching a movie.

   1. a. The speakers listened to the radio already.
       b. The speakers have been listening to the radio.

   2. a. The man lived in Dubai a year ago.
       b. The man still lives in Dubai.

   3. a. The man has called the children several times.
       b. The man called the children once.

   4. a. The speakers went to a party and are still there.
       b. The speakers went to a party and have already left.

❑ **Exercise 37. Listening and speaking.** (Chapters 1 → 4)

Part I. Listen to the phone conversation between a mother and her daughter, Lara.

A common illness

LARA: Hi, Mom. I was just calling to tell you that I can't come to your birthday party this
         weekend. I'm afraid I'm sick.

MOM: Oh, I'm sorry to hear that.

LARA: Yeah, I got sick Wednesday night, and it's just been getting worse.

MOM: Are you going to see a doctor?

LARA: I don't know. I don't want to go to a doctor if it's not serious.

MOM: Well, what symptoms have you been having?

LARA: I've had a cough, and now I have a fever.

MOM: Have you been taking any medicine?

LARA: Just over-the-counter* stuff.

MOM: If your fever doesn't go away, I think you need to call a doctor.

LARA: Yeah, I probably will.

MOM: Well, call me tomorrow and let me know how you're doing.

LARA: Okay. I'll call you in the morning.

---

over-the-counter = medicine you can buy without a prescription from a doctor

Part II. Work with a partner. Take turns being the parent and the sick person. Complete the conversation. Practice the new conversation with your partner.

Possible symptoms:

a fever	chills	a sore throat
a runny nose	achiness	a stomachache
a cough	a headache	sneezing
nausea		

A: Hi, Mom/Dad. I was just calling to tell you that I can't come to _____. I'm afraid I'm sick.

B: Oh, I'm sorry to hear that.

A: Yeah, I got sick Wednesday night, and it's just been getting worse.

B: Are you going to see a doctor?

A: I don't know. I don't want to go to a doctor if it's not serious.

B: Well, what symptoms have you been having?

A: I've had _____, and now I have _____.

B: Have you been taking any medicine?

A: Just over-the-counter stuff.

B: If your _____ doesn't go away, I think you need to call a doctor.

A: Yeah, I probably will.

B: Well, call me tomorrow and let me know how you're doing.

A: Okay. I'll call you in the morning.

❑ **Exercise 38. Looking at grammar.** (Chapter 1 and Charts 4-1 → 4-7)
Choose the correct verb. In some sentences, more than one answer may be possible. Discuss your answers.

1. I _____ the windows twice, and they still don't look clean.
    a. am washing   b. have washed   c. have been washing

2. Please tell Mira to get off the phone. She _____ for over an hour.
    a. is talking   b. has talked   c. has been talking

3. Where are you? I _____ at the mall for you to pick me up.
    a. wait   b. am waiting   c. have been waiting

4. We _____ at the Lakes Resort once. We want to go back again.
    a. stay   b. have stayed   c. have been staying

5. Where have you been? The baby _____, and I can't comfort her.
    a. cries   b. is crying   c. has been crying

□ **Exercise 39. Reading.** (Charts 4-1 → 4-7)

Answer the questions. Then read the passage and the statements that follow. Circle "T" for true and "F" for false.

Have you heard about the problem of disappearing honeybees?
Why are honeybees important to fruit and many other crops?

Where Have the Honeybees Gone?

Honeybees have been disappearing around the world for several years now. In the United States, billions of bees have already died. Europe, Australia, and Brazil have also reported losses of honeybees. This is a serious problem because bees pollinate★ crops. Without pollination, apple, orange, and other fruit trees cannot produce fruit. Other crops like nuts also need pollination. In the United States, one-third of the food supply depends on honeybees.

Scientists have a name for this problem: colony collapse disorder (CCD). Bees live in colonies or hives, and thousands of beekeepers have been finding their hives empty. A hive that once held 50,000 bees may just have a few dead or dying ones left.

There have been many theories about why this has happened; for example, disease, pests,★★ unnatural growing conditions, and damaged DNA.★★★ Scientists now think that the cause may be a combination of a virus and a fungus, but they need to do more research to find a solution to this very serious problem.

1. Honeybees have stopped disappearing.	T	F
2. Scientists expect that more bees will die.	T	F
3. Apples and other fruits depend on honeybees.	T	F
4. Bee hives have been disappearing.	T	F
5. There are only four reasons why honeybees have died.	T	F

★*pollinate* (verb) = fertilize; *pollination* (noun) = the process that causes a plant to make a new plant

★★*pest* = an insect or animal that damages crops

★★★*DNA* = deoxyribonucleic acid, a carrier of genetic information

Exercise 40. Grammar and writing. (Chapters 1, 2, and 4)

Exercise 40. Grammar and writing. (Chapters 1, 2, and 4)

Part I. Complete the sentences with the correct form of the words in parentheses.

My name (*be*) __is__ Surasuk Jutukanyaprateep. I (*be*) _____ from
1   2

Thailand. Right now I (*study*) _____ English at this school. I (*be*)
3

_____ at this school since the beginning of January. I (*arrive*)
4

_____ here January 2nd, and my classes (*begin*) _____
5   6

January 6th.

Since I (*come*) _____ here, I (*do*) _____ many
7   8

things, and I (*meet*) _____ many people. Last week, I (*go*)
9

_____ to a party at my friend's house. I (*meet*) _____ some of the
10   11

other students from Thailand at the party. Of course, we (*speak*) _____ Thai, so
12

I (*practice, not*) _____ my English that night. There (*be*)
13

_____ only people from Thailand at the party.
14

However, since I (*come*) _____ here, I (*meet*)
15

_____ a lot of other people too, including people from Latin America,
16

Africa, the Middle East, and Asia. I enjoy meeting people from other countries. Now I (*know*)

_____ people from all these places, and they (*become*) _____
17   18

my friends.

Part II. Write three paragraphs about yourself. Use the passage in Part I as a model. Answer
these questions:

PARAGRAPH I.
  1. What is your name?
  2. Where are you from?
  3. How long have you been here?

PARAGRAPH II.
  4. What have you done since you came here? OR
  5. What have you learned since you began studying English?

PARAGRAPH III.
  6. Who have you met in this class? OR
  7. Who have you met recently?
  8. Give a little information about these people.

Read Karen's statement. Which sequence of events (a. or b.) is correct?

KAREN: Jane met me for lunch. She was so happy. She had passed her driver's test.
    a. Jane talked to Karen. Then she passed her test.
    b. Jane passed her test. Then she talked to Karen.

4-8 Past Perfect

Situation: *Jack left his apartment at 2:00. Sue arrived at his apartment at 2:15 and knocked on the door.*	The PAST PERFECT is used when the speaker is talking about two different events at two different times in the past; one event ends before the second event happens.
(a) When Sue arrived, Jack wasn't there. He *had left*.	In (a): There are two events, and both happened in the past: *Jack left his apartment. Sue arrived at his apartment.*
	To show the time relationship between the two events, we use the past perfect (*had left*) to say that the first event (Jack leaving his apartment) was completed before the second event (Sue arriving at his apartment) occurred.

(b) Jack *had left* his apartment when Sue arrived.	FORM: *had* = past participle
(c) He *'d* left. I *'d* left. They *'d* left. Etc.	CONTRACTION: *I / you / she / he / it / we / they* + *'d*
(d) Jack *had left* before Sue arrived. (e) Jack *left* before Sue arrived. (f) Sue *arrived* after Jack had left. (g) Sue *arrived* after Jack left.	When *before* and *after* are used in a sentence, the time relationship is already clear so the past perfect is often not necessary. The simple past may be used, as in (e) and (g). Examples (d) and (e) have the same meaning. Examples (f) and (g) have the same meaning.
(h) Stella was alone in a strange city. She walked down the avenue slowly, looking in shop windows. Suddenly, she turned her head and looked behind her. Someone *had called* her name.	The past perfect is more common in formal writing such as fiction, as in (h).

Identify which action in the past took place first (1st) and which action took place second (2nd).

1. The tennis player **jumped** in the air for joy. She **had won** the match.

   a. __1st__ The tennis player won the match.

   b. __2nd__ The tennis player jumped in the air.

2. Before I went to bed, I **checked** the front door. My roommate **had** already **locked** it.

   a. __2nd__ I checked the door.

   b. __1st__ My roommate locked the door.

3. I **looked** for Diego, but he **had left** the building.

   a. _____ Diego left the building.

   b. _____ I looked for Diego.

4. I **laughed** when I saw my son. He **had poured** a bowl of noodles on top of his head.

   a. _____ I laughed.

   b. _____ My son poured a bowl of noodles on his head.

5. Oliver **arrived** at the theater on time, but he couldn't get in. He **had left** his ticket at home.

   a. _____ Oliver left his ticket at home.

   b. _____ Oliver arrived at the theater.

6. I **handed** Betsy the newspaper, but she didn't want it. She **had read** it during her lunch hour.

   a. _____ I handed Betsy the newspaper.

   b. _____ Betsy read the newspaper.

7. After Carl arrived in New York, he **called** his mother. He **had promised** to call her as soon as he got in.

   a. _____ Carl made a promise to his mother.

   b. _____ Carl called his mother.

Exercise 43. Listening. (Chart 4-8)

Listen to the short conversations and choose the verbs you hear.

Examples: You will hear: A: I'll introduce you to Professor Newton at the meeting tonight.
                              B: You don't need to. I have already met him.
         You will choose: has   (have)   had

         You will hear: A: Did Jack introduce you to Professor Newton?
                              B: No, it wasn't necessary. I had already met him.
         You will choose: has   have   (had)

1. has   have   had   3. has   have   had
2. has   have   had   4. has   have   had

❑ **Exercise 44. Check your knowledge.** (Chapter 4)

Edit the sentences. Correct the errors in verb tense usage.

My experience with English

1. I have been ~~studied~~ *studying* English for eight years, but I still have a lot to learn.

2. I started English classes at this school four weeks ago, and I am learning a lot of English since then.

3. I want to learn English since I am a child.

4. I have been thinking about how to improve my English skills quickly since I came here, but I hadn't found a good way.

5. Our teacher likes to give tests. We has have six tests since the beginning of the term.

6. I like learning English. When I was young, my father found an Australian girl to teach my brothers and me English, but when I move to another city, my father didn't find anyone to teach us.

7. I meet many friends in this class. I meet Abdul in the cafeteria on the first day. He was friendly and kind. We are friends since that day.

8. Abdul have been study English for three months. His English is better than mine.

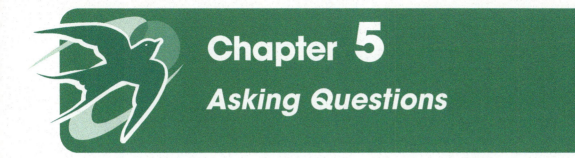

Chapter 5
Asking Questions

❑ **Exercise 1. Warm-up.** (Chart 5-1)
Choose the correct completion.

    A: _____ you need help?
        a. Are   c. Have
        b. Do   d. Were

    B: Yes, _____ .
        a. I need   c. I have
        b. I'm   d. I do

5-1 Yes/No Questions and Short Answers

Yes/No Question	Short Answer (+ Long Answer)	
(a) *Do you like* tea?	*Yes, I do.* (I like tea.) *No, I don't.* (I don't like tea.)	A **yes/no question** is a question that can be answered by *yes* or *no*.
(b) *Did Sue call?*	*Yes, she did.* (Sue called.) *No, she didn't.* (Sue didn't call.)	In an affirmative short answer (*yes*), a helping verb is NOT contracted with the subject.
(c) *Have you met* Al?	*Yes, I have.* (I have met Al.) *No, I haven't.* (I haven't met Al.)	In (c): INCORRECT: *Yes, I've.* In (d): INCORRECT: *Yes, it's.* In (e): INCORRECT: *Yes, he'll.*
(d) *Is it raining?*	*Yes, it is.* (It's raining.) *No, it isn't.* (It isn't raining.)	The spoken emphasis in a short answer is on the verb.
(e) *Will Rob be* here?	*Yes, he will.* (Rob will be here.) *No, he won't.* (Rob won't be here.)	

❑ **Exercise 2. Looking at grammar.** (Chart 5-1)
Choose the correct verbs.

A new cell phone

    1. *Is, Does*   that your new cell phone? Yes, it   *is, does.*

    2. *Are, Do*   you like it? Yes, I   *am, do.*

    3. *Were, Did*   you buy it online? Yes, I   *was, did* .

4. *Was, Did*   it expensive? No, it   *wasn't, didn't.*

5. *Is, Does*   it ringing? Yes, it   *is, does.*

6. *Are, Do*   you going to answer it? Yes, I   *am, do.*

7. *Was, Did*   the call important? Yes, it   *was, did.*

8. *Have, Were*   you turned your phone off? No, I   *haven't, wasn't.*

9. *Will, Are*   you call me later? Yes, I   *will, are.*

❑ **Exercise 3. Looking at grammar.** (Chart 5-1)
Use the information in parentheses to make yes/no questions. Complete each conversation with an appropriate short answer. Do not use a negative verb in the question.

1. A: ___*Do you know my brother?*___

   B: No, ___*I don't.*___ (I don't know your brother.)

2. A: _____

   B: No, _____ (Snakes don't have legs.)

3. A: _____

   B: Yes, _____ (Mexico is in North America.)

4. A: _____

   B: No, _____ (I won't be at home tonight.)

5. A: _____

   B: Yes, _____ (I have a bike.)*

6. A: _____

   B: Yes, _____ (Simon has left.)

7. A: _____

   B: Yes, _____ (Simon left with Kate.)

8. A: _____

   B: Yes, _____ (Acupuncture relieves pain.)

*In American English, a form of **do** is usually used when **have** is the main verb: *Do you have a car?*
In British English, a form of **do** with the main verb **have** is not necessary: *Have you a car?*

Exercise 4. Listening. (Chart 5-1)

Listen to each question and choose the correct response.

Example: You will hear: Are you almost ready?
You will choose: a. Yes, I was.   b. Yes, I do.   ⓒ Yes, I am.

Leaving for the airport

1. a. Yes, I am.   b. Yes, I do.   c. Yes, it does.
2. a. Yes, I did.   b. Yes, I was.   c. Yes, I am.
3. a. Yes, I will.   b. Yes, it will.   c. Yes, it did.
4. a. Yes, they are.   b. Yes, it did.   c. Yes, it is.
5. a. Yes, I am.   b. Yes, I will.   c. Yes, I do.

Exercise 5. Let's talk: interview. (Chart 5-1)

Interview seven students in your class. Make questions with the given words. Ask each student a different question.

1. you \ like \ animals?
2. you \ ever \ had \ a pet snake?
3. it \ be \ cold \ in this room?
4. it \ rain \ right now?
5. you \ sleep \ well last night?
6. you \ be \ tired right now?
7. you \ be \ here next year?

Exercise 6. Listening. (Chart 5-1)

In spoken English, it may be hard to hear the beginning of a yes/no question because the words are often reduced.*

Part I. Listen to these common reductions.

1. Is he absent?   →   *Ih-ze* absent? OR *Ze* absent?
2. Is she absent?   →   *Ih-she* absent?
3. Does it work?   →   *Zit* work?
4. Did it break?   →   *Dih-dit* break? OR *Dit* break?
5. Has he been sick?   →   *Ze* been sick? OR *A-ze* been sick?
6. Is there enough?   →   *Zere* enough?
7. Is that okay?   →   *Zat* okay?

Part II. Complete the sentences with the words you hear. Write the non-reduced forms.

At the grocery store

1. I need to see the manager. _____ available?

2. I need to see the manager. _____ in the store today?

3. Here is one bag of apples. _____ enough?

4. I need a drink of water. _____ a drinking fountain?

5. My credit card isn't working. Hmmm. _____ expire?

---

*See also Chapter 1, Exercise 33, p. 21, and Chapter 2, Exercise 20, p. 39.

6. Where's Simon? _____ left?

7. The price seems high. _____ include the tax?

❑ **Exercise 7. Warm-up.** (Chart 5-2)
Circle the correct answers. There may be more than one correct answer for each question.

1. Where did you go?
   a. To the hospital. b. Yes, I did. c. Outside. d. Yesterday.

2. When is James leaving?
   a. I'm not sure. b. Yes, he is. c. Yes, he does. d. Around noon.

3. Who did you meet?
   a. Tariq did. b. Sasha. c. Well, I met Sam and Mia. d. Yes, I did.

5-2 Yes / No and Information Questions

A yes/no question = a question that can be answered by "yes" or "no"
   A: *Does Ann live in Montreal?*
   B: *Yes, she does.* OR *No, she doesn't.*

An information question = a question that asks for information by using a question word:
   where, when, why, who, whom, what, which, whose, how
   A: *Where does Ann live?*
   B: *In Montreal.*

(Question Word)	Helping Verb	Subject	Main Verb	(Rest of Sentence)	
(a)	*Does*	*Ann*	*live*	in Montreal?	The same subject-verb word order is used in both yes/no and information questions:
(b) Where	*does*	*Ann*	*live*?		*Helping Verb + Subject + Main Verb*
(c)	*Is*	*Sara*	*studying*	at the library?	
(d) Where	*is*	*Sara*	*studying*?		
(e)	*Will*	*you*	*graduate*	next year?	Example (a) is a yes/no question.
(f) When	*will*	*you*	*graduate*?		Example (b) is an information question.
(g)	*Did*	*they*	*see*	Jack?	
(h) Who(m)*	*did*	*they*	*see*?		In (i) and (j): Main verb *be* in simple present and simple past (*am, is, are, was, were*) precedes the subject. It has the same position as a helping verb.
(i)	*Is*	*Heidi*		at home?	
(j) Where	*is*	*Heidi*?			
(k)		*Who*	*came*	to dinner?	When the question word (e.g., *who* or *what*) is the subject of the question, usual question word order is not used. Notice in (k) and (l) that no form of *do* is used.
(l)		*What*	*happened*	yesterday?	

*See Chart 5-4 for a discussion of *who(m)*.

❑ **Exercise 8. Looking at grammar.** (Chart 5-2)
Read the information about Irina and Paul. Then make complete questions with the given words and choose the correct short answers.

The Simple Life

Irina and Paul live a simple life. They have a one-room cabin on a lake in the mountains. They fish for some of their food. They also raise chickens. They pick fruit from trees and berries from bushes. They don't have electricity or TV, but they enjoy their life. They don't need a lot to be happy.

1. QUESTION: where \ Irina and Paul \ live?
   Where do Irina and Paul live?
   ANSWER: a. Yes, they do. (b.) On a lake.

2. QUESTION: they \ live \ a simple life?
   _____
   ANSWER: a. Yes, they live. b. Yes, they do.

3. QUESTION: what \ they \ pick \ from the trees?
   _____
   ANSWER: a. Fruit. b. Yes, they pick.

4. QUESTION: they \ have \ electricity?
   _____
   ANSWER: a. No, they don't. b. No, they don't have.

5. QUESTION: they \ enjoy \ their life?
   _____
   ANSWER: a. Yes, they do. b. Yes, they enjoy.

6. QUESTION: they \ be \ happy?
   _____
   ANSWER: a. Yes, they do. b. Yes, they are.

□ **Exercise 9. Listening.** (Chart 5-2)

Listen to the conversation. Then listen again and complete the sentences with the words you hear.

Where are Roberto and Isabel?

A: _____ Roberto and Isabel?
                    1

B: Yes, _____. They live around the corner from me.
              2

A: _____ them lately?
                  3

B: No, _____. They're out of town.
              4

A: _____ to their parents? I heard Roberto's parents are ill.
                  5

B: Yes, _____. They went to help them.
              6

A: _____ them soon?
                  7

B: Yes, _____. In fact, I'm going to pick them up at the airport.
              8

A: _____ back this weekend? I'm having a party, and I'd like
                  9

to invite them.

B: No, _____. They won't be back until Monday.
              10

□ **Exercise 10. Warm-up.** (Chart 5-3)

Complete the sentences with the most appropriate question word from the list. One sentence has two possible answers. Match the answers to the questions.

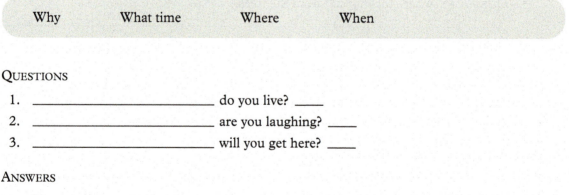

Why   What time   Where   When

QUESTIONS

1. _____ do you live? _____
2. _____ are you laughing? _____
3. _____ will you get here? _____

ANSWERS

a. At noon.

b. On Fifth Street.

c. Because the joke was funny.

5-3 Where, Why, When, What Time, How Come, What . . . For

Question	Answer	
(a) **Where** did he go?	Home.	**Where** asks about *place*.
(b) **When** did he leave?	Last night. Two days ago. Monday morning. Seven-thirty.	A question with **when** can be answered by any time expression, as in the sample answers in (b).
(c) **What time** did he leave?	Seven-thirty. Around five o'clock. A quarter past ten.	A question with **what time** asks about *time on a clock*.
(d) **Why** did he leave?	Because he didn't feel well.*	**Why** asks about *reason*.
(e) **What** did he leave *for*? (f) **How come** he left?	**Why** can also be expressed with the phrases **What** . . . **for** and **How come**, as in (e) and (f). Notice that with **How come**, usual question order is not used. The subject precedes the verb and no form of **do** is used.	

*See Chart 8-6, p. 221, for the use of *because*. *Because I didn't feel well* is an adverb clause. It is not a complete sentence. In this example, it is the short answer to a question.

❑ **Exercise 11. Looking at grammar.** (Chart 5-3)
Complete each conversation. Make questions using the information from Speaker A.

1. A: I'm going downtown in a few minutes.

   B: I didn't catch that. When _are you going downtown_____? OR

   B: I didn't catch that. Where _are you going in a few minutes_____?

2. A: My kids are transferring to Lakeview Elementary School because it's a better school.

   B: What was that? Where _____? OR

   B: What was that? Why _____?

3. A: I will meet Taka at 10:00 at the mall.

   B: I couldn't hear you. Tell me again. What time _____? OR

   B: I couldn't hear you. Tell me again. Where _____?

4. A: Class begins at 8:15.

   B: Are you sure? When _____? OR

   B: Are you sure? What time _____?

5. A: I stayed home from work because I wanted to watch the World Cup final on TV.

   B: Huh?! Why _____? OR

   B: Huh?! What _____ for?

Exercise 12. Looking at grammar. (Chart 5-3)

Restate the sentences. Use *How come* and *What for*.

1. Why are you going?
2. Why did they come?
3. Why does he need more money?
4. Why are they going to leave?

❑ **Exercise 13. Reading and grammar.** (Charts 5-2 and 5-3)

Read the passage about Nina's birthday. Make questions with the given words. Answer the questions in small groups or as a class.

The Birthday Present

Tom got home late last night, around midnight. His wife, Nina, was sitting on the couch waiting for him. She was quite worried because Tom is never late.

Tomorrow is Nina's birthday. Unfortunately, Tom doesn't think she will be happy with her birthday present. Yesterday, Tom bought her a bike and he decided to ride it home from the bike shop. While he was riding down a hill, a driver came too close to him, and he landed in a ditch. Tom was okay, but the bike was ruined. Tom found a bus stop nearby and finally got home.

Tom told Nina the story, but Nina didn't care about the bike. She said she had a better present: her husband.

1. When \ Tom \ get home
2. Where \ be \ his wife
3. What \ Tom \ buy
4. Why \ be \ Tom \ late
5. What present \ Nina \ get

❑ **Exercise 14. Listening.** (Charts 5-2 and 5-3)

Listen to each question and choose the best answer.

Example: You will hear: When are you leaving?
You will choose: a. Yes, I am. (b.) Tomorrow. c. In the city.

1. a. I am too.
   b. Yesterday.
   c. Sure.

2. a. For dinner.
   b. At 6:00.
   c. At the restaurant.

3. a. Outside the mall.
   b. After lunch.
   c. Because I need a ride.

4. a. At work.
   b. Because traffic was heavy.
   c. A few hours ago.

5. a. A pair of jeans.
   b. At the store.
   c. Tomorrow.

❑ **Exercise 15. Warm-up.** (Chart 5-4)

Match each question in Column A with the correct answer in Column B.

Column A

1. Who flew to Rome? _____
2. Who did you fly to Rome? _____
3. What did you fly to Rome? _____
4. What flew to Rome? _____

Column B

a. A small plane flew to Rome.
b. Pablo flew to Rome.
c. I flew a small plane to Rome.
d. I flew Pablo to Rome.

5-4 Questions With *Who*, *Who(m)*, and *What*

Question	Answer	
(a) **Who** came? *(S)*	**Someone** came. *(S)*	In (a): **Who** is used as the subject (S) of a question. In (b): **Who**(*m*) is used as the object (O) in a question.
(b) **Who**(*m*) did *you* see? *(O)*	*I* saw **someone**. *(S) (O)*	**Whom** is used in very formal English. In everyday spoken English, **who** is usually used instead of **whom**: UNCOMMON: Whom did you see? COMMON: Who did you see?
(c) **What** happened? *(S)*	**Something** happened. *(S)*	**What** can be used as either the subject or the object in a question.
(d) **What** did *you* see? *(O)*	*I* saw **something**. *(S) (O)*	Notice in (a) and (c): When **who** or **what** is used as the subject of a question, usual question word order is not used; no form of **do** is used: CORRECT: Who came? INCORRECT: Who did come?

❑ **Exercise 16. Looking at grammar.** (Chart 5-4)
Make questions with *who, who(m)*, and *what*. Write "S" if the question word is the subject. Write "O" if the question word is the object.

	Question	**Answer**
1.	*S* *Who knows?*	*S* **Someone** knows.
2.	*O* *Who(m) did you ask?*	*O* I asked **someone**.
3.	_____	**Someone** knocked on the door.
4.	_____	Talya met **someone**.
5.	_____	Mike learned **something**.
6.	_____	**Something** changed Gina's mind.
7.	_____	Gina is talking about **someone**.*
8.	_____	Gina is talking about **something**.

*A preposition may come at the beginning of a question in very formal English:
  About whom (NOT **who**) *is Tina talking?*
In everyday English, a preposition usually does not come at the beginning of a question.

Exercise 17. Looking at grammar. (Chart 5-4)

Complete the sentences with **who** or **what**.

1. A: _____ just called?
   B: That was Antonia.

2. A: _____ do you need?
   B: A pair of scissors. I'm cutting my hair.

3. A: _____ is Jae?
   B: My stepmom.

4. A: _____ is going on?
   B: Ben's having a party.

5. A: _____ did you call?
   B: Tracy.

6. A: _____ do you need?
   B: Dr. Smith or her nurse.

Exercise 18. Let's talk: interview. (Chart 5-4)

Walk around the room and ask your classmates questions with **who** or **what**.

Example: _____ are you currently reading?
SPEAKER A: What are you currently reading?
SPEAKER B: A book about a cowboy.

1. _____ do you like to do in your free time?
2. _____ is your idea of the perfect vacation?
3. _____ is your best friend?
4. _____ was the most memorable event of your childhood?
5. _____ stresses you out?
6. _____ do you need that you don't have?
7. _____ would you most like to invite to dinner? Why? (*The person can be living or dead.*)

Exercise 19. Listening. (Chart 5-4)

Listen to the conversation. Listen again and complete the sentences with the words you hear.

A secret

A: John told me something.

B: _____ tell you?
   ₁

A: It's confidential. I can't tell you.

B: _____ anyone else?
   ₂

A: He told a few other people.

B: _____ tell?
   ₃

A: Some friends.

B: Then it's not a secret. _____ say?
   ₄

A: I can't tell you.

B: _____ can't _____ me?
   ₅   ₆

A: Because it's about you. But don't worry. It's nothing bad.

B: Gee. Thanks a lot. That sure makes me feel better.

Exercise 20. Let's read and talk. (Chart 5-4)
Work in small groups. Ask your classmates for the meaning of the *italicized* words in the
passage. Refer to a dictionary as necessary.

Example: type
STUDENT A: What does *type* mean?
STUDENT B: *Type* means *kind* or *category*.

Types of Books

There are several different *types* of books. You may be familiar with the categories of *fiction*
and *nonfiction*. These are the two main types. *Fiction* includes *mysteries, romance, thrillers, science
fiction*, and *horror. Nonfiction* includes *biographies, autobiographies, history*, and *travel*. There are
other types, but these are some of the more common ones. Which type do you like best?

❑ **Exercise 21. Warm-up.** (Chart 5-5)
Answer the questions with information about yourself.

1. What do you do on weekends? I . . .
2. What did you do last weekend? I . . .
3. What are you going to do this weekend? I'm going to . . .
4. What will you do the following weekend? I will . . .

5-5	Using *What* + a Form of *Do*		
	Question	**Answer**	
(a)	*What **does** Bob **do** every morning?*	He *goes to class.*	***What*** + *a form of **do*** is used to ask questions about activities.
(b)	*What **did** you **do** yesterday?*	I *went downtown.*	
(c)	*What **is** Anna **doing** (right now)?*	She *'s studying.*	Examples of forms of ***do****: am doing, will do, are going to do, did, etc.*
(d)	*What **are** you **going to do** tomorrow?*	I *'m going to go to the beach.*	
(e)	*What **do** you **want to do** tonight?*	I *want to go to a movie.*	
(f)	*What **would** you **like to do** tomorrow?*	I *would like to visit Jim.*	

❑ **Exercise 22. Looking at grammar.** (Chart 5-5)
Make questions beginning with ***What*** + a form of ***do***.

1. A: ___*What are you doing*___ right now?

   B: I'm working on my monthly report.

2. A: _____ last night?

   B: I worked on my monthly report.

3. A: _____ tomorrow?

   B: I'm going to visit my relatives.

4. A: _____ tomorrow?

   B: I want to go to the beach.

5. A: _____ this evening?

   B: I would like to go to a movie.

6. A: _____ tomorrow?

   B: I'm staying home and relaxing most of the day.

7. A: _____ in your history class every day?

   B: We listen to the teacher talk.

8. A: _____ (for a living)?*

   B: I'm a teacher.

   A: _____ your wife _____ ?

   B: She designs websites. She works for an Internet company.

❏ **Exercise 23. Let's talk: interview.** (Chart 5-5)
Interview your classmates. Make questions with the given words and **what** + a form of **do**.
More than one verb tense may be possible. Share a few of your classmates' answers with the class.

Example: tomorrow
SPEAKER A: What are you going to do tomorrow? / What do you want to do tomorrow? / What would you like to do tomorrow? / Etc.
SPEAKER B: I'm going to buy a new video game. / I want to buy a new video game. / I'd like to buy a new video game. / Etc.

1. last night
2. right now
3. next Saturday
4. this afternoon
5. tonight
6. last weekend
7. after class yesterday
8. every morning
9. since you arrived in this city
10. on weekends

❏ **Exercise 24. Warm-up.** (Chart 5-6)
Answer the questions about ice-cream flavors.

blackberry	chocolate	coffee	lemon	strawberry
caramel	coconut	green tea	mint	vanilla

1. Which ice-cream flavors are popular in your country?
2. What kind of ice cream do you like?

---

*__What do you do?__ has a special meaning. It means: *What is your occupation, your job?* Another way of asking the same question: *What do you do for a living?*

5-6 Using *Which* and *What Kind Of*

Which

(a) TOM: May I borrow a pen from you?
ANN: Sure. I have two pens. This pen has black ink. That pen has red ink.
    Which pen do you want? OR
    Which one do you want? OR
    Which   do you want?
	In (a): Ann uses **which** (not **what**) because she wants Tom to choose.
	
	Which is used when the speaker wants someone to make a choice, when the speaker is offering alternatives: *this one or that one; these or those.*

(b) SUE: I like these earrings, and I like those too. BOB: **Which** (*earrings /ones*) are you going to buy? SUE: I think I'll get these.	**Which** can be used with either singular or plural nouns.
(c) JIM: Here's a photo of my daughter's class. KIM: Very nice. **Which one** is your daughter?	**Which** can be used to ask about people as well as things.
(d) SUE: My aunt gave me some money for my birthday. I'm going to take it with me to the mall. BOB: **What** are you going to buy with it? SUE: I haven't decided yet.	In (d): The question doesn't involve choosing from a particular group of items, so Bob uses **what**, not **which**.

What kind of

QUESTION	ANSWER	
		What kind of asks for information about a specific type (a specific kind) in a general category.

(e) **What kind of** *shoes* did you buy?	Boots.
	Sandals.
	Tennis shoes.
	Loafers.
	Running shoes.
	High heels.
	Etc.
		In (e): general category = shoes
		     specific kinds = boots
		                 sandals
		                 tennis shoes
		                 etc.

(f) **What kind of** *fruit* do you like best?	Apples.
	Bananas.
	Oranges.
	Grapefruit.
	Strawberries.
	Etc.
		In (f): general category = fruit
		     specific kinds = apples
		                 bananas
		                 oranges
		                 etc.

❑ **Exercise 25. Looking at grammar.** (Chart 5-6)
Make questions beginning with **Which** or **What**.

1. A: I have two books.   *Which book / Which one / Which do you want?*

    B: That one. (I want that book.)

2: A: *What did you buy when you went shopping?*

    B: A book. (I bought a book when I went shopping.)

3. A: Could I borrow your pen for a minute?

   B: Sure. I have two. _____

   A: That one. (I would like that one.)

4. A: _____

   B: A pen. (Hassan borrowed a pen from me.)

5. A: _____

   B: Two pieces of hard candy. (I have two pieces of hard candy in my hand.) Would you like one?

   A: Yes. Thanks.

   B: _____

   A: The yellow one. (I'd like the yellow one.)

6. A: Tony and I went shopping. I got some new shoes.

   B: _____

   A: A tie. (Tony got a tie.)

7. A: Did you enjoy your trip to South America?

   B: Yes, I did. Very much.

   A: _____

   B: Peru, Brazil, and Venezuela. (I visited Peru, Brazil, and Venezuela.)★

   A: _____

   B: Peru. (I enjoyed Peru the most. I have family there.)

❑ **Exercise 26. Let's talk: interview.** (Chart 5-6)
Make questions. Ask one of your classmates each question and write the answer. Share some of their answers with the class.

1. A: What kind of ___shoes___ are you wearing?

   B: Boots. *Classmate's answer:* _____

2. A: What kind of ___meat___ do you eat most often?

   B: Beef. *Classmate's answer:* _____

3. A: What kind of _____ do you like best?

   B: Rock 'n roll. *Classmate's answer:* _____

4. A: What kind of _____ do you like to watch?

   B: Comedy. *Classmate's answer:* _____

5. A: What kind of _____ do you like best?

   B: *Classmate's answer:* _____

★ The difference between **what** *country* and **which** *country* is often very small.

❑ **Exercise 27. Warm-up.** (Chart 5-7)
Answer the questions.

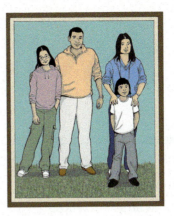

1. This is Ted's daughter. Whose daughter is that?
   a. That's Terry.   b. That's Terry's.

2. This is Ted. Who's next to him?
   a. That's Terry.   b. That's Terry's.

5-7 Using *Whose*

Question	Answer	
(a) ***Whose*** (***book***) is this?	It's John's (book).	***Whose*** asks about possession.*
(b) ***Whose*** (***books***) are those?	They're mine (OR my books).	Notice in (a): The speaker of the question may omit the noun (***book***) if the meaning is clear to the listener.
(c) ***Whose car*** did you borrow?	I borrowed Karen's (car).	
COMPARE: (d) ***Who's*** that? (e) ***Whose*** is that?	Mary Smith. Mary's.	***Who's*** and ***whose*** have the same pronunciation. ***Who's*** is a contraction of ***who is***. ***Whose*** asks about possession.

*See Charts 6-11, p. 166, and 6-12, p. 168, for ways of expressing possession.

❑ **Exercise 28. Let's talk: pairwork.** (Chart 5-7)
Work with a partner. Partner B looks at the picture below and tries to remember what the women are wearing. Then Partner B closes his/her book. Partner A asks questions by pointing to an item on page 126 and using ***whose***. Partners should change roles after four items.

Example:
PARTNER A: Whose purse is that?
PARTNER B: It's Rita's.

Nina   Rita

❑ **Exercise 29. Listening.** (Chart 5-7)

Listen to the questions and circle the correct completions.

1. Who's   Whose   3. Who's   Whose   5. Who's   Whose

2. Who's   Whose   4. Who's   Whose   6. Who's   Whose

❑ **Exercise 30. Listening.** (Chart 5-7)

Listen to the questions. Decide if the speaker is saying ***whose*** or ***who's***.

An old vacation photo

1. whose   who's   3. whose   who's   5. whose   who's

2. whose   who's   4. whose   who's   6. whose   who's

❑ **Exercise 31. Warm-up.** (Chart 5-8)

Match each question in Column A with the correct answer in Column B.

Column A

1. How tall is your sister? _____

2. How old is your brother? _____

3. How did you get here? _____

4. How soon do we need to go? _____

5. How well do you know Kazu? _____

Column B

a. By bus.

b. In five minutes.

c. I don't. I only know his sister.

d. Fifteen.

e. Five feet (1.52 meters).

5-8 Using *How*

Question	Answer	
(a) *How* did you get here?	I drove. / By car. I took a taxi. / By taxi. I took a bus. / By bus. I flew. / By plane. I took a train. / By train. I walked. / On foot.	*How* has many uses. One use of *how* is to ask about means (ways) of transportation.
(b) *How old* are you? (c) *How tall* is he? (d) *How big* is your apartment? (e) *How sleepy* are you? (f) *How hungry* are you? (g) *How soon* will you be ready? (h) *How well* does he speak English? (i) *How quickly* can you get here?	Twenty-one. About six feet. It has three rooms. Very sleepy. I'm starving. In five minutes. Very well. I can get there in 30 minutes.	*How* is often used with adjectives (e.g., *old, big*) and adverbs (e.g., *well, quickly*).

❑ **Exercise 32. Reading and grammar.** (Chart 5-8)
Read the passage about John and then answer the questions.

Long John

John is 14 years old. He is very tall for his age. He is 6 foot, 6 inches (2 meters). His friends call him "Long John." People are surprised to find out that he is still a teenager. Both his parents are average height, so John's height seems unusual.

It causes problems for him, especially when he travels. Beds in hotels are too short, and there is never enough leg room on airplanes. He is very uncomfortable. When he can, he prefers to take a train because he can walk around and stretch his legs.

1. How tall is John? _____.

2. How old is John? _____.

3. How well do you think he sleeps in hotels? _____.

4. How comfortable is he on airplanes? _____.

5. How does he like to travel? _____.

❑ **Exercise 33. Looking at grammar.** (Chart 5-8)
Make questions with *How*.

1. A: ___How old is your daughter?___
   B: Ten. (My daughter is ten years old.)

2. A: _____
   B: Very important. (Education is very important.)

3. A: _____
   B: By bus. (I get to school by bus.)

4. A: _____
   B: Very, very deep. (The ocean is very, very deep.)

5. A: _____
   B: By plane. (I'm going to get to Buenos Aires by plane.)

6. A: _____
   B: Not very. (The test wasn't very difficult.)

7. A: _____
   B: It's 29,029 feet high. (Mt. Everest is 29,029 feet high.)★

8. A: _____
   B: I ran. (I ran here.)

❑ **Exercise 34. Listening.** (Chart 5-8)
Complete the conversations with the words you hear.

1. A: _____ are these eggs?
   B: I just bought them at the Farmers' Market, so they should be fine.

2. A: _____ were the tickets?
   B: They were 50% off.

3. A: _____ was the driver's test?
   B: Well, I didn't pass, so that gives you an idea.

4. A: _____ is the car?
   B: There's dirt on the floor. We need to vacuum it inside.

5. A: _____ is the frying pan?
   B: Don't touch it! You'll burn yourself.

6. A: _____ is the street you live on?
   B: There is a lot of traffic, so we keep the windows closed a lot.

7. A: _____ are you about interviewing for the job?
   B: Very. I already scheduled an interview with the company.

★29,029 feet = 8,848 meters

❑ **Exercise 35. Warm-up: trivia.** (Chart 5-9)
Match each question in Column A with the best answer in Column B.★

Column A

1. How often does the earth go completely around the sun? _____
2. How often do the summer Olympics occur? _____
3. How often do earthquakes occur? _____
4. How many times a year can a healthy person safely donate blood? _____
5. How many times a day do the hands on a clock overlap? _____

Column B

a. About six times a year.
b. Several hundred times a day.
c. Once a year.
d. Every four years.
e. Exactly 22 times a day.

5-9 Using *How Often*

Question	Answer	
(a) **How often** do you go shopping?	Every day. Once a week. About twice a week. Every other day or so.★ Three times a month.	**How often** asks about frequency.
(b) **How many times a day** do you eat? **How many times a week** do you go shopping? **How many times a month** do you go to the post office? **How many times a year** do you take a vacation?	Three or four. Two. Once. Once or twice.	Other ways of asking **how often**: **how many times** { a day a week a month a year

Frequency Expressions		
a lot occasionally once in a while not very often hardly ever almost never never	every every other once a twice a three times a ten times a	} day / week / month / year

★*Every other day* means "Monday yes, Tuesday no, Wednesday yes, Thursday no," etc.
Or so means "approximately."

★See *Trivia Answers*, p. 421.

Exercise 36. Let's talk: pairwork. (Chart 5-9)
Work with a partner. Take turns asking and answering questions with *How often* or *How many times a day/week/month/year*.

Example: eat lunch at the cafeteria
SPEAKER A: How often do you eat lunch at the cafeteria?
SPEAKER B: About twice a week. How about you? How often do you eat at the cafeteria?
SPEAKER A: I don't. I bring my own lunch.

1. check email
2. listen to podcasts
3. go out to eat
4. cook your own dinner
5. buy a toothbrush
6. go swimming
7. attend weddings
8. download music from the Internet

❑ **Exercise 37. Reading and listening.** (Charts 5-8 and 5-9)
Read the short paragraph about Ben. Then complete the questions with the words you hear.

Ben's Sleeping Problem

Ben has a problem with insomnia. He's unable to fall asleep at night very easily. He also wakes up often in the middle of the night and has trouble getting back to sleep. Right now he's talking to a nurse at a sleep disorders clinic. The nurse is asking him some general questions.

1. _____ you?

2. _____ you?

3. _____ you weigh?

4. In general, _____ you sleep at night?

5. _____ you fall asleep?

6. _____ you wake up during the night?

7. _____ you in the mornings?

8. _____ you exercise?

9. _____ you feeling right now?

10. _____ you come in for an overnight appointment?

☐ **Exercise 38. Warm-up.** (Chart 5-10)
Look at the map and answer the questions about flying distances to these cities.

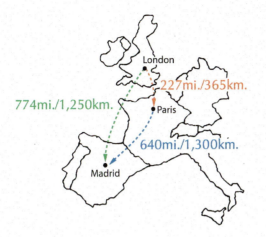

1. How far is it from London to Madrid?
2. How many miles is it from London to Paris?
3. How many kilometers is it from Paris to Madrid?

5-10 Using *How Far*

(a) **It is** 489 miles **from** Oslo **to** Helsinki by air.*	The most common way of expressing distance: **It is** + *distance* + **from/to** + **to/from**
(b) **It is** 3,605 miles { **from** Moscow **to** Beijing. **from** Beijing **to** Moscow. **to** Beijing **from** Moscow. **to** Moscow **from** Beijing.	In (b): All four expressions with **from** and **to** have the same meaning.
(c) — **How far is it** from Mumbai to Delhi? — 725 miles.	**How far** is used to ask questions about distance.
(d) — **How far do you** live from school? — Four blocks.	
(e) **How many miles** is it from London to Paris? (f) **How many kilometers** is it to Montreal from here? (g) **How many blocks** is it to the post office?	Other ways to ask **how far**: • *how many miles* • *how many kilometers* • *how many blocks*

*1 mile = 1.60 kilometers; 1 kilometer = 00.614 mile

☐ **Exercise 39. Looking at grammar.** (Chart 5-10)
Make questions with **How far**.

1. A: *How far is it from Prague to Budapest?*
   B: 276 miles. (It's 276 miles to Prague from Budapest.)

2. A: _____

   B: 257 kilometers. (It's 257 kilometers from Montreal to Quebec.)

3. A: _____

   B: Six blocks. (It's six blocks from here to the post office.)

4. A: _____

   B: A few miles. (I live a few miles from work.)

❏ **Exercise 40. Looking at grammar.** (Chart 5-10)
Write four questions with *How far* and words from the list. Use this model: *How far is it from* (___) *to* (___)? Look up the correct distances. Ask other students your questions.

the sun	the moon	the earth	Mars
Venus	Jupiter	Saturn	Neptune

❏ **Exercise 41. Warm-up.** (Chart 5-11)
Complete the sentences. Then ask three different classmates about their nighttime routine. Begin with *How long does it take you to . . . ?* Share some of their answers with the class.

1. It takes me _____ minutes to get ready for bed.

2. It takes me _____ minutes to brush my teeth.

3. It usually takes me _____ minutes/hour(s) to fall asleep.

5-11 Length of Time: *It + Take* and *How Long*

IT + TAKE + (SOMEONE) + LENGTH OF TIME + INFINITIVE	*It* + *take* is often used with time words and an infinitive to express **length of time**, as in (a) and (b).
(a) *It* takes 20 minutes *to cook* rice. (b) *It* took Al two hours *to drive* to work.	An infinitive = *to* + *the simple form of a verb.** In (a): *to cook* is an infinitive.
(c) *How long* does it take to cook rice? Twenty minutes. (d) *How long* did it take Al to drive to work today? Two hours. (e) *How long* did you study last night? Four hours. (f) *How long* will you be in Hong Kong? Ten days.	*How long* asks about *length of time*.
(g) *How many days* will you be in Hong Kong?	Other ways of asking *how long*: *how many* + { minutes / hours / days / weeks / months / years }

*See Chart 13-3, p. 346.

Exercise 42. Let's talk: pairwork. (Chart 5-11)
Work with a partner. Take turns asking and answering questions using *it* + *take*. Share a few of your answers with the class.

1. How long does it take you to . . .
    a. eat breakfast? → *It takes me ten minutes to eat breakfast.*
    b. get to class?
    c. write a short paragraph in English?
    d. read a 300-page book?

2. Generally speaking, how long does it take to . . .
    a. fly from (*a city*) to (*a city*)?
    b. get from here to your hometown?
    c. get used to living in a foreign country?
    d. commute from (*a local place*) to (*a local place*) during rush hour?

□ **Exercise 43. Looking at grammar.** (Chart 5-11)
Make questions with *How long*.

1. A: *How long did it take you to drive to Istanbul?*
   B: Five days. (It took me five days to drive to Istanbul.)

2. A: _____
   B: A week. (Mr. McNally will be in the hospital for a week.)

3. A: _____
   B: A long time. (It takes a long time to learn a second language.)

4. A: _____
   B: Six months. (I've been living here for six months.)

5. A: _____
   B: Six years. (I lived in Oman for six years.)

6. A: _____
   B: A couple of years. (I've known Mr. Pham for a couple of years.)

7. A: _____
   B: Since 2005. (He's been living in Canada since 2005.)

Listen to the questions. The verbs in *italics* are contracted with the question word. Choose the correct verb from the list for each question.

does	did	is	are	will

A birthday

1. *When's* your birthday? _____

2. *When'll* your party be? _____

3. *Where'd* you decide to have it? _____

4. *Who're* you inviting? _____

5-12 Spoken and Written Contractions with Question Words

	Spoken Only	
is	(a) "*When's* he coming?" "*Why's* she late?"	**Is, are, does, did, has, have,** and **will** are usually contracted with question words in speaking.
are	(b) "*What're* these?" "*Who're* they talking to?"	
does	(c) "*When's* the movie start?" "*Where's* he live?"	
did	(d) "*Who'd* you see?" "*What'd* you do?"	
has	(e) "*What's* she done?" "*Where's* he gone?"	
have	(f) "*How've* you been?" "*What've* I done?"	
will	(g) "*Where'll* you be?" "*When'll* they be here?"	
	(h) **What do you** → Whaddaya think? (i) **What are you** → Whaddaya thinking?	**What do you** and **What are you** both can be reduced to "Whaddaya" in spoken English.
	Written	
is	(j) *Where's* Ed? *What's* that? *Who's* he?	Only contractions with **where, what,** or **who + is** are commonly used in writing, such as in letters to friends or emails. They are generally not appropriate in more formal writing, such as in magazine articles or reference material.

❏ **Exercise 45. Listening.** (Chart 5-12)

Listen to the contractions in these questions.

1. Where is my key?
2. Where are my keys?
3. Who are those people?
4. What is in that box?
5. What are you doing?
6. Where did Bob go last night?
7. Who will be at the party?

8. Why is the teacher absent?
9. Who is that?
10. Why did you say that?
11. Who did you talk to at the party?
12. How are we going to get to work?
13. What did you say?
14. How will you do that?

❏ **Exercise 46. Listening.** (Chart 5-12)

Complete the sentences with the words you hear. Write the non-contracted forms.

On an airplane

Example: You will hear: When's the plane land?

You will write: _____*When does*_____ the plane land?

1. _____ you going to sit with?

2. _____ you going to get your suitcase under the seat?

3. _____ the flight attendant just say?

4. _____ we need to put our seat belts back on?

5. _____ the plane descending?

6. _____ we going down?

7. _____ the pilot tell us what's going on?

8. _____ meet you when you land?

9. _____ our connecting flight?

10. _____ we get from the airport to our hotel?

❏ **Exercise 47. Listening.** (Chart 5-12)

Complete the questions with the words you hear. Write the non-contracted forms.

A mother talking to her teenage daughter

1. _____ going?

2. _____ going with?

3. _____ that?

4. _____ known him?

5. _____ meet him?

Asking Questions **135**

6. _____ go to school?

7. _____ a good student?

8. _____ be back?

9. _____ wearing that outfit?

10. _____ giving me that look?

11. _____ asking so many questions?

   Because I love you!

❑ Exercise 48. Listening. (Chart 5-12)

Listen to the questions and circle the correct non-reduced forms of the words you hear.

Example: You will hear: Whaddaya want?
         You will choose: What are you   (What do you)

1. What are you   What do you

2. What are you   What do you

3. What are you   What do you

4. What are you   What do you

5. What are you   What do you

6. What are you   What do you

7. What are you   What do you

8. What are you   What do you

❑ Exercise 49. Warm-up. (Chart 5-13)

Part I. Both sentences in each pair are grammatically correct. Which question in each pair do you think is more common in spoken English?

1. a. How do you spell "Hawaii?"
   b. What is the spelling for "Hawaii?"

2. a. How do you pronounce G-A-R-A-G-E?
   b. What is the pronunciation for G-A-R-A-G-E?

Part II. Which two questions have the same meaning?

1. How are you doing?
2. How's it going?
3. How do you do?

5-13 More Questions with *How*

Question		Answer	
(a) *How do you spell* "coming"?		C-O-M-I-N-G.	To answer (a): Spell the word.
(b) *How do you say* "yes" in Japanese?		Hai.	To answer (b): Say the word.
(c) *How do you say /pronounce* this word?		——	To answer (c): Pronounce the word.
(d) *How are you getting along?*	Great. Fine. Okay. So-so.		In (d), (e), and (f): How is your life? Is your life okay? Do you have any problems? NOTE: Example (f) is also used in greetings: *Hi, Bob. How's it going?*
(e) *How are you doing?*			
(f) *How's it going?*			
(g) *How do you feel?* *How are you feeling?*	Terrific! Wonderful! Great! Fine. Okay. So-so. A bit under the weather. Not so good. Terrible! / Lousy. / Awful!		The questions in (g) ask about health or about general emotional state.
(h) *How do you do?*	How do you do?		***How do you do?*** is used by two speakers when they meet each other for the first time in a somewhat formal situation, as in (h).*

*A: *Dr. Erickson, I'd like to introduce you to a friend of mine, Rick Brown. Rick, this is my biology professor, Dr. Erickson.*
B: ***How do you do,*** *Mr. Brown?*
C: ***How do you do,*** *Dr. Erickson? I'm pleased to meet you.*

❑ **Exercise 50. Game.** (Chart 5-13)
Divide into two teams. Take turns spelling the words your teacher gives you. The team with the most correct answers wins. Your book is closed.

Example: country
TEACHER: How do you spell "country"?
TEAM A: C-O-U-N-T-R-Y.
TEACHER: Good. (*If the answer is incorrect, the other team gets a try.*)

1. together		7. beginning
2. people		8. intelligent
3. daughter		9. Mississippi
4. beautiful		10. purple
5. foreign		11. rained
6. neighbor		12. different

Walk around the room and ask your classmates how to say each item in another language (Japanese, Arabic, German, French, Korean, etc). If someone doesn't know, ask another person. Use this question: ***How do you say*** (___) ***in*** (___)**?**

Example:
SPEAKER A: How do you say "yes" in French?
SPEAKER B: "Yes" in French is "oui."

1. No.	3. Okay.	5. Good-bye.
2. Thank you.	4. How are you?	6. Excuse me.

☐ **Exercise 52. Warm-up.** (Chart 5-14)

In the conversation, the speakers are making suggestions. <u>Underline</u> their suggestions.

A: Let's invite the Thompsons over for dinner.

B: Good idea! How about next Sunday?

A: Let's do it sooner. What about this Saturday?

5-14 Using *How About* and *What About*

(a) A: We need one more player.
    B: *How about/What about Jack?*
       Let's ask him if he wants to play.
 	
(b) A: What time should we meet?
    B: *How about/What about three o'clock?*
	How about and **what about** have the same meaning and usage. They are used to make suggestions or offers.
	
	How about and **what about** are followed by a noun (or pronoun) or the **-ing** form of a verb (gerund).

(c) A: What should we do this afternoon?
    B: *How about going* to the zoo?
 	
(d) A: *What about asking* Sally over for dinner next Sunday?
    B: Okay. Good idea.
	NOTE: **How about** and **what about** are frequently used in informal spoken English, but are usually not used in writing.

(e) A: I'm tired. *How about you?*
    B: Yes, I'm tired too.
 	
(f) A: Are you hungry?
    B: No. *What about you?*
    A: I'm a little hungry.
	How about you? and **What about you?** are used to ask a question that refers to the information or question that immediately preceded it.
	
	In (e): **How about you?** = **Are you tired?**
	In (f): **What about you?** = **Are you hungry?**

☐ **Exercise 53. Grammar and listening.** (Chart 5-14)

Choose the best response. Then listen to each conversation and check your answer.

Example:
SPEAKER A: What are you going to do over vacation?
SPEAKER B: I'm staying here. What about you?
SPEAKER A: a. Yes, I will. I have a vacation too.
           (b.) I'm going to Jordan to visit my sister.
            c. I did too.

1. A: Did you like the movie?
   B: It was okay, I guess. How about you?
   A: a. I thought it was pretty good.
      b. I'm sure.
      c. I saw it last night.

2. A: Are you going to the company party?
   B: I haven't decided yet. What about you?
   A: a. I didn't know that.
      b. Why aren't you going?
      c. I think I will.

3. A: Do you like living in this city?
   B: Sort of. How about you?
   A: a. I'm living in the city.
      b. I'm not sure. It's pretty noisy.
      c. Yes, I have been.

4. A: What are you going to have?
   B: Well, I'm not really hungry. I think I might order just a salad. How about you?
   A: a. I'll have one too.
      b. I'm eating at a restaurant.
      c. No, I'm not.

❑ **Exercise 54. Let's talk: pairwork.** (Chart 5-14)
Work with a partner. The given questions are common ways to begin casual conversations or make "small talk." Partner A asks the question and Partner B answers. Both speakers look at each other, not the book, when speaking.

Example: What kind of books do you like to read?
PARTNER A: What kind of books do you like to read?
PARTNER B: I like biographies. How about you?
PARTNER A: Thrillers are my favorite.

1. How long have you been living in (*this city or country*)?
2. What are you going to do after class today?
3. What kind of movies do you like to watch?

Change roles.
4. Do you come from a large family?
5. What kind of sports do you enjoy?
6. Do you speak a lot of English outside of class?

❑ **Exercise 55. Warm-up.** (Chart 5-15)
What is the <u>expected</u> response? Circle *yes* or *no*.

1. You're studying English, aren't you?   yes   no

2. You're not a native speaker of English, are you?   yes   no

5-15 Tag Questions

(a) Jill is sick, *isn't she?* (b) You didn't know, *did you?* (c) There's enough time, *isn't there?* (d) I'm not late, *am I?* (e) I'm late, *aren't I?*	A tag question is a question that is added onto the end of a sentence. An auxiliary verb is used in a tag question. Notice that *I am* becomes *aren't I* in a negative tag, as in (e). (*Am I not* is also possible, but it is very formal and rare.

	Affirmative (+)	**Negative (−)**	**Affirmative Expected Answer**	
(d)	*You know* Bill,	*don't* you?	Yes.	When the main verb is affirmative, the tag question is negative, and the expected answer agrees with the main verb.
(e)	*Marie is* from Paris,	*isn't* she?	Yes.	

	Negative (−)	**Affirmative (+)**	**Negative Expected Answer**	
(f)	*You don't know* Tom,	*do* you?	No.	When the main verb is negative, the tag question is affirmative, and the expected answer agrees with the main verb.
(g)	*Marie isn't* from Athens,	*is* she?	No.	

THE SPEAKER'S QUESTION	THE SPEAKER'S IDEA
	Tag questions have two types of intonation: rising and falling. The intonation determines the meaning of the tag.
(h) It will be nice tomorrow, *won't it?* ↗	A speaker uses rising intonation to make sure information is correct. In (h): the speaker has an idea; the speaker is checking to see if the idea is correct.
(i) It will be nice tomorrow, *won't it?* ↘	Falling intonation is used when the speaker is seeking agreement. In (i): the speaker thinks it will be nice tomorrow and is almost certain the listener will agree.
YES/NO QUESTIONS (j) — Will it be nice tomorrow? — *Yes, it will.* OR *No, it won't.*	In (j): The speaker has no idea. The speaker is simply looking for information. Compare (h) and (i) with (j).

☐ **Exercise 56. Listening and grammar.** (Chart 5-15)

Listen to each pair of sentences and answer the question.

1. a. You're Mrs. Rose, aren't you?
    b. Are you Mrs. Rose?

    QUESTION: In which sentence is the speaker checking to see if her information is correct?

2. a. Do you take cream with your coffee?
    b. You take cream with your coffee, don't you?

    QUESTION: In which sentence does the speaker have no idea?

3. a. You don't want to leave, do you?
    b. Do you want to leave?

    QUESTION: In which sentence is the speaker looking for agreement?

❑ **Exercise 57. Grammar and listening.** (Chart 5-15)
Complete the tag questions with the correct verbs. Then listen to the questions and check your answers.

1. **Simple Present**

   a. You *like* strong coffee, ___*don't*___ you?

   b. David *goes* to Ames High School, _____ he?

   c. Leila and Sara *live* on Tree Road, _____ they?

   d. Jane *has* the keys to the storeroom, _____ she?

   e. Jane's in her office, _____ she?

   f. You're a member of this class, _____ you?

   g. Oleg *doesn't* have a car, _____ he?

   h. Lisa *isn't* from around here, _____ she?

   i. I'm in trouble, _____ I?

2. **Simple Past**

   a. Paul *went* to Indonesia, _____ he?

   b. You *didn't talk* to the boss, _____ you?

   c. Ted's parents *weren't* at home, _____ they?

   d. That *was* Pat's idea, _____ it?

3. **Present Progressive, *Be Going To*, and Past Progressive**

   a. You're *studying* hard, _____ you?

   b. Greg *isn't working* at the bank, _____ he?

   c. It *isn't going to rain* today, _____ it?

   d. Michelle and Yoko *were helping*, _____ they?

   e. He *wasn't listening*, _____ he?

4. **Present Perfect**

   a. It *has been* warmer than usual, _____ it?

   b. You've *had* a lot of homework, _____ you?

   c. We *haven't spent* much time together, _____ we?

   d. Fatima *has started* her new job, _____ she?

   e. Bruno *hasn't finished* his sales report yet, _____ he?

   f. Steve's *had to leave* early, _____ he?

❏ **Exercise 58. Let's talk: pairwork.** (Chart 5-15)

Work with a partner. Make true statements for your partner to agree with. Remember, if your partner makes an affirmative statement before the tag, the expected answer is "yes." If your partner makes a negative statement before the tag, the expected answer is "no."

1. The weather is _____ today, isn't it?

2. This book costs _____, doesn't it?

3. I'm _____, aren't I?

4. The classroom isn't _____, is it?

5. Our grammar homework wasn't _____,was it?

6. Tomorrow will be _____, won't it?

❏ **Exercise 59. Listening.** (Chart 5-15)

Listen to the tag questions and choose the <u>expected</u> responses.

Checking in at a hotel

Example: You will hear: Our room's ready, isn't it?

You will choose: (yes) no

1. yes	no	6. yes	no
2. yes	no	7. yes	no
3. yes	no	8. yes	no
4. yes	no	9. yes	no
5. yes	no	10. yes	no

❏ **Exercise 60. Check your knowledge.** (Chapter 5)

Edit the sentences. Correct the errors in question formation.

1. Who you saw? → *Who did you see?*

2. Where I buy subway tickets?

3. Whose is that backpack?

4. What kind of tea you like best?

5. It's freezing out and you're not wearing gloves, aren't you?

6. Who you studied with at school?

7. She is going to work this weekend, doesn't she?

8. How long take to get to the airport from here?

9. How much height your father have?

10. It's midnight. Why you so late? Why you forget to call?

❑ Exercise 61. Listening. (Chapter 5)

Part I. Listen to the questions and choose the correct answers.

Example: You will hear: How often do you brush your teeth?
You will choose: ⓐ Three times a day.
     b. Yes, I do.
     c. In the evening.

1. a. I love it.
    b. Jazz and rock.
    c. The radio.

2. a. I was really tired.
    b. At 7:30.
    c. A package.

3. a. A little sick.
    b. No, I'm not.
    c. Howard's fine.

4. a. Two miles.
    b. Three blocks.
    c. Ten minutes.

5. a. Amy is.
    b. Amy's.
    c. That is Amy.

6. a. Next week.
    b. A few days ago.
    c. On Fifth Street.

Part II. Listen to each conversation and choose the sentence that best completes it.

7. a. My wallet.
    b. At the box office.
    c. I think so.

8. a. It usually comes by noon.
    b. By truck.
    c. One time a day.

9. a. Yes, I am.
    b. My company is moving to another city.
    c. I loved my job.

10. a. It's great.
    b. I'm a construction supervisor.
    c. We're doing really well.

❑ Exercise 62. Let's listen and talk: pairwork. (Chapter 5)

Listen to the conversation. Then work with a partner. Take turns being the cashier and the customer. Complete the sentences with items from the menu and practice the conversation.

burger	chicken strips	soft drinks: *cola, lemon soda, iced tea*
cheeseburger	fish burger	milkshakes: *vanilla, strawberry, chocolate*
double cheeseburger	veggie burger	*(small, medium, large)*
fries	salad	

Ordering at a fast-food restaurant

CASHIER: So, what'll it be?

CUSTOMER: I'll have a _____.

CASHIER: Would you like fries or a salad with your burger?

CUSTOMER: I'll have (a) _____.

CASHIER: What size?

CUSTOMER: _____.

CASHIER: Anything to drink?

CUSTOMER: I'll have a _____.

CASHIER: Size?

CUSTOMER: _____.

CASHIER: Okay. So that's _____

_____.

CUSTOMER: About how long'll it take?

CASHIER: We're pretty crowded right now. Probably 10 minutes or so. That'll be $6.50.
Your number's on the receipt. I'll call the number when your order's ready.

CUSTOMER: Thanks.

❑ **Exercise 63. Let's read and write.** (Chapters 1 → 5)
Part I. Read the fairy tale and answer the questions at the end.

The Frog Prince

Once upon a time, there was a king with three unmarried daughters. One day while the king was thinking about his daughters' futures, he had an idea. He thought, "I'm going to drop three jewels among the young men in the village center. The men who find* the jewels will become my daughters' husbands." He announced his plan to all of the people of his kingdom.

The next day, the king took an emerald, a ruby, and a diamond into the village. He walked among the young men and dropped the jewels. A handsome man picked up the emerald. Then a wealthy prince found the ruby. But a frog hopped toward the diamond and took it. He said to the king, "I am the Frog Prince. I claim your third daughter as my wife."

When the king told Trina, his third daughter, about the Frog Prince, she refused to marry him. She hid from her friends and grew sadder every day. Meanwhile, her two sisters had grand weddings.

---

*The simple present is used here because the story is giving the king's exact words in a quotation. Notice that quotation marks ("...") are used. See Chart 14-8, p. 000, for more information about quotations.

Eventually, Trina ran away and went to live in the woods, but she was very lonely and unhappy. One day Trina went swimming in a lake. Trina became tired in the cold water and decided to give up. She didn't want to live anymore. As she was drowning, the frog suddenly appeared and pushed Trina to the shore.

"Why did you save my life, Frog?"

"Because you are very young, and you have a lot to live for."

"No, I don't," said the princess. "I am the most miserable person in the world."

"Let's talk about it," said the frog. Trina and the Frog Prince sat together for hours and hours. Frog listened and understood. He told her about his own unhappiness and loneliness. They shared their deepest feelings with each other.

One day while they were sitting near the lake, Trina felt great affection for the frog. She bent down and kissed him on his forehead. Suddenly the frog turned into a man! He took Trina in his arms and said, "You saved me with your kiss. An evil wizard changed me from a prince into a frog. I needed to find the love of a woman with a truly good heart to set me free.* You looked inside me and found the real me."

Trina and the prince returned to the castle and got married. Her two sisters, she discovered, were very unhappy because their husbands treated them poorly. But Trina and her Frog Prince lived happily ever after.

Questions:
1. What did the king want for his daughters?
2. Why did a frog claim Trina for his wife?
3. What did Trina do to escape the marriage?
4. Where did she meet the frog again?
5. Why did she kiss the frog?
6. What did an evil wizard do to the frog?
7. What kind of lives did her sisters have?
8. What kind of life did Trina and the Frog Prince have?

Part II. Write a story that begins ***Once upon a time***. Use one of the given topics.

Topics:
1. Read the story again and then retell it in your own words. Write one or two paragraphs. Do not look at the story when you write.

2. Write a fairy tale that you are familiar with, perhaps one that is well known in your culture.

3. Create a story with your classmates. Each student writes one or two sentences at a time. One student begins the story. Then he or she passes the paper on to another student, who then writes a sentence or two and passes the paper on — until everyone in the class has had a chance to write part of the story, or until the story has an ending. This story can then be reproduced for the class to edit together. The class may want to add art and "publish" the final product as a small book.

---

*set me free = give me my freedom

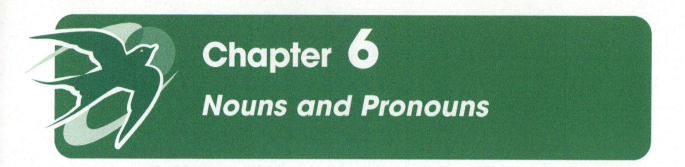

Chapter **6**
Nouns and Pronouns

❑ **Exercise 1. What do I already know?** (Chapter 6)
This exercise previews grammar terms used in this chapter. Identify the *italicized* word in each sentence as a noun, adjective, preposition, or pronoun.

1. Miki is a *student* at my school.   _____*noun*_____

2. *She* is from Kyoto, Japan.   _____*pronoun*_____

3. Kyoto is south *of* Tokyo.   _____*preposition*_____

4. It is a *beautiful* city.   _____*adjective*_____

5. This summer *I* am going there with Miki.   _____

6. I am looking forward to this *trip*.   _____

7. My parents are *happy* for me.   _____

8. I will stay *with* Miki's family.   _____

9. They have a *small* hotel.   _____

10. *It* is near a popular park.   _____

11. The park has lovely *gardens*.   _____

12. Miki has shown me postcards *of* them.   _____

❑ **Exercise 2. Warm-up.** (Chart 6-1)
Write the word **one** before the singular nouns and the word **two** before the plural nouns.

1. _____ trips   4. _____ way

2. _____ vacation   5. _____ cities

3. _____ classes   6. _____ knives

6-1 Plural Forms of Nouns

	Singular	Plural	
(a)	one bird one street one rose	two *birds* two *streets* two *roses*	To make most nouns plural, add *-s*.
(b)	one dish one match one class one box	two *dishes* two *matches* two *classes* two *boxes*	Add *-es* to nouns ending in *-sh*, *-ch*, *-ss*, and *-x*.
(c)	one baby one city	two *babies* two *cities*	If a noun ends in a consonant + *-y*, change the *y* to *i* and add *-es*, as in (c).
(d)	one toy one key	two *toys* two *keys*	If *-y* is preceded by a vowel, add only *-s*, as in (d).
(e)	one knife one shelf	two *knives* two *shelves*	If a noun ends in *-fe* or *-f*, change the ending to *-ves*. EXCEPTIONS: *beliefs, chiefs, roofs, cuffs, cliffs.*
(f)	one tomato one zoo one zero	two *tomatoes* two *zoos* two *zeroes/zeros*	The plural form of nouns that end in *-o* is sometimes *-oes* and sometimes *-os*. *-oes*: tomatoes, potatoes, heroes, echoes *-os*: zoos, radios, studios, pianos, solos, sopranos, photos, autos, videos *-oes* or *-os*: zeroes/zeros, volcanoes/volcanos, tornadoes/tornados, mosquitoes/mosquitos
(g)	one child one foot one goose one man one mouse one tooth one woman ————	two *children* two *feet* two *geese* two *men* two *mice* two *teeth* two *women* two *people*	Some nouns have irregular plural forms. NOTE: The singular form of *people* can be *person, woman, man, child*. For example, one *man* and one *child* = two *people*. (Two *persons* is also possible.)
(h)	one deer one fish one sheep	two *deer* two *fish* two *sheep*	The plural form of some nouns is the same as the singular form.
(i)	one bacterium one crisis	two *bacteria* two *crises*	Some nouns that English has borrowed from other languages have foreign plurals.

❏ **Exercise 3. Looking at grammar.** (Chart 6-1)
Write the correct singular or plural form of the given words.

1. one chair   two _____

2. a _____   a lot of windows

3. one wish   several _____

4. a _____ two dishes

5. a tax a lot of _____

6. one boy two _____

7. a hobby several _____

8. one leaf two _____

9. a _____ two halves

10. a belief many _____

11. one wolf two _____

12. a radio several _____

13. one _____ a lot of sheep

14. one _____ two feet

❏ **Exercise 4. Looking at grammar.** (Chart 6-1)
Write the plural form of each noun under the correct heading. The number of words for each
column is given in parentheses. NOTE: *fish* and *thief* can go in two places.

✓butterfly	child	hero	mouse	thief
baby	city	library	✓museum	tomato
boy	fish	✓man	potato	woman
✓bean	girl	mosquito	sandwich	zoo

People (8)	Food (5)	Things people catch (5)	Places people visit (4)
men	beans	butterflies	museums

□ **Exercise 5. Check your knowledge.** (Chart 6-1)
Edit the newspaper ad by making the appropriate nouns plural. There are eight errors.

ON SALE (while supply last)

shirt   jean   pant   dress

Outfit and shoe for babys 50% off

□ **Exercise 6. Warm-up: listening.** (Chart 6-2)

Listen to the nouns. Circle *yes* if you hear a plural ending. If not, circle *no*.

Example: You will hear: books
You will choose: (yes)   no

You will hear: class
You will choose: yes   (no)

| 1. yes | no | 3. yes | no | 5. yes | no |
| 2. yes | no | 4. yes | no | 6. yes | no |

6-2 Pronunciation of Final -s/-es

Final **-s/-es** has three different pronunciations: /s/, /z/, and /əz/.

(a)	seats	=	seat/s/	Final **-s** is pronounced /s/ after voiceless sounds. In (a): /s/ is the sound of "s" in "bus."
	maps	=	map/s/	
	lakes	=	lake/s/	Examples of voiceless* sounds: /t/, /p/, /k/.
(b)	seeds	=	seed/z/	Final **-s** is pronounced /z/ after voiced sounds. In (b): /z/ is the sound of "z" in "buzz."
	stars	=	star/z/	
	holes	=	hole/z/	Examples of voiced* sounds: /d/, /r/, /l/, /m/, /b/, and all vowel sounds.
	laws	=	law/z/	
(c)	dishes	=	dish/əz/	Final **-s/-es** is pronounced /əz/ after -sh, -ch, -s, -z, -ge/-dge sounds. In (c): /əz/ adds a syllable to a word.
	matches	=	match/əz/	
	classes	=	class/əz/	
	sizes	=	size/əz/	
	pages	=	page/əz/	
	judges	=	judge/əz/	

*See Chart 2-5, p. 39, for more information about voiceless and voiced sounds.

❏ **Exercise 7. Listening.** (Chart 6-2)

Listen to the words. Circle the sound you hear at the end of each word: /s/, /z/, or /əz/.

1. pants   /s/   /z/   /əz/   4. pens   /s/   /z/   /əz/

2. cars   /s/   /z/   /əz/   5. wishes   /s/   /z/   /əz/

3. boxes   /s/   /z/   /əz/   6. lakes   /s/   /z/   /əz/

❏ **Exercise 8. Listening.** (Chart 6-2)

Listen to each pair of words. Decide if the endings have the same sound or a different sound.

Example: You will hear: maps   streets
           You will choose: (same)   different

           You will hear: knives   forks
           You will choose: same   (different)

1. same   different   5. same   different

2. same   different   6. same   different

3. same   different   7. same   different

4. same   different   8. same   different

❏ **Exercise 9. Listening and pronunciation.** (Chart 6-2)

Listen to the words. Write the pronunciation of each ending you hear: /s/, /z/, or /əz/. Practice pronouncing the words.

1. names = name/z/   4. boats = boat/   /   7. lips = lip/   /

2. clocks = clock/s/   5. eyelashes = eyelash/   /   8. bridges = bridge/   /

3. eyes = eye/   /   6. ways = way/   /   9. cars = car/   /

❏ **Exercise 10. Listening.** (Chart 6-2)

Listen to the sentences and circle the words you hear.

1. size   sizes   3. fax   faxes   5. glass   glasses

2. fax   faxes   4. price   prices   6. prize   prizes

❏ **Exercise 11. Warm-up** (Chart 6-3)

Part I. Work in small groups. Make lists.

1. Name things people need to take with them when they travel.
2. Name things you do when you have free time.
3. Name important people in your life.

Part II. Read your lists. Make sentences using the following information. Share some of your sentences with the class.

1. People need to take _____ with them when they travel.
2. I _____ when I have free time.
3. _____ have been important in my life.

Part III. Answer these questions about your answers in Part II.

1. In which sentence did you write verbs?
2. In which two sentences did you write nouns?
3. In which sentence did you write subjects?
4. In which sentence did you write objects?

6-3 Subjects, Verbs, and Objects

(a) The **sun** **shines**. (noun) (verb)	An English sentence has a SUBJECT (S) and a VERB (V). The SUBJECT is a **noun**. In (a): **sun** is a noun; it is the subject of the verb **shines**.
(b) **Plants** **grow**. (noun) (verb)	
(c) **Plants** **need** **water**. (noun) (verb) (noun)	Sometimes a VERB is followed by an OBJECT (O). The OBJECT of a verb is a **noun**. In (c): **water** is the object of the verb **need**.
(d) **Bob** **is reading** **a book**. (noun) (verb) (noun)	

❑ **Exercise 12. Looking at grammar.** (Chart 6-3)
Complete each diagram with the correct subject, verb, and object.

1. The carpenter built a table.

The carpenter	built	a table
subject	verb	object of verb

2. Birds fly.

Birds	fly	(none)
subject	verb	object of verb

3. Cows eat grass.

subject	verb	object of verb

4. The actor sang.

subject	verb	object of verb

5. The actor sang a song.

subject	verb	object of verb

6. Accidents happen frequently.

subject	verb	object of verb

7. The accident injured a woman.

subject	verb	object of verb

❑ **Exercise 13. Looking at grammar.** (Charts 6-2 and 6-3)

If the word in *italics* is used as a noun, circle "N." If the word in *italics* is used as a verb, circle "V."

1. People *smile* when they're happy.	N	(V)
2. Maryam has a nice *smile* when she's happy.	(N)	V
3. Please don't sign your *name* in pencil.	N	V
4. People often *name* their children after relatives.	N	V
5. Airplanes *land* on runways at the airport.	N	V
6. The *land* across the street from our house is vacant.	N	V
7. People usually *store* milk in the refrigerator.	N	V
8. We went to the *store* to buy some milk.	N	V
9. I took the express *train* from New York to Washington, D.C., last week.	N	V
10. Lindsey *trains* horses as a hobby.	N	V

❑ **Exercise 14. Warm-up: pairwork.** (Chart 6-4)

Work with a partner. Make true sentences about yourself using **like** or **don't like**. Share a few of your partner's answers with the class.

I like/don't like to do my homework . . .

1. at the library.
2. at the kitchen table.
3. in my bedroom.
4. on my bed.
5. with a friend.
6. in the evening.
7. on weekends.
8. after dinner.
9. before class.
10. during class.

6-4 Objects of Prepositions

S V O PREP O OF PREP (a) Ann put her books **on** **the** **desk**. (noun)	Many English sentences have prepositional phrases. In (a): **on the desk** is a prepositional phrase.
S V PREP O OF PREP (b) A leaf fell **to** **the** **ground**. (noun)	A prepositional phrase consists of a PREPOSITION (PREP) and an OBJECT OF A PREPOSITION (O OF PREP). The object of a preposition is a NOUN.

Reference List of Prepositions

about	before	despite	of	to
above	behind	down	off	toward(s)
across	below	during	on	under
after	beneath	for	out	until
against	beside	from	over	up
along	besides	in	since	upon
among	between	into	through	with
around	beyond	like	throughout	within
at	by	near	till	without

❑ **Exercise 15. Looking at grammar.** (Chart 6-4)
Check (✓) the prepositional phrases, and underline the noun in each phrase that is the object of the preposition.

1. ✓ across the <u>street</u>
2. _____ in a minute
3. _____ daily
4. _____ down the hill

5. _____ next to the phone
6. _____ doing work
7. _____ in a few hours
8. _____ from my parents

❑ **Exercise 16. Looking at grammar.** (Charts 6-3 and 6-4)
Check (✓) the sentences that have objects of prepositions. Identify the preposition (P) and the object of the preposition (Obj. of P).

1. a. _____ Emily waited quietly.

                                                  P   Obj. of P
   b. ✓ Emily waited quietly for her mother.

                                                        P   Obj. of P
   c. ✓ Emily's mother was talking to a friend.

2. a. _____ Kimiko saw a picture on the wall.

   b. _____ Kimiko recognized the people.

   c. _____ Kimiko looked at the picture closely.

3. a. _____ Annika lost her ring yesterday.

   b. _____ Annika lost her ring in the sand.

   c. _____ Annika lost her ring in the sand at the beach.

4. a. _____ A talkative woman sat with her husband.

   b. _____ We were at a meeting.

   c. _____ She talked to her husband the entire time.

❏ **Exercise 17. Let's talk.** (Chart 6-4)
Review prepositions of place by using the given phrases in complete sentences. Demonstrate the meaning of the preposition with an action while you say the sentence. Work in pairs, in small groups, or as a class.

Example: across the room
   → *I'm walking across the room.* OR *I'm looking across the room.*

1. above the door
2. against the wall
3. toward(s) the door
4. between two pages of my book
5. in the room
6. into the room
7. on my desk
8. at my desk
9. below the window
10. beside my book
11. near the door
12. far from the door
13. off my desk
14. out the window
15. behind me
16. through the door

❏ **Exercise 18. Game: trivia.** (Chart 6-4)
Work in small groups. Answer the questions without looking at a map. After you have finished, look at a map to check your answers.* The team with the most correct answers wins.

1. Name a country directly under Russia.
2. Name the country directly above Germany.
3. What river flows through London?
4. What is a country near Haiti?
5. Name a country next to Vietnam.
6. Name a city far from Sydney, Australia.
7. What is the country between Austria and Switzerland?
8. Name the city within Rome, Italy.
9. Name two countries that have a river between them.
10. Name a country that is across from Saudi Arabia.

---

*See *Trivia Answers,* p. 421.

❑ **Exercise 19. Reading.** (Chart 6-4)
Read the passage and then answer the questions.

The Habitats of a Rainforest

Rainforests have different areas where animals live. These areas are called *habitats*. Scientists have given names to the four main habitats or layers of a rainforest.

Some animals live in the tops of giant trees. The tops of these trees are much higher than the other trees, so this layer is called the *emergent* layer*. Many birds and insects live there.

Under the emergent layer is the *canopy*. The canopy is the upper part of the trees. It is thick with leaves and vines, and it forms an umbrella over the rainforest. Most of the animals in the rainforest live in the canopy.

The next layer is the *understory*. The understory is above the ground and under the leaves. In the understory, it is very dark and cool. It gets only 2–5% of the sunlight that the canopy gets. The understory has the most insects of the four layers, and a lot of snakes and frogs also live there.

Finally, there is the *forest floor*. On the surface of this floor are fallen leaves, branches, and other debris.** In general, the largest animals in the rainforest live in this layer. Common animals in this habitat are tigers and gorillas.

1. Name two types of animals that live in the tops of giant trees.
2. Where is the understory?
3. Where do you think most mosquitoes live?
4. What are some differences between the emergent layer and the forest floor?

---

*emergent = in botany, a plant that is taller than other plants around it, like a tall tree in a forest

**debris = loose, natural material, like dirt

Complete the sentences with information about yourself.

I was born . . .

1. in _____ (*month*).
2. on _____ (*date*).

3. on _____ (*weekday*).
4. at _____ (*time*).

6-5 Prepositions of Time

in	(a) Please be on time **in** *the future*. (b) I usually watch TV **in** *the evening*.	**in** + the past, the present, the future* **in** + the morning, the afternoon, the evening
	(c) I was born **in** *October*. (d) I was born **in** *1995*. (e) I was born **in** *the 20th century*. (f) The weather is hot **in** *(the) summer*.	**in** + { a month a year a century a season
on	(g) I was born **on** *October 31st, 1995*. (h) I went to a movie **on** *Thursday*. (i) I have class **on** *Thursday morning(s)*.	**on** + a date **on** + a weekday **on** + (a) weekday morning(s), afternoon(s), evening(s)
at	(j) We sleep at night. I was asleep **at** *midnight*. (k) I fell asleep **at** *9:30* (nine-thirty). (l) He's busy **at** *the moment*. Can I take a message?	**at** + noon, night, midnight **at** + "clock time" **at** + the moment, the present time, present

*Possible in British English: *in future* (e.g., *Please be on time in future.*).

❑ **Exercise 21. Looking at grammar.** (Chart 6-5)
Complete the sentences with *in, at,* or *on*. All the sentences contain time expressions.

Studious Stan has college classes . . .

1. _____ the morning.
2. _____ the afternoon.
3. _____ the evening.
4. _____ night.
5. _____ weekdays.

6. _____ Saturdays.
7. _____ Saturday mornings.
8. _____ noon.
9. _____ midnight.

Unlucky Lisa has a birthday every four years. She was born . . .

10. _____ February 29th.
11. _____ February 29th, 2000.
12. _____ February.

13. _____ 2000.
14. _____ February 2000.
15. _____ the winter.

Cool Carlos is a fashion designer. He's thinking about clothing designs . . .

16. _____ the moment.
17. _____ the present time.
18. _____ the past.

Exercise 22. Let's talk: interview. (Chart 6-5)
Complete each question with an appropriate preposition. Interview seven classmates. Ask each person one question.

1. What do you like to do _____ the evening?

2. What do you usually do _____ night before bed?

3. What do you like to do _____ Saturday mornings?

4. What did you do _____ January 1st of this year?

5. What were you doing _____ January 1st, 2000 (the beginning of the new millennium)?

6. How do you spend your free time _____ January?

7. What will you do with your English skills _____ the future?

□ **Exercise 23. Warm-up.** (Chart 6-6)
Check (✓) all the grammatically correct sentences.

1. a. _____ I left Athens in 2005.
   b. _____ I left in 2005 Athens.
   c. _____ In 2005, I left Athens.

2. a. _____ Lee sold his car yesterday.
   b. _____ Yesterday Lee sold his car.
   c. _____ Lee sold yesterday his car.

6-6 Word Order: Place and Time

	S	V	PLACE	TIME
(a)	Ann moved		to Paris	in 2008.
	We went		to a movie	yesterday.

In a typical English sentence, "place" comes before "time," as in (a).

INCORRECT: *Ann moved in 2008 to Paris.*

		S	V	O	P	T
(b)		We bought		a house	in Miami	in 2005.

S-V-O-P-T = Subject-Verb-Object-Place-Time
          (basic English sentence structure)

	TIME	S	V	PLACE
(c)	*In 2008,*	Ann moved		to Paris.
(d)	*Yesterday*	we	went	to a movie.

Expressions of time can also come at the beginning of a sentence, as in (c) and (d).

A time phrase at the beginning of a sentence is often followed by a comma, as in (c).

□ **Exercise 24. Looking at grammar.** (Chart 6-6)
Put the given phrases in correct sentence order.

1. to Paris \ next month

   Monique's company is going to transfer her _____.

2. last week \ through Turkey

   William began a bike trip _____.

3. at his uncle's bakery \ Alexi \ on Saturday mornings \ works

_____.

4. arrived \ in the early morning \ at the airport \ my plane

_____.

❏ **Exercise 25. Warm-up.** (Chart 6-7)
Add **-s** where appropriate. If no final **-s** is necessary, write **Ø**.

1. Lions roar _____.

2. A lion roar _____.

3. Lions and tigers roar _____.

4. A tiger in the jungle roar _____.

5. Tigers in the jungle roar _____.

6. Tigers in jungles roar _____.

6-7 Subject-Verb Agreement

(a) The *sun* shine*s*. SINGULAR SINGULAR (b) *Birds sing*. PLURAL PLURAL	A singular subject takes a singular verb, as in (a). A plural subject takes a plural verb, as in (b). Notice: *verb* + **-s** = singular (*shines*) *noun* + **-s** = plural (*birds*)
(c) *My brother* **lives** in Jakarta. SINGULAR SINGULAR (d) *My brother* **and** *sister* **live** in Jakarta. PLURAL PLURAL	Two subjects connected by **and** take a plural verb, as in (d).
(e) The *glasses* over there under the window by the sink *are* clean. (f) The *information* in those magazines about Vietnamese culture and customs *is* very interesting.	Sometimes phrases come between a subject and a verb. These phrases do not affect the agreement of the subject and verb.
(g) There *is a book* on the desk. V S (h) There *are some books* on the desk. V S	**There** + **be** + *subject* expresses that something exists in a particular place. The verb agrees with the noun that follows **be**.
(i) *Every student is* sitting down. (j) *Everybody/Everyone hopes* for peace.	**Every** is a singular word. It is used with a singular, not plural, noun. INCORRECT: *Every students . . .* Subjects with **every** take singular verbs, as in (i) and (j).
(k) *People* in my country *are* friendly.	**People** is a plural noun and takes a plural verb.

❑ **Exercise 26. Looking at grammar.** (Chart 6-7)
Work in small groups. Complete the sentences with the correct form of the verb from the list.
Discuss the words you use to describe different animal sounds in your native language.

bark	chirp	hiss	meow	roar

What sounds do these animals make?

1. A dog _____.

2. Dogs _____.

3. Lions in the wild _____.

4. Lions, tigers, and leopards _____.

5. Every snake _____.

6. A bird _____.

7. Cats _____.

8. Sea lions on a beach _____.

9. A lizard _____.

10. Baby chickens _____.

❑ **Exercise 27. Looking at grammar.** (Chart 6-7)
<u>Underline</u> and identify the subject (S) and the verb (V). Correct errors in agreement.

1. The <u>students</u> in this class <u>speaks</u> English very well.

2. My aunt and uncle speak Spanish. → *OK (no error)*.

3. Every students in my class speak English well.

4. There are five student from Korea in Mr. Ahmad's class.

5. There's a vacant apartment in my building.

6. Does people in your neighborhood know each other?

7. The neighbors in the apartment next to mine is very friendly and helpful.

❑ **Exercise 28. Listening.** (Charts 6-2 and 6-7)
Listen to the passage. Listen a second time and add **-s** where necessary. Before you begin,
you may want to check your understanding of these words: *sweat, fur, paw, flap, mud.*

How Some Animals Stay Cool

How do animal ____ stay cool in hot weather? Many animal ____ don't sweat like
                        1   2
human ____, so they have other way ____ to cool themselves.
        3   4

Dog ____, for example, have a lot of fur ____ and can become very hot. They stay ____
      5   6   7
cool mainly by panting. By the way, if you don't know what *panting* means, this is the sound of

panting.

Cat _____ lick _____ their paw _____ and chest _____. When their fur _____ is wet, they
             8   9   10   11   12
become cooler.

Elephant _____ have very large ear _____. When they are hot, they can flap their huge
                13   14
ear _____. The flapping ear _____ act _____ like a fan and it cool _____ them. Elephant _____ also
     15   16   17   18   19
like to roll in the mud _____ to stay cool.
                             20

❑ **Exercise 29. Warm-up.** (Chart 6-8)
Think about the very first teacher you had. Choose words from below to describe him/her.

young	friendly	serious
middle-aged	unfriendly	patient
elderly	fun	impatient

6-8 Using Adjectives to Describe Nouns

(a) Bob is reading a ADJECTIVE NOUN *good* *book*.	Words that describe nouns are called ADJECTIVES. In (a): *good* is an adjective; it describes the book.
(b) The *tall woman* wore a *new dress*. (c) The *short woman* wore an *old dress*. (d) The *young woman* wore a *short dress*.	We say that adjectives "modify" nouns. *Modify* means "change a little." An adjective changes the meaning of a noun by giving more information about it.
(e) Roses are *beautiful flowers*. INCORRECT: *Roses are beautifuls flowers.*	Adjectives are neither singular nor plural. They do NOT have a plural form.
(f) He wore a *white shirt*. INCORRECT: *He wore a shirt white.* (g) Roses *are beautiful*. (h) His shirt *was white*.	Adjectives usually come immediately before nouns, as in (f). Adjectives can also follow main verb *be*, as in (g) and (h).

❑ **Exercise 30. Looking at grammar.** (Chart 6-8)
Check (✓) the phrases that have adjectives. <u>Underline</u> the adjectives.

1. ✓ a <u>scary</u> story
2. _____ on Tuesday
3. _____ going to a famous place

4. _____ a small, dark, smelly room
5. _____ quickly and then slowly
6. _____ long or short hair

❑ **Exercise 31. Looking at grammar.** (Chart 6-8)
Add the given adjectives to the sentences. Choose *two* of the three adjectives in each item to add to the sentence.

Example: hard, heavy, strong   A man lifted the box.
      → A strong man lifted the heavy box.

1. beautiful, safe, red   Roses are flowers.

2. empty, wet, hot   The waiter poured coffee into my cup.
3. fresh, clear, hungry   Mrs. Fields gave the kids a snack.
4. dirty, modern, delicious After our dinner, Frank helped me with the dishes.

❑ **Exercise 32. Looking at grammar.** (Chart 6-8)
Work in small groups.

Part I. Add your own nouns, adjectives, and prepositions to the list. Don't look at Part II.

1. an adjective _____old_____   6. an adjective _____

2. a person's name _____   7. an adjective _____

3. a plural noun _____   8. a preposition of place _____

4. a plural noun _____   9. an adjective _____

5. a singular noun _____   10. a plural noun _____

Part II. Complete the sentences with the same words you added in Part I. Some of your completions might sound a little odd or funny. Read your completed passage aloud to another group or to the rest of the class.

   One day a/an _____old_____ girl was walking in the city. Her name was
                        1

_____. She was carrying a package for her grandmother. It contained some
       2

_____, some _____, and a/an _____, among other
       3   4   5

things.

   As she was walking down the street, a/an _____ thief stole her package.
                                                       6

The _____ girl pulled out her cell phone and called the police, who caught the
           7

thief _____ a nearby building and returned her package to her. She took it
           8

immediately to her _____ grandmother, who was glad to get the package
                           9

because she really needed some new _____.
                                            10

❑ **Exercise 33. Warm-up.** (Chart 6-9)
Combine the word *chicken* with the words in the list.

✓fresh	hot	✓legs	recipe	soup

1. __chicken legs__   4. _____

2. __fresh chicken__   5. _____

3. _____

6-9 Using Nouns as Adjectives

(a) I have a **flower** garden.	Sometimes words that are usually used as nouns are used as adjectives.
(b) The **shoe** store also sells socks.	For example, **flower** is usually a noun, but in (a), it's used as an adjective to modify **garden**.
(c) INCORRECT: a flowers garden	When a noun is used as an adjective, it is singular in form, NOT plural.
(d) INCORRECT: the shoes store	

❑ **Exercise 34. Looking at grammar.** (Chart 6-9)
Underline and identify the nouns (N). Use one of the nouns in the first sentence as an adjective in the second sentence.

             N   N

1. This <u>book</u> is about <u>grammar</u>. It's a ___*grammar book**___ .

2. My garden has vegetables. It's a _____ .

3. The soup has beans. It's _____ .

4. I read a lot of articles in magazines. I read a lot of _____ .

5. The factory makes toys. It's a _____ .

6. The villages are in the mountains. They are _____ .

7. The lesson was about art. It was an _____ .

8. Flags fly from poles. Many government buildings have _____ .

❑ **Exercise 35. Looking at grammar.** (Chart 6-9)
Add **-s** to the *italicized* nouns if necessary. Then agree or disagree with each statement. Circle *yes* or *no*.

1.	One day, *computer* programs will make it possible for computers to think.	yes	no
2.	*Computer* make life more stressful.	yes	no
3.	*Airplane* trips are enjoyable nowadays.	yes	no
4.	*Airplane* don't have enough legroom.	yes	no
5.	*Bicycle* are better than cars for getting around in a crowded city.	yes	no
6.	It's fun to watch *bicycle* races like the *Tour de France* on TV.	yes	no
7.	*Vegetable* soups are delicious.	yes	no
8.	Fresh *vegetable* are my favorite food.	yes	no

---

*When one noun modifies another noun, the spoken stress is usually on the first noun: a ***grammar*** book.

❑ **Exercise 36. Listening and speaking.** (Charts 6-1 → 6-9)

Part I. Listen to two friends talking about finding an apartment.

Part II. Complete your own conversation. Perform it for the class. You can use words from the list. NOTE: This conversation is slightly different from Part I.

air-conditioning	an elevator	near a bus stop	a studio
a balcony	an exercise room	near a freeway	a two-bedroom
close to my job	a laundry room	parking	a walk-up

A: I'm looking for a new place to live.

B: How come?

A: _____. I need _____.

B: I just helped a friend find one. I can help you. What else do you want?

A: I want _____. Also, I _____.

    I don't want _____.

B: Anything else?

A: _____ would be nice.

B: That's expensive.

A: I guess I'm dreaming.

❑ **Exercise 37. Warm-up.** (Chart 6-10)
Read the conversation. Look at the personal pronouns in green. Decide if they are subject or object pronouns.

A: Did you hear? Ivan quit his job.
       1

B: I know. I don't understand him. Between you and me, I think it's a bad decision.
  2   3   4   5

1. you   subject   object

2. I   subject   object

3. him   subject   object

4. you   subject   object

5. me   subject   object

6-10 Personal Pronouns: Subjects and Objects

Personal Pronouns

SUBJECT PRONOUNS:	*I*	*we*	*you*	*he, she, it*	*they*
OBJECT PRONOUNS:	*me*	*us*	*you*	*him, her, it*	*them*

(a) *Kate* is married. *She* has two children. S	A pronoun refers to a noun. In (a): *she* is a pronoun; it refers to *Kate*. In (b): *her* is a pronoun; it refers to *Kate*.
(b) *Kate* is my friend. I know *her* well. O	In (a): *She* is a SUBJECT PRONOUN. In (b): *her* is an OBJECT PRONOUN.
(c) Mike has *a new blue bike*. He bought *it* yesterday.	A pronoun can refer to a single noun (e.g., *Kate*) or to a noun phrase. In (c): *it* refers to the whole noun phrase *a new blue bike*.
(d) *Eric and I* are good friends. S	Guidelines for using pronouns following *and*: If the pronoun is used as part of the subject, use a subject pronoun, as in (d).
(e) Ann met *Eric and me* at the museum. O	If the pronoun is part of the object, use an object pronoun, as in (e) and (f).
(f) Ann walked between *Eric and me*. O of PREP	INCORRECT: Eric and me are good friends. INCORRECT: Ann met Eric and I at the museum.

SINGULAR PRONOUNS:	*I*	*me*	*you*	*he, she, it*	*him, her*
PLURAL PRONOUNS:	*we*	*us*	*you*	*they*	*them*

(g) *Mike* is in class. *He* is taking a test.	Singular = one. Plural = more than one.
(h) The *students* are in class. *They* are taking a test.	Singular pronouns refer to singular nouns; plural pronouns refer to plural nouns, as in the examples.
(i) *Kate and Tom* are married. *They* have two children.	

❑ **Exercise 38. Looking at grammar.** (Chart 6-10)
Write the nouns that the pronouns in **boldface** refer to.

1. The apples were rotten, so the children didn't eat **them** even though **they** were really hungry.

   a. them = _____

   b. they = _____

2. Do bees sleep at night? Or do **they** work in the hive all night long? You never see **them** after dark. What do **they** do after night falls?

   a. they = _____

   b. them = _____

   c. they = _____

3. Table tennis began in England in the late 1800s. Today **it** is an international sport. My brother and I played **it** a lot when we were teenagers. I beat **him** sometimes, but **he** was a better player and usually won.

   a. it = _____

   b. it = _____

   c. him = _____

   d. he = _____

□ **Exercise 39. Looking at grammar.** (Chart 6-10)
Circle the correct words in *italics*.

1. Toshi ate dinner with *I, me*.

2. Toshi ate dinner with Mariko and *I, me*.

3. *I, me* had dinner with Toshi last night.

4. Jay drove Eva and *I, me* to the store. He waited for *we, us* in the car.

5. A: I want to get tickets for the soccer game.

   B: You'd better get *it, them* right away. *It, They* *is, are* selling fast.

□ **Exercise 40. Looking at grammar.** (Chart 6-10)
Complete the sentences with **she, he, it, her, him, they,** or **them**.

1. I have a grammar book. ____*It*____ is black.

2. Brian borrowed my books. _____ returned _____ yesterday.

3. Sonya is wearing some new earrings. _____ look good on _____.

4. Don't look directly at the sun. Don't look at _____ directly even if you are wearing sunglasses. The intensity of its light can injure your eyes.

5. Recently, I read about "micromachines." _____ are machines that are smaller than a grain of sand. One scientist called _____ "the greatest scientific invention of our time."

❑ **Exercise 41. Warm-up.** (Chart 6-11)
Match the phrases to the pictures that describe them.

Picture A

Picture B

1. _____ the teacher's office

2. _____ the teachers' office

6-11 Possessive Nouns

SINGULAR:	(a) I know the **student's** name.	An apostrophe (') and an **-s** are used with nouns to show possession.
PLURAL:	(b) I know the **students'** names.	
PLURAL:	(c) I know the **children's** names.	

SINGULAR	(d) the student my baby a man	→ the **student's** name → my **baby's** name → a **man's** name	SINGULAR POSSESSIVE NOUN: *noun* + *apostrophe* (') + **-s**
	(e) James	→ **James'**/**James's** name	A singular noun that ends in **-s** has two possible possessive forms: *James'* OR *James's*.
PLURAL	(f) the students my babies	→ the **students'** names → my **babies'** names	PLURAL POSSESSIVE NOUN: *noun* + **-s** + *apostrophe* (')
	(g) men the children	→ **men's** names → the **children's** names	IRREGULAR PLURAL POSSESSIVE NOUN: *noun* + *apostrophe* (') + **-s** (An irregular plural noun is a plural noun that does not end in **-s**: *children, men, people, women*. See Chart 6-1.)

Compare: (h) **Tom's** here. (i) **Tom's** brother is here.	In (h): **Tom's** is not a possessive noun. It is a contraction of *Tom is*, used in informal writing. In (i): **Tom's** is a possessive noun.

❑ **Exercise 42. Looking at grammar.** (Chart 6-11)
Decide if the meaning of the *italicized* word is "one" or "more than one."

1. The teacher answered the *student's* questions.   (one)   more than one

2. The teacher answered the *students'* questions.   one   more than one

3. Our *daughters'* bedroom is next to our room.   one   more than one

4. Our *son's* room is downstairs.　　　　　　　　　　one　　　more than one

5. *Men's* clothing is on sale at the department store.　　one　　more than one

6. This looks like a *woman's* shirt.　　　　　　　　one　　more than one

❑ ### Exercise 43. Looking at grammar. (Chart 6-11)
Look at the Nelson's family tree. Complete the sentences using the correct possessive form.

1. ___Ned's___ wife is Ella.

2. _____ husband is Sam.

3. Howard is _____ brother.

4. Howard is _____ husband.

5. _____ grandmother is Ella.

6. _____ parents are Sam and Lisa.

7. Ella and _____ grandson is William.

8. Howard and Monica are _____ aunt and uncle.

Nelson Family Tree

Ella + Ned

Lisa + Sam　　　Howard + Moni[c]

William

❑ ### Exercise 44. Game: trivia. (Chart 6-11)
Work in small groups. Use the correct possessive form of the given nouns to complete the sentences. Decide if the information is true or false. The group with the most correct answers wins.*

1. earth　　The _____ surface is about 70% water.　　　　　T　F

2. elephant　An _____ skin is pink and wrinkled.　　　　T　F

3. man　　　Pat is a _____ name.　　　　　　　　　　　T　F

4. woman　　Pat is a _____ name.　　　　　　　　　　　T　F

5. women　　The area for language is larger in _____ brains.　　T　F

6. Men　　　_____ brains are bigger than women's brains.　　T　F

7. person　　A _____ eyes blink more if he/she is nervous.　　T　F

8. People　　_____ voices always get lower as they age.　　T　F

❑ ### Exercise 45. Warm-up. (Chart 6-12)
Check (✓) all the grammatically correct responses.

Whose camera is this?

1. ____ It's my camera.

2. ____ It's mine.

3. ____ It's my.

4. ____ It's yours.

5. ____ It's your camera.

6. ____ It's your's.

7. ____ It's theirs.

8. ____ It's their camera.

*See *Trivia Answers*, p. 421.

6-12 Possessive Pronouns and Adjectives

This pen belongs to me. (a) It's **mine**. (b) It is **my** pen.	Examples (a) and (b) have the same meaning; they both show possession. **Mine** is a *possessive pronoun;* **my** is a *possessive adjective.*
POSSESSIVE PRONOUNS POSSESSIVE ADJECTIVES (c) I have **mine**. I have **my** pen. (d) You have **yours**. You have **your** pen. (e) She has **hers**. She has **her** pen. (f) He has **his**. He has **his** pen. (g) We have **ours**. We have **our** pens. (h) You have **yours**. You have **your** pen. (i) They have **theirs**. They have **their** pens. (j) ——— . I have a book. **Its** cover is black.	A POSSESSIVE PRONOUN is used alone, without a noun following it. A POSSESSIVE ADJECTIVE is used only with a noun following it. INCORRECT: *I have mine pen.* INCORRECT: *I have my.*
COMPARE **its** vs. **it's:** (k) Sue gave me a book. I don't remember **its** title. (l) Sue gave me a book. **It's** a novel.	In (k): **its** (NO apostrophe) is a possessive adjective modifying the noun *title*. In (l): **It's** (with an apostrophe) is a contraction of *it + is*.

COMPARE **their** vs. **there** vs. **they're:**
(m) The students have **their** books.
(n) My books are over **there**.
(o) Where are the students? **They're** in class.
	Their, **there,** and **they're** have the same pronunciation, but not the same meaning.
	    their = possessive adjective, as in (m)
	    there = an expression of place, as in (n)
	    they're = *they are*, as in (o)

❑ **Exercise 46. Looking at grammar.** (Chart 6-12)
Circle the correct completions.

1. Alice called (*her,*) *hers* friend.

2. Hasan wrote a letter to *his, he's* mother.

3. *It's, Its* normal for a dog to chase *it's, its* tail.

4. The bird cleaned *its, it's* feathers with *its, it's* beak.

5. Paula had to drive my car to work. *Hers, Her* had a flat tire.

6. Junko fell off her bike and broke *hers, her* arm.

7. Anastasia is a good friend of *me, mine.**

8. I met a friend of *you, yours* yesterday.

9. A: Excuse me. Is this *my, mine* pen or *your, yours?*

    B: This one is *my, mine. Your, Yours* is on *your, yours* desk.

---

*A friend of + possessive pronoun (e.g., *a friend of mine*) is a common expression.

10. a. Adam and Amanda are married. *They, Them* live in an apartment building.

b. *Their, There, They're* apartment is on the fifth floor.

c. We live in the same building. *Our, Ours* apartment has one bedroom, but *their, theirs* has two.

d. *Their, There, They're* sitting *their, there, they're* now because *their, there, they're* waiting for a visit from *their, there, they're* son.

❑ **Exercise 47. Warm-up.** (Chart 6-13)

Work in small groups. Use a mirror to demonstrate the following sentences. Take turns saying the sentences while students perform the actions.

1. I am looking at myself.
2. You are looking at yourself.
3. You are looking at yourselves.
4. He is looking at himself.

5. They are looking at themselves.
6. She is looking at herself.
7. We are looking at ourselves.

6-13 Reflexive Pronouns

myself	(a) *I* saw **myself** in the mirror.	Reflexive pronouns end in **-self**/**-selves**. They are used when the subject (e.g., *I*) and the object (e.g., *myself*) are the same person.
yourself	(b) *You* (one person) saw **yourself**.	
herself	(c) *She* saw **herself**.	
himself	(d) *He* saw **himself**.	INCORRECT: *I saw me in the mirror.*
itself	(e) *It* (e.g., the kitten) saw **itself**.	
ourselves	(f) *We* saw **ourselves**,	
yourselves	(g) *You* (plural) saw **yourselves**.	
themselves	(h) *They* saw **themselves**.	

(i) *Greg* lives **by himself**.	**By** + *a reflexive pronoun* = alone
(j) *I* sat **by myself** on the park bench.	In (i): Greg lives alone, without family or roommates.
(k) *I* **enjoyed myself** at the fair.	*Enjoy* and a few other verbs are commonly followed by a reflexive pronoun. See the list below.

Common Expressions with Reflexive Pronouns

believe in yourself	help yourself	pinch yourself	tell yourself
blame yourself	hurt yourself	be proud of yourself	work for yourself
cut yourself	give yourself (something)	take care of yourself	wish yourself (luck)
enjoy yourself	introduce yourself	talk to yourself	
feel sorry for yourself	kill yourself	teach yourself	

Complete the sentences with reflexive pronouns.

1. Are you okay, Heidi? Did you hurt ___*yourself*___?

2. Leo taught _____ to play the piano. He never had a teacher.

3. Do you ever talk to _____? Most people talk to

   _____ sometimes.

4. A newborn baby can't take care of _____.

5. It is important for all of us to have confidence in our own abilities. We need to believe in

   _____.

6. Isabel always wishes _____ good luck before a big test.

7. Kazu, there's plenty of food on the table. Please help _____.

8. I couldn't believe my good luck! I had to pinch _____ to make sure I

   wasn't dreaming.

❑ **Exercise 49. Listening.** (Chart 6-13)

Listen to the sentences and complete them with reflexive pronouns.

Example: You will hear: The accident was my fault. I caused it. I was responsible. In other
words, I blamed . . .

You will write: ___*myself*___

1. _____   4. _____

2. _____   5. _____

3. _____   6. _____

❑ **Exercise 50. Let's talk: interview.** (Chart 6-13)

Interview six students in your class. Ask each student a different question. Share some of
their answers with the class.

1. In this town, what is a good way to enjoy yourself?
2. How do people introduce themselves in your country? What do they say?
3. Have you ever wished yourself good luck? When or why?
4. Have you ever felt sorry for yourself? Or, have you ever felt proud of yourself? If so, why?
5. When athletes talk to themselves before an important event, what do you imagine they say?
6. In your country, at what age does a person usually begin living by himself or herself?

Choose the picture that matches the description.

One flower is red. Another is yellow. The other is pink.

Picture A   Picture B

6-14 Singular Forms of *Other: Another* vs. *The Other*

Another

(a) There is a large bowl of apples on the table. Paul is going to eat one apple. If he is still hungry after that, he can eat ***another*** *apple*. There are many apples to choose from.	**Another** means "one more out of a group of similar items, one in addition to the one(s) already mentioned." **Another** is a combination of *an + other,* written as one word.

The Other

(b) There are two apples on the table. Paul is going to eat one of them. Sara is going to eat ***the other*** *apple*.	**The other** means "the last one in a specific group; the only one that remains from a given number of similar items."
(c) Paul ate one apple. Then he ate { ***another*** *apple*. ***another*** *one*. ***another***.	**Another** and ***the other*** can be used as adjectives in front of a noun (e.g., *apple*) or in front of the word *one*. **Another** and ***the other*** can also be used alone as pronouns.
(d) Paul ate one apple. Sara ate { ***the other*** *apple*. ***the other*** *one*. ***the other***.	

Exercise 52. Looking at grammar. (Chart 6-14)
Complete the sentences with *another* or *the other*.

1. There are two birds in Picture A. One is an eagle. ___*The other*___ is a chicken.

    Picture A   Picture B

2. There are three birds in Picture B. One is an eagle.

    a. _____ one is a chicken.

    b. _____ bird is a crow.

3. There are many kinds of birds in the world. One kind is an eagle.

    a. _____ kind is a chicken.

    b. _____ kind is a crow.

    c. _____ kind is a sea gull.

    d. What is the name of _____ kind of bird in the world?

4. It rained yesterday, and from the look of those dark clouds, we're going to have

    _____ rainstorm today.

5. Nicole and Michelle are identical twins. The best way to tell them apart is by looking at

    their ears. One of them has pierced ears, and _____ doesn't.

6. France borders several countries. One is Spain. _____ is Italy.

❑ **Exercise 53. Warm-up.** (Chart 6-15)
Match the sentences to the correct pictures.

    Picture A   Picture B

1. _____ Some are red. Others are yellow.
2. _____ Some are red. The others are yellow.

Other(*s*)

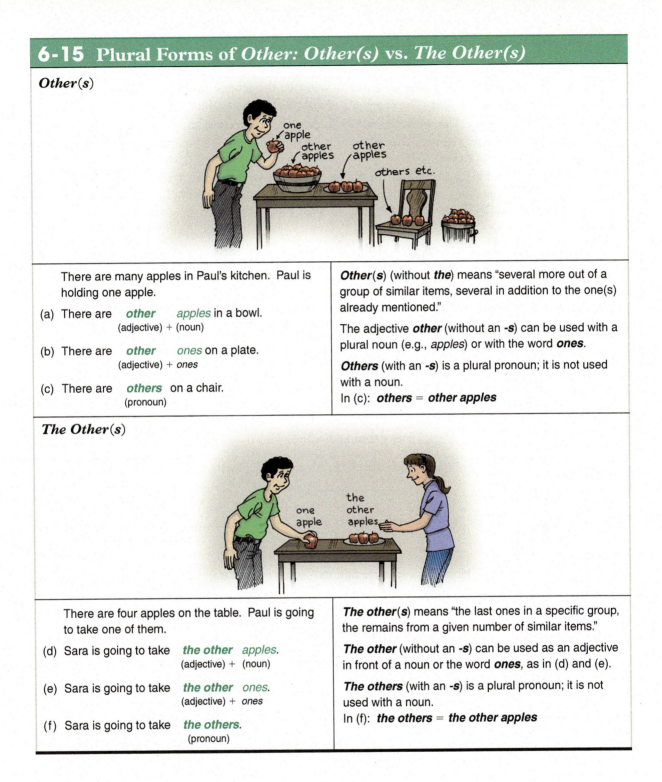

There are many apples in Paul's kitchen. Paul is holding one apple.	*Other*(*s*) (without *the*) means "several more out of a group of similar items, several in addition to the one(s) already mentioned."
(a) There are **other** *apples* in a bowl. (adjective) + (noun)	The adjective **other** (without an **-s**) can be used with a plural noun (e.g., *apples*) or with the word **ones**.
(b) There are **other** *ones* on a plate. (adjective) + *ones*	**Others** (with an **-s**) is a plural pronoun; it is not used with a noun.
(c) There are **others** on a chair. (pronoun)	In (c): **others** = **other apples**

The Other(*s*)

There are four apples on the table. Paul is going to take one of them.	**The other**(**s**) means "the last ones in a specific group, the remains from a given number of similar items."
(d) Sara is going to take **the other** *apples*. (adjective) + (noun)	**The other** (without an **-s**) can be used as an adjective in front of a noun or the word **ones**, as in (d) and (e).
(e) Sara is going to take **the other** *ones*. (adjective) + *ones*	**The others** (with an **-s**) is a plural pronoun; it is not used with a noun.
(f) Sara is going to take **the others**. (pronoun)	In (f): **the others** = **the other apples**

□ **Exercise 54. Looking at grammar.** (Charts 6-14 and 6-15)
Perform these actions.

1. Hold two pens. Use a form of ***other*** to describe the second pen.
   → *I'm holding two pens. One is mine, and the other belongs to Ahmed.*
2. Hold three pens. Use a form of ***other*** to describe the second and third pens.
3. Hold up your two hands. One of them is your right hand. Tell us about your left hand, using a form of ***other***.
4. Hold up your right hand. One of the five fingers is your thumb. Using forms of ***other***, tell us about your index finger, then your middle finger, then your ring finger, and then your little finger, the last of the five fingers on your right hand.

□ **Exercise 55. Looking at grammar.** (Chart 6-15)
Complete the sentences with ***other***(*s*) or ***the other***(*s*).

1. There are many kinds of animals in the world. The elephant is one kind. Some
   ___*others*___ are tigers, horses, and bears.

2. There are many kinds of animals in the world. The elephant is one kind. Some
   _____ kinds are tigers, horses, and bears.

3. There are three colors in the Italian flag. One of the colors is red.
   _____ are green and white.

4. There are three colors in the Italian flag. One of the colors is red.
   _____ colors are green and white.

5. Many people like to get up very early in the morning. _____ like to
   sleep until noon.

6. There are many kinds of geometric figures. Some are circles. _____
   figures are squares. Still _____ are rectangular.

7. There are four geometric figures in the above drawing. One is a square.
   _____ figures are a rectangle, a circle, and a triangle.

8. Of the four geometric figures in the drawing, only the circle has curved lines.
   _____ have straight lines.

Exercise 56. Let's read and write. (Charts 6-13→ 6-15)

Part I. Read the passage and answer the questions.

Calming Yourself

When was the last time you felt nervous or anxious? Were you able to calm yourself? There are a variety of techniques that people use to calm themselves. Here are three that many people have found helpful.

One way that people relax is by imagining a peaceful place, such as a tropical beach. Thinking about the warm water, cool breezes, and steady sounds of the ocean waves helps people calm themselves. Another popular method is deep breathing. Inhaling deeply and then slowly exhaling is an easy way for people to slow their heart rate and relax their body. Still other people find exercise helpful. Some people benefit from a slow activity like a 20-minute walk. Others prefer activities that make them tired, like running or swimming.

How about you? How do you calm yourself when you feel nervous? Do any of these methods help you, or do you do other things to relax?

1. What are three ways people relax when they are nervous? (Use **one** and ***another*** in your answer.)
2. Why do some people choose activities like running and swimming as a way to relax?
3. Imagine you are trying to relax by thinking of a peaceful place. What place would you think of?
4. How do you relax when you are nervous?

Part II. Read this paragraph by one student who tells how he relaxes when he's nervous.

How I Calm Down

Sometimes I feel nervous, especially when I have to give a speech. My body begins to shake, and I realize that I have to calm myself down. This is the technique I use: I imagine myself in a peaceful place. My favorite place in the world is the sea. I imagine myself on the water. I am floating. I feel the warm water around me. The sounds around me are very relaxing. I only hear the waves and maybe a few birds. I don't think about the past or the future. I can feel my heart rate decrease a little, and my body slowly starts to calm down.

Part III. Write a paragraph about how you relax when you are nervous. Follow the model. Give specific details about how you relax and what the results are.

Sometimes I feel nervous, especially when I have to _____. My _____ and I realize that I have to calm myself down. This is the technique I use: _____.

6-16 Summary of Forms of *Other*

	Adjective	Pronoun	
SINGULAR	another apple	another	Notice that the word **others** (**other** + *final* **-s**) is used only as a plural pronoun.
PLURAL	other apples	other**s**	
SINGULAR	the other apple	the other	
PLURAL	the other apples	the other**s**	

❑ **Exercise 57. Looking at grammar.** (Charts 6-15 and 6-16)
Complete the sentences with correct forms of *other*: *another, other, others, the other, the others*.

1. Juan has only two suits, a blue one and a gray one. His wife wants him to buy
   ___*another*___ one.

2. Juan has two suits. One is blue, and _____ is gray.

3. Some suits are blue. _____ are gray.

4. Some jackets have zippers. _____ jackets have buttons.

5. Some people keep dogs as pets. _____ have cats. Still
   _____ people have fish or birds as pets.

6. My boyfriend gave me a ring. I tried to put it on my ring finger, but it didn't fit. So I had
   to put it on _____ finger.

7. People have two thumbs. One is on the right hand. _____ is on the
   left hand.

8. Sometimes when I'm thirsty, I'll have a glass of water, but often one glass isn't enough, so
   I'll have _____ one.

9. There are five letters in the word *fresh*. One of the letters is a vowel. _____
   are consonants.

10. Smith is a common last name in English. _____ common names are
    Johnson, Jones, Miller, Anderson, Moore, and Brown.

❑ **Exercise 58. Listening.** (Charts 6-15 and 6-16)
Listen to each conversation and circle the correct statement (a. or b.).

1. a. The speaker was looking at two jackets.
   b. The speaker was looking at several jackets.

2. a. The speakers have only two favorite colors.
   b. The speakers have more than two favorite colors.

3. a. There are several roads the speakers can take.
   b. There are two roads the speakers can take.

4. a. There are only two ways to get downtown.
   b. There are more than two ways to get downtown.

5. a. The speaker had more than four pets.
   b. The speaker had only four pets.

❏ **Exercise 59. Listening.** (Charts 6-15 and 6-16)

Listen to the conversation about dealing with loneliness. Complete the sentences with the words you hear.

A: What do you do when you're feeling lonely?

B: I go someplace where I can be around _____ people. Even if they are strangers, I feel better when there are _____ around me. How about you?

A: That doesn't work for me. For example, if I'm feeling lonely and I go to a movie by myself, I look at all _____ people who are there with their friends and family, and I start to feel even lonelier. So I try to find _____ things to do to keep myself busy. When I'm busy, I don't feel lonely.

❏ **Exercise 60. Check your knowledge.** (Chapter 6)

Edit the sentences. Correct errors in nouns, pronouns, adjectives, and subject-verb agreement.

          wishes
1. Jimmy had three ~~wish~~ for his birthday.

2. I had some black beans soup for lunch.

3. The windows in our classroom is dirty.

4. People in Brazil speaks Portuguese.

5. Are around 8,600 types of birds in the world.

6. My mother and father work in Milan. Their teacher's.

7. Today many womens are carpenter, pilot, and doctor.

8. Is a new student in our class. Have you met her?

9. There are two pool at the park. The smaller one is for childs. The another is for adults.

10. The highways in my country are excellents.

11. I don't like my apartment. Its in a bad neighborhood. Is a lot of crime. I'm going to move to other neighborhood.

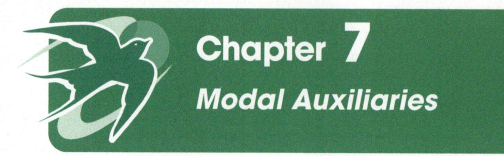

Chapter 7
Modal Auxiliaries

❑ **Exercise 1. Warm-up.** (Chart 7-1)
Check (✓) the sentences that are grammatically correct.

1. _____ I can speak English well.

2. _____ He cans speaks English well.

3. _____ She can to speak English well.

4. _____ Our neighbors can speak some English.

5. _____ My parents can't speaking English at all.

7-1 The Form of Modal Auxiliaries

The verbs listed below are called "modal auxiliaries." They are helping verbs that express a wide range of meanings (ability, permission, possibility, necessity, etc.). Most of the modals have more than one meaning.

Auxiliary + the Simple Form of a Verb

can	(a) Olga *can speak* English.	*Can, could, may, might, should, had better, must, will,* and *would* are immediately followed by the simple form of a verb.
could	(b) He *couldn't come* to class.	
may	(c) It *may rain* tomorrow.	
might	(d) It *might rain* tomorrow.	• They are not followed by *to*.
should	(e) Mary *should study* harder.	INCORRECT: *Olga can to speak English.*
had better	(f) I *had better study* tonight.	• The main verb does not have a final *-s*.
must	(g) Billy! You *must listen* to me!	INCORRECT: *Olga can speaks English.*
will	(h) I *will be* in class tomorrow.	• The main verb is not in a past form.
would	(i) *Would* you please *close* the door?	INCORRECT: *Olga can spoke English.*
		• The main verb is not in its *-ing* form.
		INCORRECT: *Olga can speaking English.*

Auxiliary + *to* + the Simple Form of a Verb

have to	(j) I *have to study* tonight.	*To* + *the simple form* is used with these auxiliaries: *have to, have got to, be able to,* and *ought to*.
have got to	(k) I *have got to study* tonight.	
be able to	(l) Kate *is able to study* harder.	
ought to	(m) Kate *ought to study* harder.	

❏ **Exercise 2. Looking at grammar.** (Chart 7-1)
Make sentences with the given verbs + *come*. Add *to* where necessary. Use this model:
Leo _____ tonight.

Example: can → *Leo can come tonight.*

1. may
2. should
3. ought
4. will not
5. could not

6. might
7. had better
8. has
9. has got
10. is not able

❏ **Exercise 3. Listening.** (Chart 7-1)
Listen to the sentences. Add *to* where necessary. If *to* isn't necessary, write **Ø**.
Notice that *to* may sound like "ta."

1. I have __*to*__ go downtown tomorrow.

2. You must __Ø__ fasten your seat belt.

3. Could you please _____ open the window?

4. May I _____ borrow your eraser?

5. I'm not able _____ sign the contract today.

6. Today is the deadline. You must _____ sign it!

7. I have got _____ go to the post office this afternoon.

8. Shouldn't you _____ save some of your money for emergencies?

9. I feel bad for Elena. She has _____ have more surgery.

10. Alexa! Stop! You must not _____ run into the street!

❏ **Exercise 4. Warm-up.** (Chart 7-2)
Circle the best completion for each sentence. Discuss your answers.

1. A newborn baby *can / can't* roll over.

2. A baby of four months *can / can't* smile.

3. A newborn baby *is able to / isn't able to* see black and white shapes.

4. A baby of six months *is able to / isn't able to* see colors.

5. When I was nine months old, I *could / couldn't* crawl.

6. When I was nine months old, I *could / couldn't* walk.

7-2 Expressing Ability: *Can* and *Could*

(a) Bob *can play* the piano. (b) You *can buy* a screwdriver at a hardware store. (c) I *can meet* you at Ted's tomorrow afternoon.	*Can* expresses *ability* in the present or future.
(d) I $\left\{ \begin{array}{l} \textbf{\textit{can't}} \\ \textbf{\textit{cannot}} \\ \textbf{\textit{can not}} \end{array} \right\}$ understand that sentence.	The negative form of *can* may be written *can't*, *cannot*, or *can not*.
(e) I *can go*. (f) I *can't go*.	In spoken English, *can* is usually unstressed and pronounced /kən/ = "kun." *Can't* is stressed and pronounced /kænʔ/, with the final sound being a glottal stop.* The glottal stop replaces the /t/ in spoken English. Occasionally native speakers have trouble hearing the difference between *can* and *can't* and have to ask for clarification.
(g) Our son *could walk* when he was one year old.	The past form of *can* is *could*.
(h) He *couldn't walk* when he was six months old.	The negative of *could* is *couldn't* or *could not*.
(i) He *can read*. (j) He *is able to read*. (k) She *could read*. (l) She *was able to read*.	Ability can also be expressed with a form of *be able to*. Examples (i) and (j) have the same meaning. Examples (k) and (l) have the same meaning.

*A glottal stop is the sound you hear in the negative "unh-uh." The air is stopped by the closing of your glottis in the back of your throat. The phonetic symbol for the glottal stop is /ʔ/.

❑ **Exercise 5. Looking at grammar.** (Chart 7-2)
Part I. Complete the sentences with *can* or *can't*.

1. A dog _____ swim, but it _____ fly.

2. A frog _____ live both on land and in water, but a cat _____ .

3. A bilingual person _____ speak three languages, but a trilingual person

   _____ .

4. People with a Ph.D. degree _____ use "Dr." in front of their name, but people

   with a master's degree _____ .

Part II. Restate the sentences in Part I. Use *be able to*.

❑ **Exercise 6. Let's talk: interview.** (Chart 7-2)
Interview your classmates. Ask each student a different question. If the answer is "yes," ask the follow-up question in parentheses. Share some of your answers with the class.

Can you . . .

1. speak more than two languages? (Which ones?)
2. play chess? (How long have you played?)
3. fold a piece of paper in half more than six times? (Can you show me?)
4. draw well — for example, draw a picture of me? (Can you do it now?)

Are you able to . . .

5. write clearly with both your right and left hands?
   (Can you show me?)
6. pat the top of your head with one hand and rub your
   stomach in a circle with the other hand at the same time?
   (Can you show me?)
7. drive a stick-shift car? (When did you learn?)
8. play a musical instrument? (Which one?)

❏ **Exercise 7. Listening.** (Chart 7-2)

Listen to the conversation. You will hear reductions for *can* and *can't*. Write the words you hear.

In the classroom

A: I _____ this math assignment.
     1

B: I _____ you with that.
     2

A: Really? _____ this problem to me?
                    3

B: Well, we _____ out the answer unless we do this part first.
                    4

A: Okay! But it's so hard.

B: Yeah, but I know you _____ it. Just go slowly.
                                  5

A: Class is almost over. _____ me after school today to finish this?
                                     6

B: Well, I _____ you right after school, but how about at 5:00?
                 7

A: Great!

❏ **Exercise 8. Let's talk.** (Chart 7-2)

Complete the sentences with *could/couldn't/be able to/not be able to* and your own words.

Example: A year ago I _____, but now I can.
     → *A year ago I couldn't speak English, but now I can.*

1. When I was a child, I _____, but now I can.
2. When I was six, I _____, but I wasn't able to do that
   when I was three.
3. Five years ago, I _____, but now I can't.
4. In the past, I _____, but now I am.

Exercise 9. Warm-up. (Chart 7-3)
Check (✓) the sentences in each group that have the same meaning.

GROUP A

1. _____ Maybe it will be hot tomorrow.

2. _____ It might be hot tomorrow.

3. _____ It may be hot tomorrow.

GROUP B

4. _____ You can have dessert, now.

5. _____ You may have dessert, now.

GROUP C

6. _____ She can't stay up late.

7. _____ She might not stay up late.

7-3 **Expressing Possibility:** *May, Might,* **and** *Maybe;* **Expressing Permission:** *May* **and** *Can*	
(a) It *may rain* tomorrow. (b) It *might rain* tomorrow. (c) — Why isn't John in class? — I don't know. He { *may* / *might* } be sick today.	*May* and *might* express *possibility* in the present or future. They have the same meaning. There is no difference in meaning between (a) and (b).
(d) It *may not rain* tomorrow. (e) It *might not rain* tomorrow.	Negative: *may not* and *might not* (Do not contract *may* and *might* with *not*.)
(f) *Maybe* it will rain tomorrow. COMPARE: (g) *Maybe* John is sick. (*adverb*) (h) John *may be* sick. (*verb*)	In (f) and (g): *maybe* (spelled as one word) is an adverb. It means "possibly." It comes at the beginning of a sentence. INCORRECT: *It will maybe rain tomorrow.* In (h): *may be* (two words) is a verb form: the auxiliary *may* + the main verb *be*. Examples (g) and (h) have the same meaning. INCORRECT: *John maybe sick.*
(i) Yes, children, you *may have* a cookie after dinner. (j) Okay, kids, you *can have* a cookie after dinner.	*May* is also used to give *permission,* as in (i). *Can* is often used to give *permission,* too, as in (j). NOTE: Examples (i) and (j) have the same meaning, but *may* is more formal than *can.*
(k) You *may not have* a cookie. You *can't have* a cookie.	*May not* and *cannot* (*can't*) are used to deny permission (i.e., to say "no").

□ **Exercise 10. Looking at grammar.** (Chart 7-3)
Complete the sentences with *can, may,* or *might*. Identify the meaning expressed by the modals: possibility or permission.

In a courtroom for a speeding ticket

1. No one speaks without the judge's permission. You ___*may / can*___ not speak until the judge asks you a question. *Meaning:* ___*permission*___

2. The judge _____ reduce your fine for your speeding ticket, or she _____ not. It depends. *Meaning:* _____

3. You _____ not argue with the judge. If you argue, you will get a fine.
Meaning: _____

4. You have a strong case, but I'm not sure if you will convince the judge. You _____ win or you _____ lose. *Meaning:* _____

□ **Exercise 11. Looking at grammar.** (Chart 7-3)
Rewrite the sentences with the words in parentheses.

1. It may snow tonight.
(might) _____
(Maybe) _____

2. You might need to wear your boots.
(may) _____
(Maybe) _____

3. Maybe there will be a blizzard.
(may) _____
(might) _____

❑ **Exercise 12. Let's talk.** (Chart 7-3)

Answer each question with *may, might,* and *maybe*. Include at least three possibilities in each answer. Work in pairs, in small groups, or as a class.

Example: What are you going to do tomorrow?
   → *I don't know. I **may** go downtown.* OR *I **might** go to the laundromat.*
   ***Maybe** I'll study all day. Who knows?*

1. What are you going to do tomorrow night?
2. What's the weather going to be like tomorrow?
3. What is our teacher going to do tonight?
4. (_____) isn't in class today. Where is he/she?
5. What is your occupation going to be ten years from now?

❑ **Exercise 13. Listening.** (Charts 7-2 and 7-3)

You will hear sentences with *can, may,* or *might*. Decide if the speakers are expressing ability, possibility, or permission.

Example: You will hear: A: Where's Victor?
                             B: I don't know. He may be sick.

You will choose: ability   (possibility)   permission

1. ability	possibility	permission		4. ability	possibility	permission
2. ability	possibility	permission		5. ability	possibility	permission
3. ability	possibility	permission				

❑ **Exercise 14. Warm-up.** (Chart 7-4)

In which sentence is the speaker expressing a past ability? a present possibility? a future possibility?

A soccer game

1. There is five minutes left and the score is 3–3. Our team could win.
2. The goalie is on the ground. He could be hurt.
3. Our team didn't win. We couldn't score another goal.

7-4 Using *Could* to Express Possibility

(a) — How was the movie? ***Could*** you ***understand*** the English? — Not very well. I ***could*** only ***understand*** it with the help of subtitles.	One meaning of ***could*** is *past ability*, as in (a).* Another meaning of ***could*** is *possibility*. In (b): ***He could be sick*** has the same meaning as *He may/might be sick*, i.e., *It is possible that he is sick.*
(b) — Why isn't Greg in class? — I don't know. He ***could be*** sick.	In (b): ***could*** expresses a *present* possibility.
(c) Look at those dark clouds. It ***could start*** raining any minute.	In (c): ***could*** expresses a *future* possibility.

*See also Chart 7-2.

Exercise 15. Looking at grammar. (Charts 7-2 and 7-4)
Does *could* express past, present, or future time? What is the meaning: ability or possibility?

Sentence	Past	Present	Future	Ability	Possibility
1. I *could be* home late tonight. Don't wait for me for dinner.			x		x
2. Thirty years ago, when he was a small child, David *could speak* Swahili fluently. Now he's forgotten a lot of it.					
3. A: Where's Alicia? B: I don't know. She *could be* at the mall.					
4. When I was a child, I *could climb* trees, but now I'm too old.					
5. Let's leave for the airport now. Yuki's plane *could arrive* early, and we want to be there when she arrives.					
6. A: What's that on the carpet? B: I don't know. It looks like a bug. Or it *could be* a piece of fuzz.					

Exercise 16. Let's talk. (Chart 7-4)
Suggest possible solutions for each situation. Use *could*. Work in pairs, in small groups, or as a class.

Example: Tim has to go to work early tomorrow. His car is completely out of gas. His bicycle is broken.
→ *He could take the bus to work.*
→ *He could get a friend to take him to a gas station to get gas.*
→ *He could try to fix his bike.*
→ *He could get up very early and walk to work.*
Etc.

1. Lisa walked to school today. Now she wants to go home. It's raining hard. She doesn't have an umbrella, and she's wearing sandals.

2. Joe and Joan want to get some exercise. They have a date to play tennis this morning, but the tennis court is covered with snow.

3. Roberto just bought a new camera. He has it at home now. He has the instruction manual. It is written in Japanese. He can't read Japanese. He doesn't know how to operate the camera.

4. Albert likes to travel around the world. He is 22 years old. Today he is alone in Paris. He needs to eat, and he needs to find a place to stay overnight. But while he was asleep on the train last night, someone stole his wallet. He has no money.

❏ **Exercise 17. Listening.** (Charts 7-3 and 7-4)
Listen to the conversation between a husband and wife. Listen again and complete the sentences with the words you hear.

In a home office

A: Look at this cord. Do you know what it's for?

B: I don't know. We have so many cords around here with all our electronic equipment. It

_____ for the printer, I guess.
         1

A: No, I checked. The printer isn't missing a cord.

B: It _____ for one of the kid's toys.
              2

A: Yeah, I _____. But they don't have many electronic toys.
              3

B: I have an idea. It _____ for the cell phone. You know — the one I
                 4

had before this one.

A: I bet that's it. We _____ probably throw this out.
              5

B: Well, let's be sure before we do that.

❏ **Exercise 18. Warm-up.** (Chart 7-5)
Check (✓) all the sentences that have the same meaning.

1. _____ May I use your cell phone?

2. _____ Can I use your cell phone?

3. _____ Could I use your cell phone?

7-5 Polite Questions: *May I, Could I, Can I*

Polite Question	Possible Answers	
(a) *May I* please borrow your pen? (b) *Could I* please borrow your pen? (c) *Can I* please borrow your pen?	Yes. Yes. Of course. Yes. Certainly. Of course. Certainly. Sure. (*informal*) Okay. (*informal*) Uh-huh (*meaning "yes"*) I'm sorry, but I need to use it myself.	People use *may I*, *could I*,* and *can I* to ask polite questions. The questions ask for someone's permission or agreement. Examples (a), (b), and (c) have basically the same meaning. NOTE: *can I* is less formal than *may I* and *could I*.
(d) *Can I* borrow your pen, *please*? (e) *Can I* borrow your pen?		*Please* can come at the end of the question, as in (d). *Please* can be omitted from the question, as in (e).

*In a polite question, *could* is NOT the past form of *can*.

☐ **Exercise 19. Looking at grammar.** (Chart 7-5)
Complete the phone conversations. Use *may I, could I*, or *can I* + a verb from the list.
NOTE: The caller is always Speaker B.

ask	help	leave	speak/talk	take

1. A: Hello?

   B: Hello. Is Ahmed there?

   A: Yes, he is.

   B: _____ to him?

   A: Just a minute. I'll get him.

2. A: Hello. Mr. Black's office.

   B: _____ to Mr. Black?

   A: _____ who is calling?

   B: Susan Abbott.

   A: Just a moment, Ms. Abbott. I'll transfer you.

3. A: Hello?

   B: Hi. This is Bob. _____ to Pedro?

   A: Sure. Hold on.

4. A: Good afternoon. Dr. Wu's office. _____ you?

   B: Yes. I have an appointment that I need to change.

   A: Just a minute, please. I'll transfer you to our appointment desk.

5. A: Hello?

   B: Hello. _____ to Emily?

   A: She's not at home right now. _____ a message?

   B: No, thanks. I'll call later.

6. A: Hello?

   B: Hello. _____ to Maria?

   A: She's not here right now.

   B: Oh. _____ a message?

   A: Sure. Just let me get a pen.

❑ **Exercise 20. Let's talk: pairwork.** (Chart 7-5)
Work with a partner. Ask and answer polite questions. Begin with *May I, Could I,* or *Can I*. Make conversations you can role-play for the class.

Example: (A), you want to see (B)'s grammar book for a minute.
SPEAKER A: May/Could/Can I (please) see your grammar book for a minute?
SPEAKER B: Of course. / Sure. / Etc.
SPEAKER A: Thank you. / Thanks. I forgot to bring mine to class today.

1. (A), you want to see (B)'s dictionary for a minute.

2. (A), you are at a restaurant. (B) is your server. You have finished your meal. You want the check.

3. (B), you run into (A) on the street. (A) is carrying some heavy packages. What are you going to say to him/her?

4. (A), you are speaking to (B), who is one of your teachers. You want to leave class early today.

5. (B), you are in a store with your good friend (A). The groceries cost more than you expected. You don't have enough money. What are you going to say to your friend?

❑ **Exercise 21. Warm-up.** (Chart 7-6)
Check the questions that are grammatically correct. Which two questions do you think are more polite than the others?

In the kitchen

1. _____ Will you help me with the dishes?

2. _____ Would you load the dishwasher?

3. _____ May you load the dishwasher?

4. _____ Can you unload the dishwasher?

5. _____ Could you unload the dishwasher?

7-6 Polite Questions: *Would You, Could You, Will You, Can You*

Polite Question	Possible Answers	
(a) *Would you* please open the door? (b) *Could you* please open the door? (c) *Will you* please open the door? (d) *Can you* please open the door?	Yes. Yes. Of course. Certainly. I'd be happy to. Of course. I'd be glad to. Sure. (informal) Okay. (informal) Uh-huh. (meaning "yes") I'm sorry. I'd like to help, but my hands are full.	People use **would you, could you, will you,** and **can you** to ask polite questions. The questions ask for someone's help or cooperation. Examples (a), (b), (c), and (d) have basically the same meaning. *Would* and *could* are generally considered more polite than *will* and *can*.
		NOTE: **May** is NOT used when **you** is the subject of a polite question. *INCORRECT:* *May you please open the door?*

☐ **Exercise 22. Looking at grammar.** (Chart 7-6)
Make two different questions for each situation. Use *you*.

1. You're in a room and it's getting very hot.

    Formal: *Would you please open the window?*

    Informal: *Can you turn on the air-conditioner?*

2. You're trying to listen to the news on TV, but your friends are talking too loud, and you can't hear it.

    Formal: _____

    Informal: _____

3. You're in a restaurant. You are about to pay and notice the bill is more than it should be. The server has made a mistake.

    Formal: _____

    Informal: _____

☐ **Exercise 23. Let's talk: pairwork.** (Charts 7-5 and 7-6)
Work with a partner. Make a conversation for one (or more) of the given situations. Perform your conversation for the rest of the class.

Example: You're in a restaurant. You want the server to refill your coffee cup.
You catch the server's eye and raise your hand slightly. He approaches your table and says: "Yes? What can I do for you?"

PARTNER A: Yes? What can I do for you?
PARTNER B: Could I please have some more coffee?
PARTNER A: Of course. Right away. Could I get you anything else?

PARTNER B: No thanks. Oh, on second thought, yes. Would you bring some cream too?
PARTNER A: Certainly.
PARTNER B: Thanks.

1. You've been waiting in a long line at a busy bakery. Finally, it's your turn. The clerk turns toward you and says: "Next!"

2. You are at work. You feel sick and you have a slight fever. You really want to go home. You see your boss, Mr. Jenkins, passing by your desk. You say: "Mr. Jenkins, could I speak with you for a minute?"

3. The person next to you on the plane has finished reading his newspaper. You would like to read it. He also has a bag on the floor that is in your space. You would like him to move it. You say: "Excuse me."

❑ **Exercise 24. Warm-up.** (Chart 7-7)
Your friend Paula has a terrible headache. What advice would you give her? Check (✓) the sentences you agree with.

1. _____ You should lie down.
2. _____ You should take some medicine.
3. _____ You ought to call the doctor.
4. _____ You should go to the emergency room.
5. _____ You ought to put an ice-pack on your forehead.

7-7 Expressing Advice: *Should* and *Ought To*

(a) My clothes are dirty. I { *should* / *ought to* } wash them.	**Should** and **ought to** have the same meaning: "This is a good idea. This is good advice."

(b) INCORRECT: *I should to wash them.*
 (c) INCORRECT: *I ought washing them.*
	FORMS:
	    should + simple form of a verb (no **to**)
	    ought + **to** + simple form of a verb

(d) You need your sleep. You **should not** (**shouldn't**) stay up late.	NEGATIVE: **should** + **not** = **shouldn't** (*Ought to* is usually not used in the negative.)
(e) A: I'm going to be late for the bus. What **should I do**? B: Run!	QUESTION: **should** + *subject* + *main verb* (*Ought to* is usually not used in questions.)

(f) A: I'm tired today.
     B: You **should/ought to** go home and take a nap.
 	
 (g) A: I'm tired today.
     B: **Maybe** you **should/ought to** go home and take a nap.
	The use of **maybe** with **should** and **ought to** "softens" advice.
	
	 COMPARE:
	 In (f): Speaker B is giving definite advice. He is stating clearly that he believes going home for a nap is a good idea and is the solution to Speaker A's problem.
	
	 In (g): Speaker B is making a suggestion: going home for a nap is one possible way to solve Speaker A's problem.

❏ **Exercise 25. Let's talk: pairwork.** (Chart 7-7)
Work with a partner. Partner A states the problem. Partner B gives advice using **should** or **ought to**. Include **maybe** to soften the advice if you wish.

Example: I'm sleepy.
PARTNER A: I'm sleepy.
PARTNER B: (Maybe) You should/ought to drink a cup of tea.

1. I can't fall asleep at night.
2. I have a sore throat.
3. I have the hiccups.
4. I sat on my friend's sunglasses. Now the frames are bent.

Change roles.
5. I'm starving.*
6. I dropped my sister's camera, and now it doesn't work.
7. Someone stole my lunch from the refrigerator in the staff lounge at work.
8. I bought some shoes that don't fit. Now my feet hurt.

❏ **Exercise 26. Warm-up.** (Chart 7-8)
Marco has lost his passport. Here are some suggestions. Check (✓) the sentences you agree with. Which sentences seem more serious or urgent?

1. _____ He had better go to the embassy.
2. _____ He should wait and see if someone returns it.
3. _____ He had better report it to the police.
4. _____ He should ask a friend to help him look for it.

7-8	Expressing Advice: *Had Better*	
(a)	My clothes are dirty. I { should / ought to / had better } wash them.	**Had better** has the same basic meaning as *should* and *ought to:* "This is a good idea. This is good advice."
(b)	You're driving too fast! You*'d better slow* down.	**Had better** has more of a sense of urgency than *should* or *ought to.* It often implies a warning about possible bad consequences. In (b): If you don't slow down, there could be a bad result. You could get a speeding ticket or have an accident.
(c)	You*'d better not eat* that meat. It looks spoiled.	NEGATIVE: **had better not**
(d)	I*'d better send* my boss an email right away.	In conversation, **had** is usually contracted: *'d.*

---

starving (informal English) = very, very hungry

Exercise 27. Looking at grammar. (Chart 7-8)
Give advice using **had better**. What are some possible bad consequences if your advice is not followed? Work in pairs, in small groups, or as a class.

1. I haven't paid my electric bill.
   → *You'd better pay it by tomorrow. If you don't pay it, the electric company will turn off the power.*
2. Joe oversleeps a lot. This week he has been late to work three times. His boss is very unhappy about that.
3. I don't feel good right now. I think I'm coming down with something.*
4. I can't remember if I locked the front door when I left for work.
5. My ankle really hurts. I think I've sprained it.
6. I can't find my credit card, and I've looked everywhere.

❑ **Exercise 28. Check your knowledge.** (Chapter 7)
Edit the sentences. Correct the verb form errors.

       had

1. You ~~will~~ better not be late.

2. Anna shouldn't wears shorts to work.

3. I should to go to the post office today.

4. I ought paying my bills today.

5. You'd had better to call the doctor today.

6. You don't should stay up too late tonight.

7. You better not leaving your key in the door.

8. Mr. Lim is having a surprise party for his wife. He ought told people soon.

❑ **Exercise 29. Let's talk.** (Charts 7-7 and 7-8)
Work in small groups. Give advice using **should, ought to,** and **had better**. The leader states the problem, and others in the group offer suggestions. Select a different leader for each item.

Example:
LEADER: I study, but I don't understand my physics class. It's the middle of the term, and I'm failing the course. I need a science course in order to graduate. What should I do?**
SPEAKER A: You**'d better** get a tutor right away.
SPEAKER B: You **should** make an appointment with your teacher and see if you can get some extra help.
SPEAKER C: Maybe you **ought to** drop your physics course and take a different science course next term.

---

*The idiom *come down with something* = get a sickness, like a cold or the flu

**Should* (NOT *ought to* or *had better*) is usually used in a question that asks for advice. The answer, however, can contain *should, ought to,* or *had better.* For example:
  A: *My houseplants always die. What **should** I do?*
  B: *You'd **better** get a book on plants. You **should** try to find out why they die. Maybe you **ought to** look on the Internet and see if you can find some information.*

1. I forgot my dad's birthday yesterday. I feel terrible about it. What should I do?

2. I just discovered that I made dinner plans for tonight with two different people. I'm supposed to meet my parents at one restaurant at 7:00, and I'm supposed to meet my boss at a different restaurant across town at 8:00. What should I do?

3. Samira accidentally left the grocery store with an item she didn't pay for. Her young daughter put it in Samira's shopping bag, but she didn't see it. What should Samira do?

4. I borrowed Karen's favorite book of poetry. It was special to her. A note on the inside cover said "To Karen." The author's signature was under it. Now I can't find the book. I think I lost it. What should I do?

❑ **Exercise 30. Warm-up.** (Chart 7-9)
Which of these statements about writing a résumé are true in your country? Check (✓) them and then decide which sentence is more common in writing and which sentences are more common in speaking.

Writing a résumé

1. _____ You must list all your previous employers.

2. _____ You have to provide references.

3. _____ You have got to include personal information, for example, whether you are married or not.

7-9 Expressing Necessity: *Have to, Have Got to, Must*

(a) I have a very important test tomorrow. I { **have to** / **have got to** / **must** } *study* tonight.	**Have to**, **have got to**, and **must** have basically the same meaning. They express the idea that something is necessary.
(b) I'd like to go with you to the movie this evening, but I can't. I **have to go** to a meeting. (c) Bye now! I**'ve got to go**. My wife's waiting for me. I'll call you later. (d) All passengers **must present** their passports at customs upon arrival. (e) Tommy, you **must hold** onto the railing when you go down the stairs.	**Have to** is used much more frequently in everyday speech and writing than **must**. **Have got to** is typically used in informal conversation, as in (c). **Must** is typically found in written instructions or rules, as in (d). Adults also use it when talking to younger children, as in (e). It sounds very strong.
(f) **Do** we **have to bring** pencils to the test? (g) Why **did** he **have to leave** so early?	QUESTIONS: **Have to** is usually used in questions, not **must** or **have got to**. Forms of **do** are used with **have to** in questions.
(h) I **had to** *study* last night.	The PAST form of **have to**, **have got to**, and **must** (meaning necessity) is **had to**.
(i) I **have to** ("hafta") *go* downtown today. (j) Rita **has to** ("hasta") *go* to the bank. (k) I've **got to** ("gotta") *study* tonight.	Notice that **have to**, **has to**, and **have got to** are commonly reduced, as in (i) through (k).

Exercise 31. Let's talk. (Charts 7-7 and 7-9)
Answer the questions. Work in pairs, in small groups, or as a class.

1. What are some things you *have to do* today? tomorrow? every day?
2. What is something you *had to do* yesterday?
3. What is something you*'ve got to do* soon?
4. What is something you*'ve got to do* after class today or later tonight?
5. What is something a driver *must do,* according to the law?
6. What is something a driver *should always do* to be a safe driver?
7. What are some things a person *should do* to stay healthy?
8. What are some things a person *must do* to stay alive?

❑ **Exercise 32. Listening.** (Chart 7-9)
Complete the sentences with the words you hear. Before you begin, you may want to check your understanding of these words: *apply, applicable, legal, nickname, previous, employer.*

```
┌─────────────────────────────────────────────────────────────┐
│              EMPLOYMENT APPLICATION                          │
│                                                             │
│  Applications are considered for all positions without regard to race, color, religion, sex, national origin, │
│  age, marital or veteran status, or in the presence of a non-related medical condition or handicap. │
│                                                             │
│   Donna          N/A          Frost      May 4, 2011        │
│   First Name    Middle Initial  Last Name      Date          │
│                                                             │
│   1443 Maple Ridge Heights              555-545-5454         │
│            Address                         Phone #           │
│                                                             │
│   Happyville     PA      05055    123-000-7890              │
│      City        State   Zip Code   Social Security #        │
└─────────────────────────────────────────────────────────────┘
```

Filling out a job application

1. The application _____ be complete. You shouldn't skip any parts. If a section doesn't fit your situation, you can write N/A (not applicable).

2. _____ type it, but your writing _____ be easy to read.

3. _____ use your full legal name, not your nickname.

4. _____ list the names and places of your previous employers.

5. _____ list your education, beginning with either high school or college.

6. _____ always _____ apply in person. Sometimes you can do it online.

7. _____ write some things, like the same telephone number, twice. You can write "same as above."

8. All spelling _____ be correct.

Exercise 33. Let's read and talk. (Charts 7-7 → 7-9)
Read the passage and then give advice.

A Family Problem

Mr. and Mrs. Hill don't know what to do about their 15-year-old son, Mark. He's very intelligent but has no interest in learning. His grades are getting worse, and he won't do any homework. Sometimes he skips school and spends the day at the mall.

His older sister Kathy is a good student, and she never causes any problems at home. Kathy hasn't missed a day of school all year. Mark's parents keep asking him why he can't be more like Kathy. Mark is jealous of Kathy and picks fights* with her.

All Mark does when he's home is stay in his room and listen to loud music. He often refuses to eat meals with his family. He argues with his parents, his room is a mess, and he won't** help around the house.

This family needs advice. Tell them what changes they should make. What should they do? What shouldn't they do?

Use each of these words at least once in the advice you give:

should	ought to
shouldn't	have to/has to
have got to/has got to	must
had better	

❑ **Exercise 34. Warm-up.** (Chart 7-10)
Which sentence (a. or b.) completes the idea of the given sentence?

We have lots of time.

   a. You must not drive so fast!
   b. You don't have to drive so fast.

7-10	Expressing Lack of Necessity: *Do Not Have To;* Expressing Prohibition: *Must Not*
(a) I finished all of my homework this afternoon. I *don't have to study* tonight. (b) Tomorrow is a holiday. Mary *doesn't have to go* to class.	*Don't/doesn't have to* expresses the idea that something is *not necessary.*
(c) Bus passengers *must not talk* to the driver. (d) Children, you *must not play* with matches!	*Must not* expresses *prohibition* (DO NOT DO THIS!).
(e) You *mustn't play* with matches.	*Must* + *not* = *mustn't* (NOTE: The first "t" is not pronounced.)

**pick a fight* = start a fight

***won't* is used here to express refusal: *He refuses to help around the house.*

❑ **Exercise 35. Looking at grammar.** (Chart 7-10)
Complete the sentences with **don't have to, doesn't have to,** or **must not.**

1. You ___must not___ drive when you are tired. It's dangerous.

2. I live only a few blocks from my office. I ___don't have to___ drive to work.

3. Liz finally got a car, so now she drives to work. She _____ take the bus.

4. Mr. Murphy is very wealthy. He _____ work for a living.

5. You _____ tell Daddy about the birthday party. We want it to be a surprise.

6. A: Did Professor Acosta give an assignment?

   B: Yes, she assigned Chapters 4 and 6, but we _____ read Chapter 5.

7. A: Listen carefully, Kristen. If a stranger offers you a ride, you _____ get in the car. Never get in a car with a stranger. Do you understand?

   B: Yes, Mom.

❑ **Exercise 36. Warm-up.** (Chart 7-11)
Read the situation and the conclusions that follow. Which conclusion(s) seems logical to you? Explain your answers, if necessary.

SITUATION: Mr. Ellis is a high school gym teacher. He usually wears gym clothes to work. Today he is wearing a suit and tie.

1. He must have an important meeting.
2. He must be rich.
3. He must need new clothes.
4. He must want to make a good impression on someone.
5. His gym clothes must not be clean.

7-11 Making Logical Conclusions: *Must*

(a) A: Nancy is yawning. 　　B: She ***must be*** sleepy.	In (a): Speaker B is making a logical guess. He bases his guess on the information that Nancy is yawning. His logical conclusion, his "best guess," is that Nancy is sleepy. He uses ***must*** to express his logical conclusion.
(b) LOGICAL CONCLUSION: Amy plays tennis every day. She ***must like*** to play tennis. (c) NECESSITY: If you want to get into the movie theater, you ***must buy*** a ticket.	COMPARE: ***Must*** can express 　• a logical conclusion, as in (b). 　• necessity, as in (c).
(d) NEGATIVE LOGICAL CONCLUSION: Eric ate everything on his plate except the pickle. He ***must not like*** pickles. (e) PROHIBITION: There are sharks in the ocean near our hotel. We ***must not go*** swimming there.	COMPARE: ***Must not*** can express 　• a negative logical conclusion, as in (d). 　• prohibition, as in (e).

❑ **Exercise 37. Looking at grammar.** (Chart 7-11)
Complete the conversations with ***must*** or ***must not***.

1. A: Did you offer our guests something to eat?
   B: Yes, but they didn't want anything. They ___*must not*___ be hungry yet.

2. A: You haven't eaten since breakfast? That was hours ago. You ___*must*___ be hungry.
   B: I am.

3. A: Gregory has already had four glasses of water, and now he's having another.
   B: He _____ be really thirsty.

4. A: I offered Holly something to drink, but she doesn't want anything.
   B: She _____ be thirsty.

5. A: The dog won't eat.
   B: He _____ feel well.

6. A: Brian has watery eyes and has been coughing and sneezing.
   B: Poor guy. He _____ have a cold.

7. A: Erica's really smart. She always gets above 95 percent on her math tests.
   B: I'm sure she's pretty bright, but she _____ also study a lot.

8. A: Listen. Someone is jumping on the floor above us.
   B: It _____ be Sam. Sometimes he does exercises in his apartment.

□ **Exercise 38. Looking at grammar.** (Chart 7-11)
Make a logical conclusion for each situation. Use **must**.

1. Alima is crying. → *She must be unhappy.*
2. Mrs. Chu has a big smile on her face.
3. Samantha is shivering.
4. Olga watches ten movies a week.
5. James is sweating.
6. Toshi can lift one end of a compact car by himself.

□ **Exercise 39. Let's talk.** (Chart 7-11)
Make logical conclusions with **must** or **must not**. Use the suggested completions and/or your own words.

1. I am at Cyril's apartment door. I've knocked on the door and have rung the doorbell several times. Nobody has answered the door. *be at home? be out somewhere?*
   → *Cyril must not be at home. He must be out somewhere.*

2. Jennifer reads all the time. She sits in a quiet corner and reads even when people come to visit her. *love books? like books better than people? like to talk to people?*

3. Lara has a full academic schedule, plays on the volleyball team, has the lead in the school play, is a volunteer at the hospital, takes piano lessons, and has a part-time job at an ice-cream store. *be busy all the time? have a lot of spare time? be a hard worker?*

4. Simon gets on the Internet every day as soon as he gets home from work. He stays at his computer until he goes to bed. *be a computer addict? have a happy home life? have a lot of friends?*

□ **Exercise 40. Looking at grammar.** (Charts 7-9 and 7-11)
Complete the sentences with **must, have to,** or **had to** and the correct form of the verbs in parentheses.

At work

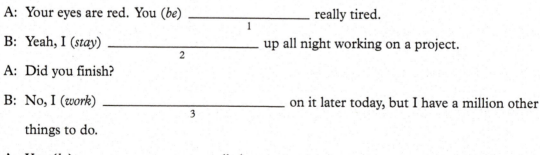

A: Your eyes are red. You (*be*) _____ really tired.
                                          1

B: Yeah, I (*stay*) _____ up all night working on a project.
                         2

A: Did you finish?

B: No, I (*work*) _____ on it later today, but I have a million other
                        3
things to do.

A: You (*be*) _____ really busy.
                    4

B: I am!

□ **Exercise 41. Warm-up.** (Chart 7-12)
Complete the questions with the correct words from the list. Two words don't fit any questions.

can't	couldn't	do	does	will	wouldn't

1. You can work this weekend, _____ you?

2. He won't be late, _____ he?

3. We'd like you to stay, _____ we?

4. They don't have to leave, _____ they?

7-12 Tag Questions with Modal Auxiliaries

(a) You *can* come, ***can't you*** ? (b) She *won't* tell, ***will she*** ? (c) He *should* help, ***shouldn't he*** ? (d) They *couldn't* do it, ***could they*** ? (e) We *would like* to help, ***wouldn't we*** ?	Tag questions are common with these modal auxiliaries: ***can, will, should, could,*** and ***would.****
(f) They *have to leave*, ***don't they*** ? (g) They *don't have to leave*, ***do they*** ? (h) He *has to leave*, ***doesn't he*** ? (i) He *doesn't have to leave*, ***does he*** ? (j) You *had to leave*, ***didn't you*** ? (k) You *didn't have to leave*, ***did you*** ?	Tag questions are also common with ***have to, has to,*** and ***had to.*** Notice that forms of ***do*** are used for the tag in (f) through (k).

*See Chart 5-15, p. 140, for information on how to use tag questions.

□ **Exercise 42. Looking at grammar.** (Chart 7-12)
Complete the tag questions.

1. You can answer these questions, _____ you?

2. Melinda won't tell anyone our secret, _____ she?

3. Alice would like to come with us, _____ she?

4. I don't have to do more chores, _____ I?

5. Steven shouldn't come to the meeting, _____ he?

6. Flies can fly upside down, _____ they?

7. You would rather have your own apartment, _____ you?

8. Jill has to renew her driver's license, _____ she?

9. If you want to catch your bus, you should leave now, _____ you?

10. Ms. Baxter will be here tomorrow, _____ she?

11. You couldn't hear me, _____ you?

12. We have to be at the doctor's early tomorrow, _____ we?

❑ **Exercise 43. Warm-up.** (Chart 7-13)
Read each group of sentences. Decide who the speaker is and a possible situation for each group.

GROUP A
1. Show me your driver's license.
2. Take it out of your wallet, please.
3. Step out of the car.

GROUP B
1. Open your mouth.
2. Stick out your tongue.
3. Say "ahhh."
4. Let me take a closer look.
5. Don't bite me!

7-13 Giving Instructions: Imperative Sentences

COMMAND: (a) Captain: *Open* the door! Soldier: Yes, sir! REQUEST: (b) Teacher: *Open* the door, please. Student: Sure. DIRECTIONS: (c) Barbara: Could you tell me how to get to the post office? Stranger: Certainly. *Walk* **two blocks down this street.** *Turn* **left and** *walk* **three more blocks.** It's on the right-hand side of the street.	Imperative sentences are used to give commands, make polite requests, and give directions. The difference between a command and a request lies in the speaker's tone of voice and the use of *please*. *Please* can come at the beginning or end of a request: *Open the door, please.* *Please open the door.*
(d) *Close* the window. (e) Please *sit* down. (f) *Be* quiet! (g) *Don't walk* on the grass. (h) Please *don't wait* for me. (i) *Don't be* late.	The simple form of a verb is used in imperative sentences. In (d): The understood subject of the sentence is *you* (meaning the person the speaker is talking to): *Close the window = You close the window.* NEGATIVE FORM: *Don't* + *the simple form of a verb*

Exercise 44. Let's talk. (Chart 7-13)

Part I. Read the steps for cooking rice. Put them in a logical order (1–9). Work with a partner or in small groups.

1. Measure the rice. _____
2. Cook for 20 minutes. _____
3. Pour water into a pan. _____
4. Bring the water to a boil. _____
5. Put the rice in the pan. _____
6. Don't burn yourself. _____
7. Set the timer. _____
8. Turn off the heat. _____
9. Take the pan off the stove. _____

Part II. Write instructions for cooking something simple. Share your recipe with the class.

Exercise 45. Listening. (Chart 7-13)

Part I. Listen to the steps in this number puzzle and write the verbs you hear. Before you begin, you may want to check your understanding of these words: *add, subtract, multiply, double*.

Puzzle steps:

1. _____ down the number of the month you were born. For example,

   _____ the number 2 if you were born in February.

   _____ 3 if you were born in March, etc.

2. _____ the number.

3. _____ 5 to it.

4. _____ it by 50.

5. _____ your age.

6. _____ 250.

Part II. Now follow the steps in Part I to complete the puzzle. In the final number, the last two digits on the right will be your age, and the one or two digits on the left will be the month you were born.

Part I. Read the passage. Cross out suggestions that don't work for a job interview in your country. Then add more suggestions until there are ten.

How to Make a Good Impression in a Job Interview

Do you want to know how to make a good impression when you interview for a job? Here are some suggestions for you to consider.

1. Dress appropriately for the company. Flip-flops and shorts, for example, are usually not appropriate.
2. Be sure to arrive early. Employers like punctual workers.
3. Bring extra copies of your résumé and references. There may be more than one interviewer.
4. Make eye contact with the interviewer. It shows confidence.
5. Don't chew gum during the interview.
6. Research the company before you go. That way you can show your knowledge and interest in the company.

If you follow these suggestions, you will have a better chance of making a good impression when you go for a job interview.

Part II. Write three paragraphs. Use the topic in Part I, or give general advice to people who want to . . .

1. improve their health.
2. get good grades.
3. improve their English.
4. find a job.
5. get a good night's sleep.
6. protect the environment by recycling.

Use this model.
  I. Introductory paragraph: *Do you want to . . . ? Here are some suggestions for you to consider.*
 II. Middle paragraph: (List the suggestions and add details.)
III. Final paragraph: *If you follow these suggestions, you will . . . .*

□ **Exercise 47. Warm-up.** (Chart 7-14)
Check (✓) the items that are suggestions.

1. _____ Why do bears hibernate?
2. _____ I have a day off. Why don't we take the kids to the zoo?
3. _____ Let's go see the bears at the zoo.

7-14 Making Suggestions: *Let's* and *Why Don't*

(a) — It's hot today. ***Let's*** *go to the beach.* — Okay. Good idea. (b) — It's hot today. ***Why don't we*** *go to the beach?* — Okay. Good idea.	***Let's*** and ***Why don't we*** are used to make suggestions about activities for you and another person to do. Examples (a) and (b) have the same meaning. ***Let's*** = *let us*
(c) — I'm tired. — ***Why don't you*** *take a nap?* — That's a good idea. I think I will.	In (c): ***Why don't you*** is used to make a friendly suggestion or to give friendly advice.

□ **Exercise 48. Let's talk.** (Chart 7-14)
Make suggestions beginning with ***Let's*** and ***Why don't we***.

1. Where should we go for dinner tonight?
2. Who should we ask to join us for dinner tonight?
3. What time should we meet at the restaurant?
4. Where should we go afterwards?

□ **Exercise 49. Let's talk.** (Chart 7-14)
Work in small groups. The leader states the problem, and then others in the group offer suggestions beginning with ***Why don't you***.

1. I'm freezing.
2. I'm feeling dizzy.
3. I feel like doing something interesting and fun this weekend. Any ideas?
4. I need to get more exercise, but I get bored with indoor activities. Any suggestions?
5. I haven't done my assignment for Professor Lopez. It will take me a couple of hours, and class starts in an hour. What am I going to do?
6. I've lost the key to my apartment, so I can't get in. My roommate is at the library. What am I going to do?
7. My friend and I had an argument, and now we aren't talking to each other. I've had some time to think about it, and I'm sorry for what I said. I miss her friendship. What should I do?

Exercise 50. Listening. (Chart 7-14)
Listen to the conversation about a couple making suggestions for the evening. Listen a second time and put the suggestions in the correct order (1–3).

Suggestions:

1. go to a restaurant _____

2. go dancing _____

3. go to a movie _____

❏ **Exercise 51. Warm-up.** (Chart 7-15)
Check (✓) the statements that are true for you.

1. _____ I prefer fruit to vegetables.

2. _____ I like raw vegetables better than cooked.

3. _____ I would rather eat vegetables than meat.

7-15 Stating Preferences: *Prefer, Like … Better, Would Rather*

(a) I *prefer* apples *to* oranges.	*prefer* + *noun* + *to* + *noun*
(b) I *prefer* watching TV *to* studying.	*prefer* + *-ing* verb + *to* + *-ing* verb
(c) I *like* apples *better than* oranges.	*like* + *noun* + *better than* + *noun*
(d) I *like* watching TV *better than* studying.	*like* + *-ing* verb + *better than* + *-ing* verb
(e) Ann *would rather have* an apple than an orange.	*Would rather* is followed immediately by the simple form of a verb (e.g., *have, visit, live*), as in (e).
(f) INCORRECT: *Ann would rather has an apple.*	
(g) I'd rather visit a big city *than live* there.	Verbs following *than* are also in the simple form, as in (g).
(h) INCORRECT: *I'd rather visit a big city than to live there.* INCORRECT: *I'd rather visit a big city than living there.*	
(i) *I'd / You'd / She'd / He'd / We'd / They'd* rather have an apple.	Contraction of *would* = *'d*
(j) *Would you rather* have an apple *or* an orange?	In (j): In a polite question, *would rather* can be followed by *or* to offer someone a choice.

❏ **Exercise 52. Looking at grammar.** (Chart 7-15)
Complete the sentences with *than* or *to*.

1. When I'm hot and thirsty, I **prefer** cold drinks __*to*__ hot drinks.

2. When I'm hot and thirsty, I **like** cold drinks **better** __*than*__ hot drinks.

3. When I'm hot and thirsty, **I'd rather have** a cold drink __*than*__ a hot drink.

4. I **prefer** tea _____ coffee.

5. I **like** tea **better** _____ coffee.

6. I'd **rather** drink tea _____ coffee.

7. When I choose a book, I **prefer** nonfiction _____ fiction.

8. I **like** folk music music **better** _____ rock and roll.

9. My parents **would rather work** _____ retire. They enjoy their jobs.

10. Do you **like** spring **better** _____ fall?

11. I **prefer visiting** my friends in the evening _____ watching TV by myself.

12. I **would rather read** a book in the evening _____ visit with friends.

❑ **Exercise 53. Let's talk: pairwork.** (Chart 7-15)
Work with a partner. Take turns asking and answering questions. Be sure to answer in complete sentences.

Examples: Which do you prefer: apples or oranges?*
→ *I prefer oranges to apples.*

Which do you like better: bananas or strawberries?
→ *I like bananas better than strawberries.*

Which would you rather have right now: an apple or a banana?
→ *I'd rather have a banana.*

1. Which do you like better: rice or potatoes?
2. Which do you prefer: peas or corn?
3. Which would you rather have for dinner tonight: fish or chicken?
4. Name two sports. Which do you like better?
5. Name two movies. Which one would you rather see?
6. What kind of music would you rather listen to: rock or classical?
7. Name two vegetables. Which do you prefer?
8. Name two TV programs. Which do you like better?

❑ **Exercise 54. Let's talk: interview.** (Chart 7-15)
Interview your classmates. Use **would rather . . . than** in your answers.

Would you rather . . .

1. live in an apartment or in a house?** Why?
2. be an author or an artist? Why?
3. drive a fast car or fly a small plane? Why?
4. be rich and unlucky in love or poor and lucky in love? Why?
5. surf the Internet or watch TV? Why?
6. have a big family or a small family? Why?
7. be a bird or a fish? Why?
8. spend your free time with other people or be by yourself? Why?

_____

*Use a rising intonation on the first choice and a falling intonation on the second choice: *Which do you prefer, apples or oranges?*

It is possible but not necessary to repeat a preposition after **than.
CORRECT: *I'd rather live in an apartment **than in a house**.*
CORRECT: *I'd rather live in an apartment **than a house**.*

Choose the best completion for each sentence.

Example: A: My cat won't eat.
      B: You _____ call the vet.
        a.   will   (b.) had better   c. may

1. A: Does this pen belong to you?
    B: No. It _____ be Susan's. She was sitting at that desk.
       a. had better   b. will   c. must

2. A: Let's go to a movie this evening.
    B: That sounds like fun, but I can't. I _____ finish a report before I go to bed tonight.
       a. have got to   b. would rather   c. ought to

3. A: Hey, Pietro. What's up* with Ken? Is he upset about something?
    B: He's angry because you recommended Ann instead of him for the promotion. You
       _____ sit down with him and explain your reasons. At least that's what I think.
       a. should   b. will   c. can

4. A: Does Omar want to go with us to the film festival tonight?
    B: No. He _____ go to a wrestling match than the film festival.
       a. could   b. would rather   c. prefers

5. A: I did it! I did it! I got my driver's license!
    B: Congratulations, Michelle. I'm really proud of you.
    A: Thanks, Dad. Now _____ I have the car tonight? Please, please?
    B: No. You're not ready for that quite yet.
       a. will   b. should   c. may

6. A: I just tripped on your carpet and almost fell. It's loose right by the door. You _____ fix
    it before someone gets hurt.
    B: Yes, Uncle Ben. I should. I will. I'm sorry. Are you all right?
       a. can   b. ought to   c. may

7. A: Are you going to the conference in Atlanta next month?
    B: I _____. It's sort of iffy** right now. I've applied for travel money, but who knows what
    my supervisor will do.
       a. will   b. have to   c. might

8. A: What shall we do after the meeting this evening?
    B: _____ pick Jan up and all go out to dinner together.
       a. Why don't   b. Let's   c. Should

9. A: What shall we do after that?
    B: _____ we go back to my place for dessert.
       a. Why don't   b. Let's   c. Should

---

*What's up? = What's going on?

**iffy = uncertain; doubtful

10. A: Have you seen my denim jacket? I _____ find it.
    B: Look in the hall closet.
        a. may not   b. won't   c. can't

11. A: Bye, Mom. I'm going to go play soccer with my friends.
    B: Wait a minute, young man! You _____ do your chores first.
        a. had better not   b. have to   c. would rather

12. A: Do you think that Scott will quit his job?
    B: I don't know. He _____. He's very angry. We'll just have to wait and see.
        a. must   b. may   c. will

13. A: The hotel provides towels, you know. You _____ pack a towel in your suitcase.
    B: This is my bathrobe, not a towel.
        a. don't have to   b. must not   c. couldn't

14. A: Did you climb to the top of the Statue of Liberty when you were in New York?
    B: No, I didn't. My knee was very sore, and I _____ climb all those stairs.
        a. might not   b. couldn't   c. must not

15. A: Rick, _____ work for me this evening? I'll take your shift tomorrow.
    B: Sure. I was going to ask you to work for me tomorrow anyway.
        a. should you   b. could you   c. do you have to

16. A: What are you children doing? Stop! You _____ play with sharp knives.
    B: Why not?
        a. must not   b. couldn't   c. don't have to

17. A: Don't wait for me. I _____ late.
    B: Okay.
        a. maybe   b. can be   c. may be

18. A: The Bensons are giving their daughter a new skateboard for her birthday.
    B: They _____ give her a helmet, too. She does some dangerous things on a skateboard.
        a. had better   b. can't   c. would rather

Appendix

Supplementary Grammar Charts

UNIT A

A-1 The Present Perfect vs. The Past Perfect

Present Perfect	(a) I am not hungry now. I *have* already *eaten*.	The PRESENT PERFECT expresses an activity that *occurred before now, at an unspecified time in the past,* as in (a).
before now / now (timeline: ✗ before now, ✗ now)		
Past Perfect	(b) I was not hungry at 1:00 P.M. I *had* already *eaten*.	The PAST PERFECT expresses an activity that *occurred before **another** time in the past.* In (b): I ate at noon. I was not hungry at 1:00 P.M. because I had already eaten before 1:00 P.M.
before 1:00 / 1:00 P.M. (timeline: ✗ before 1:00, ✗ 1:00 P.M.)		

I laughed when I saw my son.
He *had poured* a bowl of noodles on top of his head.

A-2 The Past Progressive vs. The Past Perfect

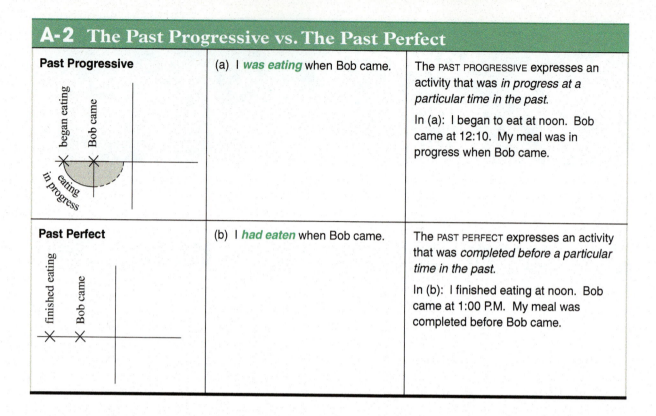

Past Progressive	(a) I *was eating* when Bob came.	The PAST PROGRESSIVE expresses an activity that was *in progress at a particular time in the past.* In (a): I began to eat at noon. Bob came at 12:10. My meal was in progress when Bob came.
Past Perfect	(b) I *had eaten* when Bob came.	The PAST PERFECT expresses an activity that was *completed before a particular time in the past.* In (b): I finished eating at noon. Bob came at 1:00 P.M. My meal was completed before Bob came.

A-3 *Still* vs. *Anymore*

Still

(a) It was cold yesterday. **It is *still* cold** today. **We *still* need to wear coats.** (b) The mail didn't come an hour ago. **The mail *still* hasn't come.**	***Still*** = A situation continues to exist from past to present without change. ***Still*** is used in either affirmative or negative sentences. Position: midsentence*

Anymore

(c) I lived in Chicago two years ago, but then I moved to another city. **I don't live in Chicago *anymore.***	***Anymore*** = A past situation does not continue to exist at present; a past situation has changed. ***Anymore*** has the same meaning as *any longer.* ***Anymore*** is used in negative sentences. Position: end of sentence

*See Chart 1-3, p. 10. A midsentence adverb
  (1) precedes a simple present verb: *We **still need** to wear coats.*
  (2) follows *am, is, are, was, were: It **is still** cold.*
  (3) comes between a helping verb and a main verb: *Bob **has already arrived.***
  (4) precedes a negative helping verb: *Ann **still hasn't** come.*
  (5) follows the subject in a question: *Have **you already** seen that movie?*

A-4 Additional Verbs Followed by *That*-Clauses

conclude that	guess that	pretend that	show that
demonstrate that	imagine that	recall that	suspect that
fear that	indicate that	recognize that	teach that
figure out that	observe that	regret that	
find out that	presume that	reveal that	

Scientists *have **concluded that*** dolphins can communicate with each other.

A-5 Additional Expressions with *Be* + *That*-Clauses

be ashamed that	be furious that	be proud that
be amazed that	be horrified that	be terrified that
be astounded that	be impressed that	be thrilled that
be delighted that	be lucky that	
be fortunate that	be positive that	

UNIT B: Phrasal Verbs

NOTE: See the *Fundamentals of English Grammar Workbook* appendix for more practice exercises for phrasal verbs.

B-1 Phrasal Verbs

(a) We ***put off*** our trip. We'll go next month instead of this month. (*put off = postpone*)	In (a): ***put off*** = a phrasal verb A PHRASAL VERB = a verb and a particle that together have a special meaning. For example, *put off* means "postpone."
(b) Jimmy, ***put on*** your coat before you go outdoors. (*put on = place clothes on one's body*)	
(c) Someone left the scissors on the table. They didn't belong there. I ***put*** them ***away***. (*put away = put something in its usual or proper place*)	A PARTICLE = a "small word" (e.g., *off, on, away, back*) that is used in a phrasal verb.
(d) After I used the dictionary, I ***put*** it ***back*** on the shelf. (*put back = return something to its original place*)	Notice that the phrasal verbs with ***put*** in (a), (b), (c), and (d) all have different meanings.
Separable	Some phrasal verbs are **separable**: a NOUN OBJECT can either

(e) We *put **off** our trip*. = (vb + **particle** + NOUN)
(f) We *put our trip **off***. = (vb + NOUN + **particle**)
(g) We *put **it** off*.   = (vb + PRONOUN + **particle**)
	(1) follow the particle, as in (e), OR
	  (2) come between (separate) the verb and the particle, as in (f).
	
	If a phrasal verb is separable, a PRONOUN OBJECT comes between the verb and the particle, as in (g).
	   INCORRECT: We put off it.

Nonseparable	If a phrasal verb is **nonseparable**, a NOUN or PRONOUN always follows (never precedes) the particle, as in (h) and (i).
(h) I *ran **into** Bob*. = (vb + **particle** + NOUN) (i) I *ran **into** him*. = (vb + **particle** + PRONOUN)	*INCORRECT: I ran Bob into.* *INCORRECT: I ran him into.*
Phrasal Verbs: Intransitive	Some phrasal verbs are intransitive; i.e., they are not followed by an object.
(j) The machine *broke down*. (k) Please *come in*. (l) I *fell down*.	
Three-Word Phrasal Verbs	Some two-word verbs (e.g., *drop in*) can become three-word verbs (e.g., *drop in on*).
(m) Last night some friends ***dropped in***.	In (m): ***drop in*** is not followed by an object. It is an intransitive phrasal verb (i.e., it is not followed by an object).
(n) Let's ***drop in on*** Alice this afternoon.	In (n): ***drop in on*** is a three-word phrasal verb. Three-word phrasal verbs are transitive (they are followed by objects).
(o) We *dropped in on **her*** last week.	In (o): Three-word phrasal verbs are nonseparable (the noun or pronoun follows the phrasal verb).

A **ask out** = ask (someone) to go on a date

B **blow out** = extinguish (a match, a candle)
break down = stop functioning properly
break out = happen suddenly
break up = separate, end a relationship
bring back = return
bring up = (1) raise (children)
(2) mention, start to talk about

C **call back** = return a telephone call
call off = cancel
call on = ask (someone) to speak in class
call up = make a telephone call
cheer up = make happier
clean up = make neat and clean
come along (with) = accompany
come from = originate
come in = enter a room or building
come over (to) = visit the speaker's place
cross out = draw a line through
cut out (of) = remove with scissors or knife

D **dress up** = put on nice clothes
drop in (on) = visit without calling first or
without an invitation
drop out (of) = stop attending (school)

E **eat out** = eat outside of one's home

F **fall down** = fall to the ground
figure out = find the solution to a problem
fill in = complete by writing in a blank space
fill out = write information on a form
fill up = fill completely with gas, water, coffee,
etc.
find out (about) = discover information
fool around (with) = have fun while wasting
time

G **get on** = enter a bus/an airplane/a train/a
subway
get out of = leave a car, a taxi

get over = recover from an illness or a shock
get together (with) = join, meet
get through (with) = finish
get up = get out of bed in the morning
give away = donate, get rid of by giving
give back = return (something) to (someone)
give up = quit doing (something) or quit trying
go on = continue
go back (to) = return to a place
go out = not stay home
go over (to) = (1) approach
(2) visit another's home
grow up (in) = become an adult

H **hand in** = give homework, test papers, etc., to
a teacher
hand out = give (something) to this person,
then to that person, then to
another person, etc.
hang around/out (with) = spend time relaxing
hang up = (1) hang on a hanger or a hook
(2) end a telephone conversation
have on = wear
help out = assist (someone)

K **keep away (from)** = not give to
keep on = continue

L **lay off** = stop employment
leave on = (1) not turn off (a light, a machine)
(2) not take off (clothing)
look into = investigate
look over = examine carefully
look out (for) = be careful
look up = look for information in a dictionary,
a telephone directory, an
encyclopedia, etc.

P **pay back** = return borrowed money to
(someone)
pick up = lift
point out = call attention to

(continued)

print out = create a paper copy from a computer

put away = put (something) in its usual or proper place

put back = return (something) to its original place

put down = stop holding or carrying

put off = postpone

put on = put clothes on one's body

put out = extinguish (stop) a fire, a cigarette

R **run into** = meet by chance

run out (of) = finish the supply of (something)

S **set out (for)** = begin a trip

shut off = stop a machine or a light, turn off

sign up (for) = put one's name on a list

show up = come, appear

sit around (with) = sit and do nothing

sit back = put one's back against a chair back

sit down = go from standing to sitting

speak up = speak louder

stand up = go from sitting to standing

start over = begin again

stay up = not go to bed

T **take back** = return

take off = (1) remove clothes from one's body
(2) ascend in an airplane

take out = invite out and pay

talk over = discuss

tear down = destroy a building

tear out (of) = remove (paper) by tearing

tear up = tear into small pieces

think over = consider

throw away/out = put in the trash, discard

try on = put on clothing to see if it fits

turn around
turn back } change to the opposite direction

turn down = decrease the volume

turn off = stop a machine or a light

turn on = start a machine or a light

turn over = turn the top side to the bottom

turn up = increase the volume

W **wake up** = stop sleeping

watch out (for) = be careful

work out = solve

write down = write a note on a piece of paper

❑ **EXERCISE 1. Looking at grammar.** (Charts B-1 and B-2)
Underline the second part of the phrasal verb in each sentence.

1. I picked <u>up</u> a book and started to read.

2. The teacher called on me in class.

3. I get up early every day.

4. I feel okay now. I got over my cold last week.

5. I woke my roommate up when I got home.

6. I turned the radio on to listen to some music.

7. When I don't know how to spell a word, I look it up.

☐ EXERCISE 2. Looking at grammar. (Charts B-1 and B-2)
Check (✓) the correct sentences. In some cases, both are correct.

1. _____ I turned the light on.

   _____ I turned on the light.

2. _____ I ran into Mary.

   _____ I ran Mary into.

3. _____ Joe looked up the definition.

   _____ Joe looked the definition up.

4. _____ I took off my coat.

   _____ I took my coat off.

5. _____ I got in the car and left.

   _____ I got the car in and left.

6. _____ I figured out the answer.

   _____ I figured the answer out.

☐ EXERCISE 3. Looking at grammar. (Charts B-1 and B-2)
Complete the sentences with particles and the pronouns *it* or *them*. If the phrasal verb is separable, circle SEP. If it is nonseparable, circle NONSEP.

1. I got over my cold. → I got ___over it___.   SEP   (NONSEP)

2. I made up the story. → I made _____.   SEP   NONSEP

3. I put off my homework. → I put _____.   SEP   NONSEP

4. I wrote down the numbers. → I wrote _____.   SEP   NONSEP

5. I looked up the answer. → I looked _____.   SEP   NONSEP

6. I got on the bus. → I got _____.   SEP   NONSEP

7. I looked into the problem. → I looked _____.   SEP   NONSEP

8. I shut off the engine. → I shut _____.   SEP   NONSEP

9. I turned off the lights. → I turned _____.   SEP   NONSEP

10. I got off the subway. → I got _____.   SEP   NONSEP

NOTE: See the *Fundamentals of English Grammar Workbook* appendix for more practice exercises for phrasal verbs.

UNIT C: Prepositions

NOTE: See the *Fundamentals of English Grammar Workbook* appendix for practice exercises for preposition combinations.

C-1 Preposition Combinations: Introduction

ADJ + PREP (a) Ali is ***absent from*** class today. V + PREP (b) This book ***belongs to*** me.	*At, from, of, on,* and *to* are examples of prepositions. Prepositions are often combined with adjectives, as in (a), and verbs, as in (b).

C-2 Preposition Combinations: A Reference List

A
be absent from
be accustomed to
   add (*this*) to (*that*)
be acquainted with
   admire (*someone*) for (*something*)
be afraid of
   agree with (*someone*) about (*something*)
be angry at / with (*someone*) about / over (*something*)
   apologize to (*someone*) for (*something*)
   apply for (*something*)
   approve of
   argue with (*someone*) about / over (*something*)
   arrive at (*a building / a room*)
   arrive in (*a city / a country*)
   ask (*someone*) about (*something*)
   ask (*someone*) for (*something*)
be aware of

B
be bad for
   believe in
   belong to
be bored with / by
   borrow (*something*) from (*someone*)

C
be clear to
   combine with
   compare (*this*) to / with (*that*)
   complain to (*someone*) about (*something*)
be composed of
   concentrate on
   consist of
be crazy about
be crowded with
be curious about

D
   depend on (*someone*) for (*something*)
be dependent on (*someone*) for (*something*)

be devoted to
   die of / from
be different from
   disagree with (*someone*) about (*something*)
be disappointed in
   discuss (*something*) with (*someone*)
   divide (*this*) into (*that*)
be divorced from
be done with
   dream about / of
   dream of

E
be engaged to
be equal to
   escape from (*a place*)
be excited about
   excuse (*someone*) for (*something*)
   excuse from
be exhausted from

F
be familiar with
be famous for
   feel about
   feel like
   fill (*something*) with
be finished with
   forgive (*someone*) for (*something*)
be friendly to / with
be frightened of / by
be full of

G
   get rid of
be gone from
be good for
   graduate from

H
happen to
be happy about (*something*)
be happy for (*someone*)
    hear about / of (*something*) from (*someone*)
    help (*someone*) with (*something*)
    hide (*something*) from (*someone*)
    hope for
be hungry for

I
    insist on
be interested in
    introduce (*someone*) to (*someone*)
    invite (*someone*) to (*something*)
be involved in

K
be kind to
    know about

L
    laugh at
    leave for (*a place*)
    listen to
    look at
    look for
    look forward to
    look like

M
be made of
be married to
    matter to
be the matter with
    multiply (*this*) by (*that*)

N
be nervous about
be nice to

O
be opposed to

P
    pay for
be patient with
be pleased with / about
    play with
    point at
be polite to
    prefer (*this*) to (*that*)

be prepared for
    protect (*this*) from (*that*)
be proud of
    provide (*someone*) with

Q
be qualified for

R
    read about
be ready for
be related to
    rely on
be resonsible for

S
be sad about
be satisfied with
be scared of / by
    search for
    separate (*this*) from (*that*)
be similar to
    speak to / with (*someone*) about (*something*)
    stare at
    subtact (*this*) from (*that*)
be sure of / about

T
    take care of
    talk about (*something*)
    talk to / with (*someone*) about (*something*)
    tell (*someone*) about (*something*)
be terrified of / by
    thank (*someone*) for (*something*)
    think about / of
be thirsty for
be tired from
be tired of
    translate from (*one language*) to (*another*)

U
be used to

W
    wait for
    wait on
    warn about / of
    wonder about
be worried about

Listening Script

NOTE: You may want to pause the audio after each item or in longer passages so that there is enough time to complete each task.

Chapter 1: Present Time

Exercise 1, p. 1.

SAM: Hi. My name is Sam.
LISA: Hi. I'm Lisa. It's nice to meet you.
SAM: Nice to meet you too. Where are you from?
LISA: I'm from Boston. How about you?
SAM: I'm from Quebec. So, how long have you been here?
LISA: Just one day. I still have a little jet lag.
SAM: Me too. I got in yesterday morning. So we need to ask each other about a hobby. What do you like to do in your free time?
LISA: I spend a lot of time outdoors. I love to hike. When I'm indoors, I like to surf the Internet.
SAM: Me too. I'm studying Italian right now. There are a lot of good websites for learning languages on the Internet.
LISA: I know. I found a good one for Japanese. I'm trying to learn a little. Now, when I introduce you to the group, I have to write your full name on the board. What's your last name and how do you spell it?
SAM: It's Sanchez. S-A-N-C-H-E-Z.
LISA: My last name is Paterson — with one "t": P-A-T-E-R-S-O-N.
SAM: It looks like our time is up. Thanks. It's been nice talking to you.
LISA: I enjoyed it too.

Exercise 5, p. 4.

Lunch at the Fire Station

It's 12:30, and the firefighters are waiting for their next call. They are taking their lunch break. Ben, Rita, and Jada are sitting at a table in the fire station. Their co-worker Bruno is making lunch for them. He is an excellent cook. He often makes lunch. He is fixing spicy chicken and rice. Their captain isn't eating. He is doing paperwork. He skips lunch on busy days. He works in his office and finishes his paperwork.

Exercise 6, p. 5.

1. Irene designs video games.
2. She is working on a new project.
3. She is sitting in front of her computer.
4. She spends her weekends at the office.
5. She's finishing plans for a new game.

Exercise 9, p. 6.

A problem with the printer

1. Does it need more paper?
2. Does it have enough ink?
3. Are you fixing it yourself?
4. Do you know how to fix it?
5. Do we have another printer in the office?
6. Hmmm. Is it my imagination or is it making a strange noise?

Exercise 21, p. 14.

Natural disasters: a flood

1. The weather causes some natural disasters.
2. Heavy rains sometimes create floods.
3. A big flood causes a lot of damage.
4. In towns, floods can damage buildings, homes, and roads.
5. After a flood, a town needs a lot of financial help for repairs.

Exercise 24, p. 15.

1. talks
2. fishes
3. hopes
4. teaches
5. moves
6. kisses
7. pushes
8. waits
9. mixes
10. bows
11. studies
12. buys
13. enjoys
14. tries
15. carries

Exercise 33, p. 21.

Part I.

At the doctor's office

1.	Do you	becomes	Dyou	Do you have an appointment?
2.	Does he	becomes	Dze	Does he have an appointment?
3.	Does she	becomes	Duh-she	Does she have an appointment?
4.	Do we	becomes	Duh-we	Do we have an appointment?
5.	Do they	becomes	Duh-they	Do they have an appointment?
6.	Am I	becomes	Mi	Am I late for my appointment?
7.	Is it	becomes	Zit	Is it time for my appointment?
8.	Does it	becomes	Zit	Does it hurt?

Part II.

1. Do you have pain anywhere?
2. Does it hurt anywhere else?
3. Does she have a cough or sore throat?
4. Does he have a fever?
5. Does she need lab tests?
6. Am I very sick?
7. Is it serious?
8. Does he need to make another appointment?
9. Do they want to wait in the waiting room?
10. Do we pay now or later?

Exercise 35, p. 22.

1. We have a few minutes before we need to leave. Do you want a cup of coffee?
2. We need to leave. Are you ready?
3. Look outside. Is it raining hard?
4. Do we need to take an umbrella?
5. Mr. Smith has his coat on. Is he leaving now?
6. I'm looking for the office supplies. Are they in here?

Exercise 37, p. 24.

Aerobic Exercise

Jeremy and Nancy believe exercise is important. They go to an exercise class three times a week. They like aerobic exercise.

Aerobic exercise is a special type of exercise. It increases a person's heart rate. Fast walking, running, and dancing are examples of aerobic exercise. During aerobic exercise, a person's heart beats fast. This brings more oxygen to the muscles. Muscles work longer when they have more oxygen.

Right now Jeremy and Nancy are listening to some lively music. They are doing special dance steps. They are exercising different parts of their body.

How about you? Do you like to exercise? Do your muscles get exercise every week? Do you do some type of aerobic exercise?

Chapter 2: Past Time

Exercise 4, p. 27.

1. We studied . . .
2. Mr. Green wrote a magazine article . . .
3. The sun sets . . .
4. A substitute teacher taught . . .
5. Mr. Watson drove a sports car . . .

Exercise 5, p. 28.

Part I.

1. I was in a hurry. I wasn't in a hurry.
2. They were on time. They weren't on time.
3. He was at the doctor's. He wasn't at the doctor's.
4. We were early. We weren't early.

Part II.

At a wedding

1. The bride wasn't nervous before the ceremony.
2. The groom was nervous before the ceremony.
3. His parents weren't nervous about the wedding.
4. The bride and groom were excited about their wedding.
5. The ceremony was in the evening.
6. The wedding reception wasn't after the wedding.
7. It was the next day.
8. It was at a popular hotel.
9. A lot of guests were there.
10. Some relatives from out of town weren't there.

Exercise 8, p. 30.

1. Shhh. The movie is beginning.
2. Oh, no. The elevator door is stuck. It isn't opening.
3. Here's a letter for you. I opened it accidentally.
4. I'm listening to the phone message that you aready listened to.
5. Are you lying to me or telling me the truth?
6. We enjoyed the party.
7. I'm enjoying the nice weather today.
8. You look upset. What happened?

Exercise 16, p. 37.

Part I.

1.	Did you	becomes	Did-ja	Did you forget something? OR
	Did you	becomes	Did-ya	Did you forget something?
2.	Did I	becomes	Dih-di	Did I forget something? OR
	Did I	becomes	Di	Did I forget something?
3.	Did he	becomes	Dih-de	Did he forget something? OR
	Did he	becomes	De	Did he forget something?

4. Did she   becomes   Dih-she   Did she forget something?

5. Did we   becomes   Dih-we   Did we forget something?

6. Did they   becomes   Dih-they   Did they forget something?

Part II.

1. Alex hurt his finger. Did he cut it with a knife?
2. Ms. Jones doesn't have any money in her wallet. Did she spend it all yesterday?
3. Karen's parents visited. Did you meet them yesterday?
4. The Browns don't have a car anymore. Did they sell it?
5. I dropped the glass. Did I break it?
6. Ann didn't throw away her old clothes. Did she keep them?
7. John gave a book to his son. Did he read it to him?
8. You don't have your glasses. Did you lose them?
9. Mr. Jones looked for his passport in his desk drawer. Did he find it?
10. The baby is crying. Did I upset her?

Exercise 17, p. 37.

Luka wasn't home last night.

1. Did he go to a party last night?
2. Did he have a good time?
3. Did he eat a lot of food?
4. Did he drink a lot of soda?
5. Did he meet some new people?
6. Did he shake hands with them when he met them?
7. Did he dance with friends?
8. Did he sit with his friends and talk?

Exercise 19, p. 38.

A Deadly Flu

Every year, the flu kills 200,000 to 300,000 people around the world. But in 1918, a very strong flu virus killed millions of people. This flu began in 1918 and lasted until 1920. It spread around the world, and between 20 million and 100 million people died. Unlike other flu viruses that usually kill the very young and the very old, many of the victims were healthy young adults. This was unusual and made people especially afraid.

Exercise 20, p. 39.

Part I.

1. watch, watched
2. studied, studied
3. works, worked
4. decided, decided

Part II.

1. We watched a movie.
2. They studied in the morning.
3. She worked at the library.
4. They decided to leave.

Exercise 21, p. 39.

1. We agree with you.
2. We agreed with you.
3. I arrived on time.
4. The teacher explains the answers well.
5. My doctor's appointment ended late.
6. The train stopped suddenly.
7. You touched a spider!

Exercise 22, p. 40.

1. It rains in the spring . . .
2. It rained a lot . . .
3. The mail carrier walks to our house . . .
4. My friend surprised me with a birthday present . . .
5. The taxi picks up passengers at the airport . . .
6. I passed my final exam in math . . .

Exercise 23, p. 40.

1. cooked	5. started	9. added
2. served	6. dropped	10. passed
3. wanted	7. pulled	11. returned
4. asked	8. pushed	12. pointed

Exercise 24, p. 40.

A: Did you have a good weekend?
B: Yeah, I went to a waterslide park.
A: Really? That sounds like fun!
B: It was great! I loved the fast slides. How about you? How was your weekend?
A: I visited my aunt.
B: Did you have a good time?
A: Not really. She didn't like my clothes or my haircut.

Exercise 31, p. 46.

At a checkout stand in a grocery store

1. A: Hi. Did you find what you needed?
   B: Almost everything. I was looking for sticky rice, but I didn't see it.
   A: It's on aisle 10, in the Asian food section.

2. A: This is the express lane. Ten items only. It looks like you have more than ten. Did you count them?
   B: I thought I had ten. Oh, I guess I have more. Sorry.
   A: The checkout stand next to me is open.

3. A: Do you have any coupons you wanted to use?
   B: I had a couple in my purse, but I can't find them now.
   A: What were they for? I might have some extras here.
   B: One was for eggs, and the other was for ice cream.
   A: I think I have those.

Exercise 39, p. 51.

Jennifer's Problem

Jennifer works for an insurance company. When people need help with their car insurance, they call her. Right now it is 9:05 A.M., and Jennifer is sitting at her desk.

She came to work on time this morning. Yesterday Jennifer was late to work because she had a minor auto accident. While she was driving to work, her cell phone rang. She reached for it.

While she was reaching for her phone, Jennifer lost control of the car. Her car ran into a row of mailboxes beside the road and stopped. Fortunately, no one was hurt in the accident.

Jennifer is okay, but her car isn't. It needs repairs. Jennifer feels very embarrassed now. She made a bad decision, especially since it is illegal to talk on a cell phone and drive at the same time where she lives.

Exercise 43, p. 53.

1. I used to stay up past midnight, but now I often go to bed at 10:00 because I have an 8:00 class.
2. What time did you used to go to bed when you were a child?
3. Tom used to play tennis after work every day, but now he doesn't.
4. I used to skip breakfast, but now I always have something to eat in the morning because I read that students who eat breakfast do better in school.
5. I didn't used to like grammar, but now I do.

Chapter 3: Future Time

Exercise 2, p. 56.

At the airport

1. The security line will take about a half hour.
2. The plane is going to arrive at Gate 10.
3. Your flight is already an hour late.
4. Your flight will be here soon.
5. Did you print your boarding pass?
6. Are you printing my boarding pass too?
7. Are we going to have a snack on our flight?
8. We will need to buy snacks on the flight.

Exercise 6, p. 58.

Part I.

Looking for an apartment

A: We're going to look for an apartment to rent this weekend.
B: Are you going to look in this area?
A: No, we're going to search in an area closer to our jobs.
B: Is the rent going to be cheaper in that area?
A: Yes, apartment rents are definitely going to be cheaper.

B: Are you going to need to pay a deposit?
A: I'm sure we're going to need to pay the first and last month's rent.

Part II.

A: Where are you going to move to?
B: We're going to look for something outside the city. We're going to spend the weekend apartment hunting.
A: What fees are you going to need to pay?
B: I think we are going to need to pay the first and last month's rent.
A: Are there going to be other fees?
B: There is probably going to be an application fee and a cleaning fee. Also, the landlord is probably going to run a credit check, so we are going to need to pay for that.

Exercise 10, p. 60.

Part I.

1. I'll be ready to leave soon.
2. You'll need to come.
3. He'll drive us.
4. She'll come later.
5. We'll get there a little late.
6. They'll wait for us.

Part II.

1. Don't wait up for me tonight. I'll be home late.
2. I paid the bill this morning. You'll get my check in the next day or two.
3. We have the better team. We'll probably win the game.
4. Henry twisted his ankle while running down a hill. He'll probably take a break from running this week.
5. We can go to the beach tomorrow, but it'll probably be too cold to go swimming.
6. I invited some guests for dinner. They'll probably get here around seven.
7. Karen is doing volunteer work for a community health-care clinic this week. She'll be gone a lot in the evenings.

Exercise 11, p. 61.

Part I.

At the doctor's office

1. The doctor'll be with you in a few minutes.
2. Your appointment'll take about an hour.
3. Your fever'll be gone in a few days.
4. Your stitches'll disappear over the next two weeks.
5. The nurse'll schedule your tests.
6. The lab'll have the results next week.
7. The receptionist at the front desk'll set up your next appointment.

Part II.

At the pharmacy

1. Your prescription'll be ready in ten minutes.
2. The medicine'll make you feel a little tired.
3. The pharmacist'll call your doctor's office.

4. This cough syrup'll help your cough.
5. Two aspirin'll be enough.
6. The generic drug'll cost less.
7. This information'll explain all the side effects for this medicine.

Exercise 13, p. 62.

My day tomorrow

1. I'm going to go to the bank tomorrow.
2. I'll probably do other errands too.
3. I may stop at the post office.
4. I will probably pick up groceries at the store.
5. It is going to be hot.
6. Maybe I'll do my errands early.

Exercise 17, p. 64.

Predictions about the future

1. People'll have flying cars.
2. Cars'll use solar power or energy from the sun instead of gas.
3. Some people'll live underwater.
4. Some people may live in outer space.
5. Maybe creatures from outer space'll live here.
6. Children'll learn on computers in their homes, not at school.
7. Robots may clean our homes.
8. Maybe computers'll have feelings.
9. People won't die.
10. The earth'll be too crowded.

Exercise 23, p. 67.

1. Could someone please open the window?
2. Do you have plans for the weekend?
3. Do you have a car?
4. I feel sick. I need to leave.

Exercise 33, p. 73.

Going on vacation

A: I'm going on vacation tomorrow.
B: Where are you going?
A: To San Francisco.
B: How are you getting there? Are you flying or driving your car?
A: I'm flying. I have to be at the airport by seven tomorrow morning.
B: Do you need a ride to the airport?
A: No, thanks. I'm taking a taxi. What about you? Are you planning to go somewhere over vacation?
B: No. I'm staying here.

Exercise 44, p. 79.

At a Chinese restaurant

A: Okay, let's all open our fortune cookies.
B: What does yours say?
A: Mine says, "You will receive an unexpected gift." Great! Are you planning to give me a gift soon?

B: Not that I know of. Mine says, "Your life will be long and happy."
Good. I want a long life.
C: Mine says, "A smile solves all communication problems." Well, that's good! After this, when I don't understand someone, I'll just smile at them.
D: My fortune is this: "If you work hard, you will be successful."
A: Well, it looks like all of us will have good luck in the future!

Chapter 4: Present Perfect and Past Perfect

Exercise 2, p. 82.

1. call, called, called
2. speak, spoke, spoken
3. do, did, done
4. know, knew, known
5. meet, met, met
6. come, came, come
7. eat, ate, eaten
8. cut, cut, cut
9. read, read, read
10. be, was/were, been

Exercise 12, p. 88.

1. I saw a two-headed snake once. Have you ever . . . ?
2. I flew in a small plane last year. Have you ever . . . ?
3. I rode in a limousine once. Have you ever . . . ?
4. I did volunteer work last month. Have you ever . . . ?
5. I accidentally tore my shirt yesterday. Have you ever . . . ?
6. I had a scary experience on an airplane last year. Have you ever . . . ?
7. I fell out of a boat last week. Have you ever . . . ?
8. I felt very, very embarrassed once, and my face got hot. Have you ever . . . ?
9. I spoke to a famous person yesterday. Have you ever . . . ?
10. I wanted to be famous once. Have you ever . . . ?

Exercise 17, p. 91.

1. Lori holds the baby a lot.
2. Richard gives the baby a bath at the end of the day.
3. Lori changes the baby's diapers.
4. Richard has taken lots of pictures of the baby.
5. Lori wakes up when the baby cries.
6. Richard does some of the household chores.
7. Lori is tired during the day.

Exercise 19, p. 92.

At a restaurant

1. My coffee's a little cold.
2. My coffee's gotten a little cold.
3. Your order's not ready yet.
4. Wow! Our order's here already.
5. Excuse me, I think our waiter's forgotten our order.
6. Actually, your waiter's just gone home sick. I'll take care of you.

Exercise 20, p. 93.

A job interview

Mika is a nurse. She is interviewing for a job with the manager of a hospital emergency room. He is looking at her resume and asking her some general questions.

INTERVIEWER: It looks like you've done a lot of things since you became a nurse.

MIKA: Yes, I've worked for a medical clinic. I've worked in a prison. I've worked in several area hospitals. And I've done volunteer work at a community health center for low-income patients.

INTERVIEWER: Very good. But, let me ask you, why have you changed jobs so often?

MIKA: Well, I like having new challenges and different experiences.

INTERVIEWER: Why have you applied for this job?

MIKA: Well, I'm looking for something more fast-paced, and I've been interested in working in an E.R. for a long time. I've heard that this hospital provides great training for its staff, and it offers excellent patient care.

INTERVIEWER: Thank you for coming in. I'll call you next week with our decision.

MIKA: It was good to meet you. Thank you for your time.

Exercise 26, p. 97.

1. Every day, I spend some money. Yesterday, I spent some money. Since Friday, I have . . .
2. I usually make a big breakfast. Yesterday, I made a big breakfast. All week, I have . . .
3. Every day, I send emails. Yesterday I sent an email. Today I have already . . .
4. Every time I go to a restaurant, I leave a nice tip. Last night I left a nice tip. I just finished dinner, and I have . . .
5. Every weekend, I sleep in late. Last weekend, I slept in late. Since I was a teenager, I have . . .
6. I drive very carefully. On my last trip across the country, I drove very carefully. All my life, I have . . .
7. Every morning, I sing in the shower. Earlier today, I sang in the shower. Since I was little, I have . . .

Exercise 31, p. 100.

Part I.

1. Jane's been out of town for two days.
2. My parents've been active in politics for 40 years.
3. My friends've moved into a new apartment.
4. I'm sorry. Your credit card's expired.
5. Bob's been traveling in Montreal since last Tuesday.
6. You're the first one here. No one else's come yet.

Part II.

1. The weather's been warm since the beginning of April.

2. This month's been unusually warm.
3. My parents've been living in the same house for 25 years.
4. My cousins've lived in the same town all their lives.
5. You slept late. Your friend's already gotten up and made breakfast.
6. My friends've planned a going-away party for me. I'm moving back to my hometown.
7. I'm afraid your work's been getting a little sloppy.
8. My roommate's traveled a lot. She's visited many different countries.

Exercise 34, p. 103.

Today's Weather

The weather has certainly been changing today. Boy, what a day! We've already had rain, wind, hail, and sun. So, what's in store for tonight? As you have probably seen, dark clouds have been building. We have a weather system moving in that is going to bring colder temperatures and high winds. We've been saying all week that this system is coming, and it looks like tonight is it! We've even seen snow down south of us, and we could get some snow here too. So hang onto your hats! We may have a rough night ahead of us.

Exercise 36, p. 104.

1. A: What song is playing on the radio?
   B: I don't know, but it's good, isn't it?
2. A: How long have you lived in Dubai?
   B: About a year.
3. A: Where are the kids?
   B: I don't know. I've been calling them for ten minutes.
4. A: Who have you met tonight?
   B: Actually, I've met a few people from your office. How about you? Who have you met?
   A: I've met some interesting artists and musicians.

Exercise 37, p. 104.

A common illness

LARA: Hi, Mom. I was just calling to tell you that I can't come to your birthday party this weekend. I'm afraid I'm sick.

MOM: Oh, I'm sorry to hear that.

LARA: Yeah, I got sick Wednesday night, and it's just been getting worse.

MOM: Are you going to see a doctor?

LARA: I don't know. I don't want to go to a doctor if it's not serious.

MOM: Well, what symptoms have you been having?

LARA: I've had a cough, and now I have a fever.

MOM: Have you been taking any medicine?

LARA: Just over-the-counter stuff.

MOM: If your fever doesn't go away, I think you need to call a doctor.

LARA: Yeah, I probably will.
MOM: Well, call me tomorrow and let me know how you're doing.
LARA: Okay. I'll call you in the morning.

Exercise 43, p. 110.

1. A: Oh, no! We're too late. The train has already left.
   B: That's okay. We'll catch the next one.

2. A: Last Thursday we went to the station to catch the train, but we were too late.
   B: Yeah, the train had already left.

3. A: You sure woke up early this morning!
   B: Well, I wasn't sleepy. I had already slept for eight hours.

4. A: Go back to sleep. It's only six o'clock in the morning.
   B: I'm not sleepy. I'm going to get up. I have already slept for eight hours.

Chapter 5: Asking Questions

Exercise 4, p. 113.

Leaving for the airport

1. Do you have your passport?
2. Did you remember to pack a snack for the plane?
3. Will your carry-on bag fit under the seat?
4. Is your taxi coming soon?
5. Will you call me when you get there?

Exercise 6, p. 113.

Part I.

1. Is he absent?	becomes	*Ih-ze* absent? OR *Ze* absent?
2. Is she absent?	becomes	*Ih-she* absent?
3. Does it work?	becomes	*Zit* work?
4. Did it break?	becomes	*Dih-dit* break? OR *Dit* break?
5. Has he been sick?	becomes	*Ze* been sick? OR *A-ze* been sick?
6. Is there enough?	becomes	*Zere* enough?
7. Is that okay?	becomes	*Zat* okay?

Part II.

At the grocery store

1. I need to see the manager. Is she available?
2. I need to see the manager. Is he in the store today?
3. Here is one bag of apples. Is that enough?
4. I need a drink of water. Is there a drinking fountain?
5. My credit card isn't working. Hmmm. Did it expire?
6. Where's Simon? Has he left?
7. The price seems high. Does it include the tax?

Exercise 9, p. 116.

Where are Roberto and Isabel?

A: Do you know Roberto and Isabel?
B: Yes, I do. They live around the corner from me.
A: Have you seen them lately?
B: No, I haven't. They're out of town.
A: Did they go to their parents? I heard Roberto's parents are ill.
B: Yes, they did. They went to help them.
A: Are you going to see them soon?
B: Yes, I am. In fact, I'm going to pick them up at the airport.
A: Will they be back this weekend? I'm having a party, and I'd like to invite them.
B: No, they won't. They won't be back until Monday.

Exercise 14, p. 118.

1. Do you want to go to the mall?
2. When are the Waltons coming?
3. Where will I meet you?
4. Why were you late?
5. What did you buy?

Exercise 19, p. 120.

A secret

A: John told me something.
B: What did he tell you?
A: It's confidential. I can't tell you.
B: Did he tell anyone else?
A: He told a few other people.
B: Who did he tell?
A: Some friends.
B: Then it's not a secret. What did he say?
A: I can't tell you.
B: Why can't you tell me?
A: Because it's about you. But don't worry. It's nothing bad.
B: Gee. Thanks a lot. That sure makes me feel better.

Exercise 29, p. 126.

1. Who's ringing the doorbell?
2. Whose coat is on the floor?
3. Whose glasses are those?
4. Who's sitting next to you?
5. Whose seat is next to yours?
6. Who's out in the hallway?

Exercise 30, p. 126.

An old vacation photo

1. Whose picture is this?
2. Who's in the picture?
3. Who's standing in back?
4. You don't wear glasses. Whose glasses are you wearing?
5. Who's the woman in the purple jacket?
6. Whose cabin are you at?

Exercise 34, p. 128.

1. A: How fresh are these eggs?
   B: I just bought them at the Farmers' Market, so they should be fine.

2. A: How cheap were the tickets?
   B: They were 50% off.

3. A: How hard was the driver's test?
   B: Well, I didn't pass, so that gives you an idea.

4. A: How clean is the car?
   B: There's dirt on the floor. We need to vacuum it inside.

5. A: How hot is the frying pan?
   B: Don't touch it! You'll burn yourself.

6. A: How noisy is the street you live on?
   B: There is a lot of traffic, so we keep the windows closed a lot.

7. A: How serious are you about interviewing for the job?
   B: Very. I already scheduled an interview with the company.

Exercise 37, p. 130.

Questions:

1. How old are you?
2. How tall are you?
3. How much do you weigh?
4. In general, how well do you sleep at night?
5. How quickly do you fall asleep?
6. How often do you wake up during the night?
7. How tired are you in the mornings?
8. How many times a week do you exercise?
9. How are you feeling right now?
10. How soon can you come in for an overnight appointment?

Exercise 44, p. 134.

A birthday

1. When's your birthday?
2. When'll your party be?
3. Where'd you decide to have it?
4. Who're you inviting?

Exercise 45, p. 135.

1. Where's my key?
2. Where're my keys?
3. Who're those people?
4. What's in that box?
5. What're you doing?
6. Where'd Bob go last night?
7. Who'll be at the party?
8. Why's the teacher absent?
9. Who's that?
10. Why'd you say that?
11. Who'd you talk to at the party?

12. How're we going to get to work?
13. What'd you say?
14. How'll you do that?

Exercise 46, p. 135.

On an airplane

1. Who're you going to sit with?
2. How're you going to get your suitcase under the seat?
3. What'd the flight attendant just say?
4. Why'd we need to put our seat belts back on?
5. Why's the plane descending?
6. Why're we going down?
7. When'll the pilot tell us what's going on?
8. Who'll meet you when you land?
9. When's our connecting flight?
10. How'll we get from the airport to our hotel?

Exercise 47, p. 135.

A mother talking to her teenage daughter

1. Where're you going?
2. Who're you going with?
3. Who's that?
4. How long've you known him?
5. Where'd you meet him?
6. Where's he go to school?
7. Is he a good student?
8. What time'll you be back?
9. Why're you wearing that outfit?
10. Why're you giving me that look?
11. Why am I asking so many questions? Because I love you!

Exercise 48, p. 136.

1. What do you want to do?
2. What are you doing?
3. What are you having for dinner?
4. What are you doing that for?
5. What do you think about that?
6. What are you laughing for?
7. What do you need?
8. What do you have in your pocket?

Exercise 53, p. 138.

1. A: Did you like the movie?
   B: It was okay, I guess. How about you?

2. A: Are you going to the company party?
   B: I haven't decided yet. What about you?

3. A: Do you like living in this city?
   B: Sort of. How about you?

4. A: What are you going to have?
   B: Well, I'm not really hungry. I think I might order just a salad. How about you?

Exercise 56, p. 140.

1. a. You're Mrs. Rose, aren't you?
   b. Are you Mrs. Rose?
2. a. Do you take cream with your coffee?
   b. You take cream with your coffee, don't you?
3. a. You don't want to leave, do you?
   b. Do you want to leave?

Exercise 57, p. 141.

1. Simple Present
   a. You like strong coffee, don't you?
   b. David goes to Ames High School, doesn't he?
   c. Leila and Sara live on Tree Road, don't they?
   d. Jane has the keys to the storeroom, doesn't she?
   e. Jane's in her office, isn't she?
   f. You're a member of this class, aren't you?
   g. Oleg doesn't have a car, does he?
   h. Lisa isn't from around here, is she?
   i. I'm in trouble, aren't I?

2. Simple Past
   a. Paul went to Indonesia, didn't he?
   b. You didn't talk to the boss, did you?
   c. Ted's parents weren't at home, were they?
   d. That was Pat's idea, wasn't it?

3. Present Progressive, *Be Going To,* and Past Progressive
   a. You're studying hard, aren't you?
   b. Greg isn't working at the bank, is he?
   c. It isn't going to rain today, is it?
   d. Michelle and Yoko were helping, weren't they?
   e. He wasn't listening, was he?

4. Present Perfect
   a. It has been warmer than usual, hasn't it?
   b. You've had a lot of homework, haven't you?
   c. We haven't spent much time together, have we?
   d. Fatima has started her new job, hasn't she?
   e. Bruno hasn't finished his sales report yet, has he?
   f. Steve's had to leave early, hasn't he?

Exercise 59, p. 142.

Checking in at a hotel

1. You have our reservation, don't you?
2. We have a non-smoking room, don't we?
3. There's a view of the city, isn't there?
4. I didn't give you my credit card yet, did I?
5. The room rate doesn't include tax, does it?
6. Breakfast is included in the price, right?
7. Check-out time's noon, isn't it?
8. You don't have a pool, do you?
9. There are hair dryers in the rooms, aren't there?
10. Kids aren't allowed in the hot tub, are they?

Exercise 61, p. 143.

Part I.

1. What kind of music do you enjoy listening to?
2. I just saw you for a few minutes last night. What did you leave so early for?

3. How are you feeling?
4. How long does the bus ride take?
5. Whose children are those?
6. When did the Browns move into their new apartment?

Part II.

7. A: We only have a few minutes before the movie starts.
   B: I'm hurrying.
   A: Do you have enough money for the tickets?

8. A: Is the mail here yet?
   B: No, I just checked.
   A: I'm expecting a package. How soon will it be here?

9. A: I start my new job next week.
   B: Wow, that's soon.
   A: Yeah, I wanted to start as soon as possible.
   B: Now, how come you're changing jobs?

10. A: Are you new to the area?
    B: Yes, I moved here last month. My company transferred me here.
    A: Oh, so what do you do?

Exercise 62, p. 143.

Ordering at a fast-food restaurant

Cashier: So, what'll it be?
Customer: I'll have a burger.
Cashier: Would you like fries or a salad with your burger?
Customer: I'll have fries.
Cashier: What size?
Customer: Medium.
Cashier: Anything to drink?
Customer: I'll have a vanilla shake.
Cashier: Size?
Customer: Medium.
Cashier: Okay. So that's a burger, fries, vanilla shake.
Customer: About how long'll it take?
Cashier: We're pretty crowded right now. Probably 10 minutes or so. That'll be $6.50. Your number's on the receipt. I'll call the number when your order's ready.
Customer: Thanks.

Chapter 6: Nouns and Pronouns

Exercise 6, p. 149.

1. hat   3. pages   5. keys
2. toys   4. bridge   6. dish

Exercise 7, p. 150.

1. pants   3. boxes   5. wishes
2. cars   4. pens   6. lakes

Exercise 8, p. 150.

1. prizes	ways
2. lips	pants
3. glasses	matches
4. taxes	shirts
5. pills	stars
6. toes	fingers
7. laws	maps
8. lights	places

Exercise 9, p. 150.

1. names	4. boats	7. lips
2. clocks	5. eyelashes	8. bridges
3. eyes	6. ways	9. cars

Exercise 10, p. 150.

1. This shirt comes in three sizes: small, medium, and large.
2. I found this fax on my desk. It's for you.
3. I found these faxes on my desk. They're for you.
4. I'm not going to buy this car. The price is too high.
5. I can't find my glasses anywhere. Have you seen them?
6. The prize for the contest is a new bike.

Exercise 28, p. 159.

How Some Animals Stay Cool

How do animals stay cool in hot weather? Many animals don't sweat like humans, so they have other ways to cool themselves.

Dogs, for example, have a lot of fur and can become very hot. They stay cool mainly by panting. By the way, if you don't know what panting means, this is the sound of panting.

Cats lick their paws and chests. When their fur is wet, they become cooler.

Elephants have very large ears. When they are hot, they can flap their huge ears. The flapping ear acts like a fan and it cools them. Elephants also like to roll in the mud to stay cool.

Exercise 36, p. 163.

A: I'm looking for a new place to live.
B: How come?
A: My two roommates are moving out. I can't afford my apartment. I need a one-bedroom.
B: I just helped a friend find one. I can help you. What else do you want?
A: I want to be near the subway . . . within walking distance. But I want a quiet location. I don't want to be on a busy street.
B: Anything else?
A: A small balcony would be nice.
B: That's expensive.
A: Yeah. I guess I'm dreaming.

Exercise 49, p. 170.

1. Be careful with that knife! It's very sharp. If you're not careful, you'll cut . . .
2. My wife and I have our own business. We don't have a boss. In other words, we work for . .
3. Rebecca is home in bed because she has the flu. She's resting and drinking plenty of fluids. She's being careful about her health. In other words, she is taking care of . . .
4. In a cafeteria, people walk through a section of the restaurant and pick up their food. They are not served by waiters. In other words, in a cafeteria people serve. . .
5. When Joe walked into the room, he didn't know anyone. He smiled confidently and began introducing . . .
6. When I didn't get the new job, I felt sad and depressed. I sat in my apartment and felt sorry for . . .

Exercise 58, p. 176.

1. A: Did you buy the black jacket?
   B: No. I bought the other one.

2. A: One of my favorite colors is dark blue. Another one is red.
   B: Me too.

3. A: This looks like the wrong street. Let's go back and take the other road.
   B: Okay.

4. A: What's the best way to get downtown from here?
   B: It's pretty far to walk. Some people take the bus. Others prefer the subway.

5. A: When I was a kid, I had lots of pets. One was a black dog. Another was an orange cat. Some others were a goldfish and a turtle.
   B: Pets are great for kids.

Exercise 59, p. 177.

A: What do you do when you're feeling lonely?
B: I go someplace where I can be around other people. Even if they are strangers, I feel better when there are others around me. How about you?
A: That doesn't work for me. For example, if I'm feeling lonely and I go to a movie by myself, I look at all the other people who are there with their friends and family, and I start to feel even lonelier. So I try to find other things to do to keep myself busy. When I'm busy, I don't feel lonely.

Chapter 7: Modal Auxiliaries

Exercise 3, p. 179.

1. I have to go downtown tomorrow.
2. You must fasten your seat belt.
3. Could you please open the window?

4. May I borrow your eraser?
5. I'm not able to sign the contract today.
6. Today is the deadline. You must sign it!
7. I have got to go to the post office this afternoon.
8. Shouldn't you save some of your money for emergencies?
9. I feel bad for Elena. She has to have more surgery.
10. Alexa! Stop! You must not run into the street!

Exercise 7, p. 181.

In the classroom

A: I can't understand this math assignment.
B: I can help you with that.
A: Really? Can you explain this problem to me?
B: Well, we can't figure out the answer unless we do this part first.
A: Okay! But it's so hard.
B: Yeah, but I know you can do it. Just go slowly.
A: Class is almost over. Can you meet me after school today to finish this?
B: Well, I can't meet you right after school, but how about at 5:00?
A: Great!

Exercise 13, p. 184.

1. A: Mom, are these oranges sweet?
   B: I don't know. I can't tell if an orange is sweet just by looking at it.

2. A: What are you going to order?
   B: I'm not sure. I might have pasta, or I might have pizza.

3. A: Mom, can I have some candy?
   B: No, but you can have an apple.

4. A: What are you doing this weekend?
   B: I don't know yet. I may go snowboarding with friends, or I may try to fix my motorcycle.

5. May I have everyone's attention? The test is about to begin. If you need to leave the room during the examination, please raise your hand. You may not leave the room without asking. Are there any questions? No? Then you may open your test booklets and begin.

Exercise 17, p. 186.

In a home office

A: Look at this cord. Do you know what it's for?
B: I don't know. We have so many cords around here with all our electronic equipment. It could be for the printer, I guess.
A: No, I checked. The printer isn't missing a cord.
B: It might be for one of the kid's toys.

A: Yeah, I could ask. But they don't have many electronic toys.
B: I have an idea. It may be for the cell phone. You know—the one I had before this one.
A: I bet that's it. We can probably throw this out.
B: Well, let's be sure before we do that.

Exercise 32, p. 194.

Filling out a job application

1. The application has to be complete. You shouldn't skip any parts. If a section doesn't fit your situation, you can write N/A (not applicable).
2. You don't have to type it, but your writing has to be easy to read.
3. You've got to use your full legal name, not your nickname.
4. You've got to list the names and places of your previous employers.
5. You have to list your education, beginning with either high school or college.
6. You don't always have to apply in person. Sometimes you can do it online.
7. You don't have to write some things, like the same telephone number, twice. You can write "same as above."
8. All spelling has to be correct.

Exercise 45, p. 201.

Puzzle steps

1. Write down the number of the month you were born. For example, write the number 2 if you were born in February. Write 3 if you were born in March, etc.
2. Double the number.
3. Add 5 to it.
4. Multiply it by 50.
5. Add your age.
6. Subtract 250.

Exercise 50, p. 204.

A: Why don't we go dancing tonight?
B: I don't know how to dance.
A: Oh. Then why don't we go to a movie?
B: I don't like movies.
A: You don't like movies?!
B: No.
A: Well then, let's go to a restaurant for dinner.
B: That's a waste of money.
A: Well, you do what you want tonight, but I'm going to go out and have a good time.

Trivia Answers

Chapter 1, Exercise 10, p. 7.

1. T
2. T
3. F [According to a 1993 study: the death rate for right-handed people = 32.2%; for left-handed people = 33.8%, so the death rate is about the same.]
4. T
5. F [The official Eiffel Tower Web site says 1,665.]
6. F [Honey never spoils.]
7. T
8. T
9. T
10. T

Chapter 5, Exercise 35, p. 129.

1. c
2. d
3. b
4. a
5. e

Chapter 6, Exercise 18, p. 154.

1. Georgia, Azerbaijan, Kazakhstan, China, Mongolia
2. Denmark
3. The Thames
4. The Dominican Republic, Cuba, Puerto Rico, Jamaica
5. Laos, Thailand, Cambodia, China
6. (*Answers will vary.*)
7. Liechtenstein
8. Vatican City
9. (*Answers will vary.*)
10. Egypt, Sudan, Eritrea, Iran

Chapter 6, Exercise 44, p. 167.

1. T
2. F [gray and wrinkled]
3. T
4. T
5. T
6. T [about 11% to 12% bigger]
7. T
8. F [Men's voices have a higher pitch.]

Index

After, 48, 68, 153 (*Look on pages 48, 68 and 153.*)	The numbers following the words listed in the index refer to page numbers in the text.
Consonants, 14*fn.* (*Look at the footnote on page 14.*)	The letters *fn.* mean "footnote." Footnotes are at the bottom of a chart or the bottom of a page.

NOTES